DAVID WATKINS & PHIL L

Colour artwork : Malcolm Laird

Layout & project design : Phil Listemann

Copyright © David Watkins and Phil Listemann 2007

ISBN 978-295-26-3813-5

Edited by Phil H. Listemann

philedition@wanadoo.fr

www.raf-in-combat.com

Printed in France by
GRAPHIC SUD
BP44 - ZAC de Rigoulet
47552 Boé Cedex, France
Tél : (33).5.53.48.20.30 - Fax : (33).5.53.48.20.35
igs@wanadoo.fr

ACKNOWLEDGEMENTS

Vernon Benner, Ron Bennett, Graham Berry, Neil Crabtree, Wg Cdr C F "Bunny" Currant, Wg Cdr Paul Farnes, DFM, Sqn Ldr J.A.A. Gibson, DSO, DFC, W J Green, Reverend A.J. Grottick, A.E. "Ben" Gunn, AFRAeS, Colin Hodgkinson, AVM H.A.V. "Harry" Hogan, CB, DFC, W.B. Holroyd, L.R. "Beans" Knight, Sheila Lacey, AM Ian D Macfadyen, CB, OBE, FRAeS, Wg Cdr K W "Mac" Mackenzie, DFC, AFC, AE, Kenneth "Hawkeye" Lee, Eric Moore, A D Pickup, OBE, Gilbert Wild, Peter Winston.
André Bar (Belgians in RAF & SAAF), Jim Halley, Hugh Halliday (relative to Canadian pilots), Errol Martyn & Paul Sortehaug (relative to NZ pilots), Wojtek Matusiak (relative to Polish pilots), Jiri Rajlich (relative to Czech pilots), Andy Thomas, Chris Thomas.

GLOSSARY OF TERMS

ADF : Aircraft Delivery Flight
ADGB : Air Defense of Great Britain
AFC : Air For...
AFDU : Air F...
(BEL)/RAF : ...g ...e RAF
(CAN)/RAF : Canadian serving in the RAF
Cz : Czech
(CZ)/RAF : Czechoslovak serving in the RAF
CzAF : Czechoslovakian Air Force
(DAN) : Dane serving in the RAF
DFC : Distinguished Flying Cross
DFM : Distinguished Flying Medal
DSO : Distinguished Service Order
Eva : Evaded
FE : Far East
FFAF : Free French Air Force
F/L : Flight Lieutenant
FLS : Fighter Leaders School
F/O : Flying Officer
(FR)/RAF : French serving in the RAF
F/Sgt : Flight Sergeant
FTS : Flying Training School
G/C : Group Captain
HQ : Headquarters
HQFC : Headquarters Fighter Command
LAC : Leading Aircraftman
LG : London Gazette
MBE : Member of British Empire
ME : Middle East
MU : Maintenance Unit
(NZ)/RAF : New Zealander serving in the RAF
ORB : Operational Record Book
OTU : Operational Training Unit
PAF : Polish Air Force
P/O : Pilot Officer
(POL)/RAF : Pole serving in the RAF
PoW : Prisoner of War
RAAF : Royal Australian Air Force
RCAF : Royal Canadian Air Force
RNZAF : Royal New Zealand Air Force
SA : South African
Sgt : Sergeant
S/L : Squadron Leader
Sqn : Squadron
SSC : Short Service Commission
RAF : Royal Air Force
W/C : Wing Commander
W/O : Warrant Officer

Background : A No.501 Squadron Hurricane being serviced by ground crew in France in May 1940. (IWM C1731)

Now is War! But if the pilots of those Hurricanes Mk.Is are starting their engine in September 1939, it is for another training flight. But things will change soon. (501 Squadron Association)

MAIN EQUIPMENT 1939-1945			
HURRICANE I	09.39 - 06.41	SPITFIRE V	09.41 - 08.44
HURRICANE X	08.40 - 11.40	SPITFIRE IX	11.43 - 05.44
SPITFIRE I	04.41 - 06.41	TEMPEST V	07.44 - 04.45
SPITFIRE II	05.41 - 10.41		

As part of the general re-organisation of the RAF during the late 1930s, No.501 Squadron became a fighter squadron in No.11 Group, Fighter Command, on 1st December 1938, and selected to receive the RAF's first, eight-gun monoplane fighter aircraft - the Hawker Hurricane.

It would be another three months before the squadron took delivery of its first Hawker Hurricane when, on 10th March 1939, L1866 was flown direct from the manufacturers at Brooklands by Flying Officer Jackson of No.2 Ferry Pilots Pool. No.501 Squadron's pilots eagerly sought the opportunity to fly the new fighter, and a handful of Fairey Battle trainers were loaned to the squadron to assist with the conversion training and to provide dual instruction.

Fully equipped with the Hurricane by June, the follo-wing month the squadron went to Manston for its summer camp. The annual summer camp at Manston would, however, be the last for another eight years as European political relations had deteriorated to the extent that some form of major conflict was inevita-ble. In March 1939, Germany's self-assumed Supreme Commander, Adolph Hitler broke his 1938 Munich Agreement by invading Czechoslovakia; six months later, on 1st September 1939, without prior declaration of war, he then struck at Poland. Britain's Prime Minister, Neville Chamberlain issued an ulti-matum to Germany which was ignored and ten days later, Europe was once more at war.

On 23rd August, orders were received for the squadron to be embodied into the RAF. Squadron personnel immediately reported for duty and to bring the unit up to strength, RAFVR and NCO pilots were drafted in to supplement the "part-timers". By midnight on 24th August the squadron was complete.

Very quickly No.501 Squadron settled down to a rou-tine, carrying out convoy patrols and anti-submarine searches over the Bristol Channel, together with end-less hours of night flying practice. It was during one of these periods of night flying training that Flight Lieutenant Brian Hewett crashed and seriously dama-ged his Hurricane; although the pilot was uninjured, it

TERRITORIAL AND AUXILIARY FORCES

The concept of the Territorial and Auxiliary Forces dated from 1907, when the Territorial and Reserve Forces Act was passed, followed by the Air Force (Constitution) Act in November 1917 which made provision for the creation of an Auxiliary Air Force. In 1919, Air Marshal, Sir Hugh Trenchard (Chief of the Air Staff and later Marshal of the Royal Air Force) formulated a plan that would reconstitute the post-war RAF, which was presented to Parliament in the form of a White Paper in the November of that year.

Contained in his study, Trenchard called for the creation of a Citizen Air Force, made up of Special Reserve and Auxiliary Air Force units which would operate on a territorial basis and act as a back-up to the Regular squadrons. Trenchard also insisted that the non-Regular squadrons - soon to be dubbed "weekend flyers" - would be a necessary part of the RAF, but with their roots firmly established in the civil life of the country.

There was much opposition to the draft Bill of 1922 to implement Trenchard's plan and it was temporarily shelved on the grounds that modern aeroplanes were far too sophisticated to be operated by a part-time organisation. Two years later, following the Labour party's defeat of 1924, the new Secretary of State for Air, Sir Samuel Hoare, a staunch supporter of the Bill effected immediate plans for such a force. The Auxiliary Air Force and Air Force Reserves Act of 14th July 1924 made provision for raising seven Reserve squadrons - to be numbered from 500 Squadron (the first of which, No.502 (Ulster) Squadron was formed at Aldergrove, N. Ireland, in May 1925) - and six Auxiliary squadrons - to be numbered from 600 Squadron with the formation of No.602 (City of Glasgow) Squadron at Renfrew in September 1925. Auxiliary Air Force squadrons were raised by the County Territorial Associations and manned by locally-recruited non-Regular personnel to be commanded by a non-Regular officer, with a small cadre of Regulars acting as permanent staff. Special Reserve squadrons differed in that they would be directly administered by the RAF and raised in certain localities as part of the Air Defence of Great Britain at an aerodrome in the vicinity of the town from which the personnel were recruited. Commanded by a Regular officer, the SR squadrons were complemented by a larger proportion of Regular airmen to reservists. A town HQ would provide a centre for recruitment, training and social activities, while flying training would be carried out a nearby airfield.

On 14th June 1929, No.501 (Bomber) Squadron was officially formed at Filton airfield, Bristol, as a cadre unit of the Special Reserve and received its first aircraft, an Avro 504N trainer, the following August. The squadron took delivery of the first of its DH 9A two-seat, light day bombers in March 1930 and was renamed as No.501 (City of Bristol) (Bomber) Squadron the following May. In September 1930 the squadron re-equipped with the Westland Wapiti, having previously undertaken the first of its annual, two-week period of intensive training - summer camps - at Manston in July. Westland Wallaces were received in March 1933, and these were continued to be flown in the day bomber role until 1st May 1936, when the unit became an Auxiliary squadron as part of the RAF Expansion Plan. With a change in title to that of No.501 (County of Gloucester) (Bomber) Squadron, AAF, the unit was subsequently re-equipped with Hawker Hart and Hind light day bombers.

was considered that the Hurricane was the first squadron "victim" of WWII.

At 10.50 hrs on 11th November, the squadron carried out its first operational patrol of the war when two sections were scrambled to intercept an enemy aircraft reported over the Bristol Channel. The first section, led by Flight Lieutenant Williams and comprising Sergeants Crabtree and Dafforn, were relieved by Flight Lieutenant Hewett , Pilot Officers Sylvester and Cridland. Unfortunately no contact was made and the last aircraft returned to Filton, two hours later.

Following Fighter Command's decision that the squadron was now fully operational, No.501 Squadron left Filton on 27th November 1939 and flew to its designated war station at Tangemere in Sussex. Tangmere was a well-run aerodrome, situated on the English Channel coast, which the squadron shared with No.92 Squadron, RAF, and No.601 Squadron, Auxiliary Air Force, both flying Bristol Blenheims. Despite everyone's optimism for immediate action, Tangmere proved to be another anti-climax and the squadron continued the monotonous routine of night-flying training, formation flying practice, searchlight co-operation and practice interceptions against "friendly" bombers.

By the spring of 1940, the pace of the so-called *Phoney War* was increasing and the squadron crews grew impatient as every day, news filtered back regarding the successes of the other RAF fighter squadrons in France. Finally, orders were received for the squadron to prepare for a move to Norway and establish an advance party in support of the forces resisting the German invasion of their country.

SERIALS OF HURRICANE I IN USE ON 3RD SEPTEMBER 1939.

L : 1866, 1867, 1868, 1870, 1910, 1949, 1953, 2052, 2053, 2054, 2055, 2056

Total : 12

THE *PHONEY WAR* IS OVER

The ill-conceived plan to send the squadron to Norway was eventually cancelled. On 10th May 1940, the Germans bombed Rotterdam and invaded Belgium, Holland and North-East France; the *Phoney War* was over and No.501 Squadron was ordered to France to re-inforce the Advanced Air Striking Force. Hitler's lightning attack had surprised everyone and within hours of the Dutch and Belgian Ministers appealing for help, No.501 Squadron was preparing to move. By 14.40 hrs, the squadron CO, Squadron Leader Monty Clube, was leading a formation of sixteen Hurricanes from Tangmere to a forward base at Betheniville to join No.67 Wing of the AASF. Two other RAF Hurricane squadrons, 3 and 79, were also detached from No.11 Group to support the Force.

The squadron landed in France ninety minutes later and was immediately ordered up again to familiarise the pilots with the local countryside. Within hours of arriving it would claim its first enemy victory when,

at 18.20 hrs, Flying Officer Derrick Pickup shot down a Do17, 15 miles north-west of Vouziers after a burst of 140 rounds.

Ordered up on a reconnaissance patrol at 17.15 hrs with two other aircraft flown by Flying Officer Smith and Flight Sergeant Payne, Pickup became separated from his section and spotted a Do17 slightly below him. Pulling himself together, he attacked the enemy bomber and was surprised to see smoke streaming from it and that parachutes began to appear. His first thought was to return to base to re-arm and re-fuel, and, although he did not see the Do17 crash, it was later confirmed as destroyed by the French authorities.

Located north-east of Rheims, on the borders of the Provinces of the Marne and the Ardennes, Betheniville consisted of a series of flat, grass fields, two kilometres from the village. There was few facilities available other than two small Nissen huts which constituted the working accommodation, two petrol bowsers and a small van. The groundcrews

The Phoney War ended abrutly on 10th May 1940 with the invasion of the Low Countries, Belgium, Luxembourg and France. Reinforcements are called in the first hours and No.501 Squadron is sent in France and rushed into the battle at once.
(501 Squadron Association)

Hawker Hurricane Mk.I L2052, No.501 (County of Gloucester) Squadron, Filton, October 1939.

The wreck of the Bombay which crashed on 11.05.40 at Betheniville. Two members of the Squadron were killed in the crash.
(501 Squadron Association)

were billeted in tents in the village, whilst the officers managed to requisition a small cafe. Tents were also erected to act as the Operations Room and, despite initial refuelling and rearming problems, the crews settled in alongside the Fairey Battles of No.103 Squadron to await the squadron rear party.

The following day, the rear party set off for France in Ensign and Bombay transport aircraft, arriving after lunch. The first of the Bombay transports landed, followed by the Imperial Airway's Ensign. As the ground crews disembarked, a second Bombay (L5813) made its approach to the tiny French field. Suddenly the aircraft began to climb, hold itself on the edge of a stall, before the nose and wingtip fell and it hit the ground with a terrifying crash. Fortunately there was no explosion, which enabled the remaining crews to come to the assistance of their comrades. The medical team worked relentlessly throughout the rest of the day and night, tending the injured passengers which included not only ground crews but also the spare squadron pilots.

Together with the crew of the Bombay, the Squadron's casualty list included: Flying Officer A.C.J. Percy[1], Sergeants H.J. Barnwell (from No.103 Squadron, also based at Betheniville) and W.H. Whitfield killed, and Flying Officer MacGevor, Pilot Officer Brady, Duckenfield, Flight Sergeant Avent, Sergeants

Adams, Crabtree and Davis injured. The cause of the crash was eventually established as an incorrect distribution of passengers and cargo, resulting in the fatal stall.

Faced with the grim realities of war and a determination to prove itself as a fighter squadron, No.501 Squadron was back in action later that day, shooting down five enemy aircraft without loss. An early morning patrol by six Hurricanes encountered a formation of Do17Zs of 2./KG 2 south of Rheims, which was attacked and resulted in one bomber being shot down by Sergeant Bob Dafforn near Arcis le Ponsart (Marne) and another slightly damaged by Flight Lieutenant Edward Williams. In the afternoon, 30 He111s of KG 53 escorted by Bf110s of ZG 2 were engaged by the Hurricanes of Nos.1 and 73 Squadrons over Mourmelon. No.501 Squadron joined in the action and quickly claimed four aircraft as shot down: two Bf110s by Pilot Officer Dickie Hulse and Sergeant Ronnie Morfill near Cornay and Tourteron, respectively, whilst a further two He111s were despatched by Flying Officer Cam Malfroy and Flight Sergeant Jammy Payne close to Betheniville and Mourmelon.

[1] Alister C.J. Percy (service number 90025), was the Squadron Adjutant. His father was the Major-General Sir Jocelyn Percy, K.B.E, C.B., C.M.G., D.S.O.

SERIALS OF HURRICANE I IN USE ON 1ST MAY 1940.

L : 1605, 1659, 1865, 1866, 1868, 1910, 1949, 1953, 1991, 2037, 2038, 2045, 2052
2053, 2054, 2055, 2056, 2124

N : 2586

Total : 19

On 12th May, the squadron was rudely awakened by an early morning bombing raid on targets near the village. However, the day's almost continuous activity resulted in twelve more Luftwaffe aircraft being shot down. Taking off at 06.50 hrs to intercept a formation of He111s of II./KG 53 returning from a raid on Mourmelon airfield, two sections encountered 18 of the bombers near Vouziers. Three aircraft were shot down by Pilot Officer Rayner, Sylvester and Flight Sergeant Payne, whilst a fourth was badly damaged by Flying Officer Gus Holden and forced to make an emergency landing near the Luxembourg border.

A further patrol by four aircraft in the afternoon encountered four Do17s near Sedan, one of which was shot down by Pilot Officer "Hawkeye" Lee near the Belgian border. The rest of section was immediately bounced by the Bf110 escort, damaging Flying Officer Michael Smith's Hurricane and forcing him to bale out. He was again attacked by a Bf110 as he floated to the ground and raked by machine gun fire, his body coming down close to the village of Artaise le Vivier. Flying Officer Cam Malfroy's aircraft was also hit and he was fortunate to make a successful forced-landing at Mourmelon. With the loss of Flying Officer Peter Rayner who was shot down by a Bf110 and killed during the morning's fighting when his aircraft crashed near Seuil (Ardennes), the score-sheet for the day amounted to twelve enemy aircraft destroyed for the loss of two pilots.

Monday, 13th May, 1940, brought the inevitable early morning raid when 42 Luftwaffe bombers attacked the railhead in the village, causing considerable damage and loss of life. Several bombs exploded near the airfield but fortunately there were no casualties. 501's

Some of the No.501 Squadron pilots who went to France in May 1940. This photograph taken on 12.05.40 at Betheniville shows from to right, the New Zealander Flying Officer C.E. Malfroy, Pilot Officer C.L. Hulse (background), Sergeant J.H. Lacey (background with helmet), Flying Officer A.D. Pickup and Flying Officer M.F.C. Smith. Sadly M.F.C. Smith will be killed in action before the end of the day, becoming the first war casualty of the Squadron. C.L. Hulse won't return to the UK either, being also killed in action on 08.06.40. (501 Squadron Association)

Hawker Hurricane Mk.I L2045, No.501 (County of Gloucester) Squadron, Squadron Leader M.V.M. Clube, Tangmere, February 1940.

Hurricane Mk.I L2124/SD-H, taken during the first weeks of the war at Filton. This aircraft will be later shot down during a bomber escort on 31.05.40, flown by Pilot Officer E.J.H. Sylverster.
(501 Squadron Association)

The Hawker HURRICANE

The Hawker Hurricane was the first of the RAF's monoplane fighters and the prototype flew for the first time on 6th November 1935.

The initial version, powered by a Merlin II of 1,030 hp, was designated the **Hurricane Mk.I** and was ordered in quantity during the summer of 1936 to rearm the RAF's fighter squadrons. The first aircraft were delivered during the Autumn of 1937 and the type became operational in January 1938. On the eve of the Second World War, nearly 500 Hurricanes had been delivered to the RAF and was the backbone of Fighter Command until late 1940, supplemented by **Hurricanes Mk.X**, the Canadian version of the Hurricane Mk.I.

After the Battle of Britain, the Hurricane gave way to the Spitfire as the main fighter of Fighter Command, as squadrons were gradually re-equipped.

It was at that time that the Hurricane Mk.II, with the more powerful Merlin XX of 1,390 hp engine appeared, but its performance remained inferior to that of German fighters, and the Hurricane seemed to have reached its limit of development. Because of this the Hurricane I and II would remain the two main production versions.

From mid-1941, the Hurricane was used, briefly, as a night fighter and with more success as a fighter-bomber. Considerable numbers were shipped to other theatres for service in this role. It gradually disappeared from active operations in Europe as the RAF introduced new types into service. The Hurricane remained in first-line service in North Africa and the Far East until the end of the war. In January 1947, No.6 Squadron at Palestine became the last RAF squadron to operate the type when it re-equipped with Spitfires.

Hurricanes were quick to respond, inflicting a heavy toll on the Luftwaffe by adding another six aircraft to its increasing score-sheet with a Do17 shot down near Auberive and Flight Lieutenant Charles Griffiths and Pilot Officer "Hawkeye" Lee each claiming a Bf110 of 1./ZG 26 near Le Chesne. Three of the day's total were claimed by Sergeant Ginger Lacey, who opened his personal tally when he shot down a Bf109 and He111 in the same action near Stenay. Later in the morning he went on to claim a Bf110, which dived into the ground near Le Chesne following a two-second burst of fire into the port engine.

By the following day, the German Panzer Divisions had crossed the River Meuse and, despite an ill-fated attack on the pontoon bridges by the Fairey Battles of No.103 Squadron, the German Army continued its relentless advance. Betheniville was bombed three times that morning, killing 14 civilians. During a morning patrol over the Meuse, Flying Officer Ryan Cridland was able to open his score-sheet when he shot down a Do17, while a section of No.501 Squadron's Hurricanes attacked a formation of He111s from KG 51 during later patrol in the morning over Rheims. Three of the bombers were shot down

Being damaged by enemy action on 12.05.40, while flown by Flying Officer E. Holden, Hurricane L2045 was sent to No.21 Aircraft Depot for repairs. Unlike many other Hurricanes engaged in France, it could make the way back to the UK.

by Flight Sergeant Jammy Payne, Sergeants John Proctor and Bob Dafforn.

Refugees had now begun pouring into the village, packing the narrow French roads as they fled from the advancing German forces. A further raid on the airfield damaged several of the squadron's aircraft and, despite three more Do17s shot down by Flight Lieutenant Charles Griffiths, Flying Officer Ryan Cridland and Flight Sergeant Jammy Payne, a further two Hurricanes were wrecked as the result of flying accidents.

The Dornier shot down over Betheniville Station by Flight Lieutenant Charles Griffiths was of particular interest as it brought the squadron into personal contact with one of the Luftwaffe crew members. Badly damaged by the concentrated attack of the No.501 Squadron's Hurricanes, one of the air gunners was able to bale out before the crippled Do17Z of 5./KG 3 plunged into a nearby field. An angry crowd of French civilians awaited his landing, and his inevitable fate was only avoided by the timely intervention of two passing RAF officers, who took him to the airfield and gave him a meal.

By Thursday, 16th May, the German Panzer Divisions had overrun the Meuse bridges, forcing the defending French troops to withdraw. With the fighting getting nearer and with the airfield only twelve miles away from the front line it was decided to withdraw both RAF Squadrons; No.103 Squadron was the first to leave, followed by No.501 Squadron which flew to

Anglure, some 50 miles away, to support the beleaguered British Army retreating from Dunkirk.

The Squadron's new base was small in comparison to Betheniville, which again necessitated operations to be conducted from tents and with the aircraft dispersed around the edge of the field. The following days were relatively quiet, and despite large formations of enemy bombers being observed by No.501 Squadron's patrols they were not engaged as orders had been received to only attack fighters. As most formations were usually too high for an effective interception, the squadron continued with fruitless scrambles or reconnaissance patrols over the Soissons sector.

It was during one of these latter patrols near Aizy on 23rd May, that Flight Sergeant Jammy Payne's Hurricane was completely overturned by the concussion of intense German anti-aircraft fire; it was later estimated that at least 150 rounds had been fired at him. On 25th May, the Squadron took off to patrol the Hesdin area with orders to provide an escort for RAF bombers attacking enemy troop movements. Arriving over the Abbeville, the Hurricanes came under a sustained and accurate barrage of enemy fire which claimed Pilot Officer Sylvester, who was last seen diving away with glycol streaming from his engine. Although originally reported as missing, he was able to return to the squadron on foot the following day; his Hurricane so badly damaged by the return fire from a Do17 and flak that his survival was considered little short of a miracle.

No.501Squadron's forward operating airfield at Boos was close to the important industrial town: a centre for road and rail communications for French and British military operations. On 27th May, while operating from Boos, the unit was able to inflict a severe blow to the Luftwaffe when, led by Flight Lieutenant Gus Holden, thirteen squadron Hurricanes on patrol over the Blangy/Albancourt area spotted an unescorted formation of 12 He111 bombers.

No.501Squadron's pilots were ordered into echelon formation and singled out their targets. The Squadron Operational Book sums up the attack: Sylvester fired all his ammunition into a Heinkel which was seen to be falling by Farnes who was able to fire further rounds into it. In addition, Lacey and McKay saw two other Heinkels going down with their undercarriage down and trailing smoke. Hewitt also saw another falling away after firing at it. Our own machines suffered hardly any damage in the encounter, all pilots returning safely. During the attack the Heinkels had taken no evasive action or offered return fire, and as the squadron pilots flew away they noted the French countryside littered with the smoke of twelve burning aircraft. Many were later to recall that the bombers were probably on a training flight, with pilots of limited experience and without the protection of rear gunners.

Claims were submitted by all the pilots taking part in the action, with Flying Officer Cam Malfroy and Sergeant Ginger Lacey shooting down two apiece, and with Pilot Officer John Gibson and Sergeant Bob Dafforn sharing another and Sgt Paul Farnes claiming a possible.

This had been the first combat patrol for Pilot Officer Duncan Hewitt and Sergeant Lewis, who had joined the squadron a few days previously with Pilot Officer John Gibson. Three days later, Pilot Officer Gibson was able to repeat his success of the 27th May when he shot down a He111 and damaged another near Rouen. Replacement aircraft were delivered very quickly and were readied for operational service at such a rate that they were often flown with the squadron code letters simply chalked on the fuselage until time and opportunity allowed for the usual painting.

Pilots, on the other hand, were not as easy to replace and on 3rd June, Pilot Officer Peter Hairs was fortunate to escape serious injury when his Hurricane was badly damaged by cannon fire from an attack by a Bf109. Bellylanding his aircraft in a field at St Leger aux Bois, near Soissons, he was detained by a French soldier until "liberated" by British soldiers and eventually returned to the squadron. Two days later, Pilot Officer Claydon was shot down and killed near Le Mans, while on 8th June Pilot Officer Dickie Hulse was also killed in action while the squadron was operating from Boos.

At tea-time, on Sunday, 2nd June, 501 was ordered to move once more and by 03.30 hrs the following mor-

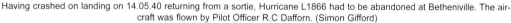

Having crashed on landing on 14.05.40 returning from a sortie, Hurricane L1866 had to be abandoned at Betheniville. The aircraft was flown by Pilot Officer R.C Dafforn. (Simon Gifford)

Within two weeks, it became clear to many that the Battle of France was already lost. Most of the British Expedionary Force (BEF) was evacuated to the United Kingdom from Dunkirk at the end of May, and the AASF was living its last days in France. So did the No.501 Squadron seen retreating on the French roads in June 1940. (501 Squadron Association)

ning was packed and on the road to Le Mans. The squadron spent its first night in the pits of the Grand Prix Course but the next day it was moved into the nearby woods because of its vulnerability from air attack. From the airfield at Le Mans, No.501 Squadron continued its dawn-to-dusk patrols, together with the occasional close escort missions to Allied bombers attacking enemy troop concentrations, railway lines, roads and bridges.

By 4th June, 1940, the evacuation of British and French troops from the beaches of Dunkirk was complete. The squadron had been able to cover the operation by flying countless defensive patrols and was now exhausted. Two more victories claimed by Pilot Officer John Gibson of a Bf109 near Abbeville on 8th June, together with another at Le Havre, two days later, brought the squadron tally to 51 enemy aircraft destroyed for the loss of 18 Hurricanes and eight pilots.

Fighting a continued rearguard action from small French airfields found the squadron operating under the most primitive of conditions, and by 15th June it was flying from a field at Dinard near the English Channel. On 17th June, 1940, Marshal Petain approached Germany for honourable peace terms: this was the signal to the British for the complete evacuation of its forces from France.

Air Vice Marshal Barrett, Commander of the AASF, immediately ordered Nos.17 and 501 Squadrons to Dinard to protect St Malo and Cherbourg, where they found a handful of French Potez fighters managing a defiant but desperate action against the Luftwaffe. The following day, No.501Squadron's ground crews moved to St Malo, where they sailed for the Channel Islands to join the squadron's Hurricanes at Jersey. At 09.00 hrs on 20th June 1940, the squadron finally arrived at Southampton Docks and proceeded to Yatesbury; the air party left St Helier the same day, arriving at Tangmere at 21.00 hrs.

THE BATTLE OF BRITAIN - THE OPEN PHASE

On 21st June, 1940, the squadron moved to the pre-war civil aerodrome at Croydon to re-organise itself and replace its equipment. New pilots were posted in, together with a new CO, Squadron Leader Harry Hogan, who appointed Flight Lieutenants George Stoney and "Pan" Cox as his Flight Commanders.

By the beginning of July the squadron was declared as operational and moved to Middle Wallop, near Andover, on 4th July, where it was immediately placed on Night Readiness in anticipation of an all-out attack by the Luftwaffe; a minor air raid on its first night strengthened the belief that it would be imminent.It is generally accepted that the Battle of Britain is divided into five major phases. The first phase, from 10th July to 7th August 1940 involved concentrated attacks on the Channel ports and convoys as a show of force by Goering's Luftwaffe.

Despite a low cloudbase on 11th July, three aircraft of

Green Section were scrambled to intercept a raid on Portland harbour. An enemy force of at least ten Dornier bombers and twenty escorting Bf109s were encountered, and in the ensuing fight, Sergeant Frederick Dixon was attacked and shot down by a Bf109 of III./JG 27 flown by *Oberleutnant* Franziket, ten miles off Portland Bill. Although he was seen to bale out, a search by the Weymouth lifeboat failed to find Dixon and he was presumed to have drowned. During the engagement, Pilot Officer Duncan Hewitt was also reported to have shot down a "Hurricane with Luftwaffe markings".

The following afternoon, No.501 Squadron flew down to Warmwell, where it was to operate for the first time as part of No.11 Group's decision to deploy a whole squadron to a forward operating base. At 15.15 hrs, Squadron Leader Hogan led the unit to counter another shipping attack by Dornier bombers off Portland. Despite atrocious weather conditions, Flight Lieutenant Holden and Pilot Officer Hewitt pursued a reconnaissance Do17 into cloud, which was claimed as damaged by Holden. During this action, Pilot Officer Duncan Hewitt was seen to crash in the Channel. His body was not recovered. The squadron continued to operate from Warmwell, and on the morning of 20th July it was scrambled to intercept a large raid on the convoy "Bosom" in Lyme Bay. A force of Ju87s and Bf109s was engaged near Portland Bill, resulting in two enemy fighters being shot down by Squadron Leader Holden and Sergeant Lacey, with a further half-kill going to Flight Lieutenant "Pan" Cox.

Unfortunately, one of the squadron veterans, Pilot Officer Sylvester was killed after being attacked and shot down near Cherbourg by a Bf109 flown by *Leutnant* Zirkenbach of I./JG 27.

On 25th July, the squadron moved to Gravesend on the south bank of the River Thames, opposite Tilbury Docks, to become part of the Biggin Hill Sector of No.11 Group. The following day it flew down to its forward operating base at Hawkinge, near Folkestone, and was scrambled at 17.20 hrs to intercept an enemy formation over Dover harbour. After attacking and damaging a Bf109, Flight Lieutenant "Pan" Cox baled out over the sea and was reported as missing, although a post-war Luftwaffe combat report officially credits him to *Feldwebel* Fernsebner of III./JG 52, it was generally believed at the time that Cox was shot down by the Anti-Aircraft defences at Dover.

An early morning attack on Dover harbour on 29th July by a large force of Ju87s, escorted by an equally large number of Bf109s, found the squadron being scrambled at 07.20 hrs to assist the Spitfires of No.41 Squadron from Manston. Six enemy aircraft were shot down by the squadron, together with a further six claimed as damaged, including two Ju87s by Flight Lieutenant "Johnny" Gibson, a Ju87 by Flight Lieutenant George Stoney, and a Bf109 by Ronnie Morfill. Pilot Officer "Hawkeye" Lee and Sergeant Don McKay also claimed a Ju87 apiece as damaged, with Pilot Officer Leonard Duckenfield sharing a further dive bomber.

On the last day of July 1940, Flight Lieutenant

In the beginning of June, the situation in France was no more under control, the total collapse of France approaching very fast. No.501 Squadron was caught in the middle, retreating with a flow of refugees, like on the military field of Le Mans in June 1940. (501 Squadron Association)

FIGHTER COMMAND

After experiencing Zeppelin and bomber attacks during the First World War, Britain was well aware that they were vulnerable from the air and the German re-armament programme of the thirties did nothing but further increase this fear. Despite an expansion programme process Fighter Command could only boast 25 regular squadrons, two from the Special Reserve and 12 Auxiliary squadrons when war was declared in September 1939. Not only was this number well short of the 57 squadrons deemed necessary for the Air Defence of Great Britain but, of the existing 39, not all were fully operational.

During the first year of the war Fighter Command was expanded and at the successful conclusion of the Battle of Britain, which would be it's greatest achievement, had almost 70 squadrons on its Order of Battle. When the planning for the Invasion of Europe commenced squadrons were divided into defensive and offensive roles and Fighter Command disappeared on 15th November 1943. It was superseded by Air Defence of Great Britain (ADGB), which was responsible for the defence of the British Isles, and the 2nd Tactical Air Force, which was in charge of the offensive actions.

At the time of the restructuring Fighter Command had approximately 100 squadrons under its umbrella but this was reduced by a third with the inception of the 2nd TAF, which would become the RAF's spear-head for the Invasion. In October 1944 when the advance of Allied troops appeared irreversible, and the Luftwaffe's effort was concentrated mainly on the Eastern front, ADGB re-adopted its original name of Fighter Command. However its needs had become largely obsolete and at the German surrender barely 40 squadrons remained under its control.

From its inception Fighter Command was organised into Groups, with geographical boundaries, which would vary in accordance with the changing circumstances of the time. Originally just three Groups, No's 11, 12 and 13 were responsible for the defence of the whole of British Isles, but resources were too thinly spread and by the end of 1940, another three had been re-activated.

Chronologically the Groups were:

<u>No.11 Group</u>: Reformed at Uxbridge on 1st May 1936, it fell under the control of Fighter Command on 14th July. This Group was responsible for the South and, later, the Southeast region of England, which included London. During the Battle of Britain it was situated closest to the enemy and controlled the largest number of squadrons. It went onto the offensive when Fighter Command began attacks across the English Channel in 1941.

<u>No.12 Group</u>: Reformed at Hucknall on 1st April 1937 and was immediately placed under Fighter Command control to defend the central area of England. This included protecting the region located immediately north of No.11 Group, and the Midland industrial area, including the east and west parts south of the Humber.

<u>No.13 Group</u>: Reformed at Newcastle on 15th March 1939 and immediately placed under the control of Fighter Command to ease the pressure on No.12 Group. Its zone initially comprised industrial areas north of the Humber and southern Scotland.

<u>No.10 Group</u>: Reformed at Rudlow Manor on 1st June 1940 primarily to cover the Southwest of England and protect shipping in the western half of the channel. It was absorbed into No.11 Group on 2nd May 1945.

<u>No.14 Group</u>: Reformed at Inverness on 29th June 1940 to protect Scotland. It was absorbed into No.13 Group on 15th July 1943.

<u>No.9 Group</u>: Reformed at Preston on 9th August 1940 to protect the north-west of England and Northern Ireland. It was absorbed into No.12 Group on 15th September 1944.

SERIALS OF HURRICANE I IN USE ON 7ᵀᴴ JULY 1940.

L : 2038

N : 2495

P : 2549, 2691, 2760, 2986, 3040, 3041, 3082, 3083, 3084, 3349, 3397, 3646, 3803, 3808

Total : 16

Gibson was in action again when he damaged a Do17 bomber during a short scrap near Hawkinge. Returning to Gravesend later that evening, Pilot Officers Ralph Don and Gordon Parkin were both seriously injured in flying accidents; Don was forced to bale out of his Hurricane when the engine caught fire and crashed on Lydden Marshes, while Parkin undershot the approach to Gravesend in poor visibility and crash-landed.

The first week of August brought a slight lull in the fighting, although the squadron managed to lose two aircraft when Sergeants Howarth and Wilkinson collided in poor visibilty whilst landing at Gravesend; both pilots being fortunate to escape serious injury.

The brief respite enabled No.501 Squadron to re-establish its pilot strength with the arrival of the first Polish aircrew, Flying Officers Stefan Witorzenc and Kazimierz Lukaszewicz, and Pilots Officers Pawal Zenker and Franciszek Kozlowski, all of whom had recently been absorbed into the RAF following the invasion of their country.

THE REAL BATTLE BEGINS

Phase Two of the Battle of Britain began on 8ᵗʰ August and involved the Luftwaffe's all-out attack on coastal aerodromes and radar stations with the aim of weakening Britain's defences. The heaviest of the fighting, however, was away from Gravesend and it was not until the 12ᵗʰ August that No.501 Squadron was back in action when a force of between thirty and forty Ju87s and Bf109s were intercepted at 4,000 feet whilst attacking a destroyer in the Thames Estuary between Deal and Ramsgate.

Several enemy aircraft were destroyed in the savage fight that ensued, including three Ju87s by Sergeant Anton Glowacki, who also claimed a further enemy aircraft as damaged. Sergeant Ginger Lacey also submitted claims for a Ju87 as shot down and damage to another. Newcomer, Flying Officer Lukaszewicz was lost when he was bounced by a Bf109 and crashed into the sea west of Ramsgate. During the afternoon a Bf110 was shot down by Sergeant Lacey near Ramsgate, with Flight Lieutenant "Johnny" Gibson claiming a Ju87 during further fighting in the evening whilst the squadron was operating from Gravesend.

On 15ᵗʰ August, the bitterest fighting of the whole Battle was encountered when *Reichmarschall* Goering committed his *Luftflotten* to its greatest effort so far, with airfields as the main targets.

At 11.00 hrs, a large force of Ju87s of IV(St)./LG 1, with an escort of Bf109s from JG 26 was picked up on radar, destined for Hawkinge. No.501 Squadron Hurricanes were late being scrambled but, together with the Spitfires of No.54 Squadron, were able to intercept the raiders over Folkestone. The formation was broken up and No.501 Squadron was credited with at least fourteen aircraft as either destroyed or damaged. Flight Lieutenant Johnny Gibson shot down a Ju87 and damaged another before his Hurricane was severely mauled by cannon fire from a Bf109. Struggling with the controls of his aircraft, Gibson slipped out of his brand-new shoes and threw them out of the cockpit before descending to a thousand feet and joining them. An immediate DFC and the return of his shoes completed his day. Flight Lieutenant Putt was also shot down during this engagement but was able to bale out and land in the sea, unharmed.

Airborne again at 15.00 hrs to join battle with waves of upwards of 100 raiders over Deal and Folkestone, No.501 Squadron had just returned to base when it was immediately ordered back into action. Already low on fuel, the Hurricanes pounced on a formation of at least 70 aircraft. Forced to split up, the enemy bombers missed their primary targets of Biggin Hill and Kenley, attacking instead West Malling where they inflicted heavy damage to the runways and buildings. Following an eight-second burst, Sergeant Paul Farnes shot down a Ju87 of 10./LG 1, which crashed at Folkestone. Further Ju87s were claimed when Sergeant Don McKay crippled a machine which then flew through HT cables and ploughed into a row of houses at Shorncliffe Crescent, Folkestone. Flying Officer Witorzenc sent another Ju87 into the Channel near the lightship at Folkestone Gate, killing one crew

Pilots of B Flight, No.501 Squadron at Hawkinge, August 1940, left to right :
Standing, F/O S. Witorzenc (Polish), F/L G.E.B. Stoney, P/O F. Kozlowski (Polish). Sitting, F/O R.C. Dafforn, Sgt P.C.P. Farnes
P/O K.N.T. Lee, J.A.A. Gibson (NZ) and Sgt H.C. Adams. (501 Sqn Association)

member and injuring the other after a short burst of fire following a chase at sea-level.

With a further eight claims by the squadron, including a Dornier Do215 near Tunbridge Wells by Pilot Officer Duckenfield to add to his claim earlier in the day of another Dornier near Detling as a probable, the German losses for the day were far heavier than anticipated and altered the whole course of the Battle.

At tea-time the following day, No.501 Squadron was ordered up to intercept a raid by Dorniers and Bf110s with fighter escort that was building up in the Dungeness/Hastings area. During the sharp engagement that followed three Do17s were damaged, one by Sqn Ldr Hogan who attacked the rearmost, outside aircraft of the formation from beneath with a short burst of fire.

The 18th August was a miserable day for No.501 Squadron. At lunch-time, nine Hurricanes were returning to Gravesend in a tight formation when, at 17,000 feet over Canterbury, they were bounced by Bf109s of Gerhard Schöpfel's III/JG.26, based near Calais. Recently promoted to succeed Major Adolph Galland, Schöpfel fell on the two weavers, Pilot Officers Kozlowski and Bland. Bland was killed instantly when his Hurricane plunged into the ground at Calcott Hill, Sturry. Kozlowski was seriously injured but managed to bale out before his aircraft crashed on Raynham's Farm, near Whitstable.

Schöpfel then turned on Sergeant McKay, whom he shot down in flames over Dargate, forcing the pilot to bale out, slightly injured, before pouring a burst of fire into Pilot Officer "Hawkeye" Lee's Hurricane. Wounded in the leg, Lee was fortunate that debris and oil from his damaged aircraft had obliterated Schöpfel's windscreen, forcing him to break off his attack and enable Lee to safely abandon his aircraft over Whitchurch.

The ease of which Schöpfel had managed to shoot down four Hurricanes in as many minutes during his surprise attack was quickly blamed on the strict formations that Fighter Command had ordered them to fly and, although squadron claims also included a Bf109 by Sergeant Glowacki and a Do17 by Sergeant Farnes, the tragic event over Canterbury that morning had shocked everyone on No.501 Squadron.

Biggin Hill was heavily bombed at lunch-time on the 18th by waves of Do17s and Ju88s, inflicting considerable damage and loss of life. No.501 Squadron had just returned to Gravesend and was immediately ordered up again with only seven serviceable Hurricanes to intercept a force of almost 60 bombers with an escort of Bf110s crossing the Kent coast. Although two enemy fighters were quickly shot down by Flying

Officer Witorzenc and Pilot Officer Zenker, Flight Lieutenant Stoney was singled out by a Bf109 and shot down over Stile Farm, Chilham; he died later of his injuries. Pilot Officer Bob Dafforn was slightly more fortunate when his Hurricane was badly damaged over Biggin Hill and he was forced to bale out; his aircraft crashing at Cronk's Farm, East Seal. The day's losses included six Hurricanes, two pilots killed and a further three in hospital with serious injuries. Low cloud on the 19th August gave Fighter Command a chance to lick its wounds and prepare for the next and critical phase.

THE CRITICAL WEEKS

Phase Three of the Battle - the attack on Fighter Stations and aircraft factories began on 24th August, during which Red Section intercepted a force of 30 Dornier bombers with fighter escort four miles north-west of Dover. The enemy formation was broken up, forcing the bombers to jettison their loads before retreating. Although one Bf109 was destroyed and a Do215 was seriously damaged during the fight, Pilot Officer Zenker was jumped by a Bf109 over Dover and last seen heading towards the French coast with his Hurricane in obvious difficulties.

Heavy fighting later in the afternoon brought the Polish pilots back into the action when Sergeant Glowacki and the rest of his section pounced on a formation of enemy bombers which had just carried out a devastating attack on Manston. Glowacki tore into the Ju88s and shot down two in quick succession, plus one of the escorting Bf109s. A few hours later he notched up his fifth kill of the day when he downed a Bf109 near Graystone. Pilot Officer Aldridge was forced to bale out near Ryarsh after attacking a Ju 88 when his Hurricane was badly damaged by A-A fire. He came down close to the hop fields at Pells Farm, West Kingsdown, suffering a broken shoulder and arm in the process.

Sergeant Bill Green was also hit by A-A fire during a raid on Manston, suffering considerable damage to his Hurricane. Gliding into Hawkinge with half of his undercarriage shot away, the aircraft's nose dug into the ground on landing and left Green to clamber down from his first "write-off".

Five days later, on 29th August, Sergeant Green was scrambled along with his section at 18.00 hrs to maintain a standing patrol over Dover. Circling at 20,000 feet, Green was bounced by a Bf109, which shattered his bullet-proof windscreen with a burst of fire and sent the Hurricane out of control. At 16,000 feet he baled out and found to his horror that the parachute cords had been damaged by cannon splinters. Falling helplessly, at 500 feet a sudden gust of wind opened the parachute folds and he gently drifted into a field at Elham Valley. Shocked and slightly injured, Green was later taken to hospital.

Flight Lieutenant Gibson was also shot down during the same action as Green and was fortunate to suc-

At the height of the Battle of Britain, two Hurricanes of No.501 Squadron are taking off from Hawkinge on 15.08.40, most probably flown by P/O K.N.T. Lee (P3059/SD-N) and P/O R.C. Dafforn (P3208/SD-T). That day, the Squadron shot down two Ju87s near Folkestone. Both aircraft were shot down three days later by *Obertleutnant* G. Schöpfel of JG26. (501 Sqn Association)

Gravesend, August 1940, left to right :
Sgt T.G. Pickering, Sgt R.J. Gent, F/Sgt P.F. Morfill, Sgt P.C. Farnes, Sgt A. Glowacki (Polish), Sgt H.C.Adams, Sgt A.H. Whitehouse, Sgt L.H. Lacey, Sgt R.C. Dafforn. (501 Squadron Association)

cessfully bale out over Ottinge before his Hurricane plunged into the ground at Acrise. The day's fighting on the 29th ended with two He111s shot down by No.501 Squadron, with a further two Bf110s as damaged. A Bf109 of 3./JG 3 was also claimed by Sergeant Lacey during a hectic scrap near Hawkinge aerodrome, which had burst into flames and crashed into the sea killing its pilot.

On 30th August, Pilot Officer Stanislaw Skalski, one of the squadron's replacement pilots, claimed his first kill with No.501 Squadron when he shot down a He111 near Dungeness and damaged another near Southend. Although he was shot down and injured during the action over Herne Bay on 5th September, between these dates Skalski also managed to claim three Bf109s, with another Bf110 as damaged. Later in the war he would lead the Polish Fighting Team - "Skalski's Circus" - in North Africa and become Poland's top-scoring fighter pilot, with 21 kills to his credit.

The last day of August found seven Hurricanes taking-off at 12.59 hrs and engaging an enemy fighter escort over Gravesend. At least two Bf109s were shot down in exchange for Sergeant Anton Glowacki, who was forced to bale out after being injured by a Bf109. His aircraft crashing on Gravesend aerodrome.

Biggin Hill had been repeatedly bombed by the Luftwaffe during the last days of August and early September. To defend its neighbour against these attacks the squadron had been constantly in action, but on 2nd September, 1940 the squadron found itself defending Gravesend, which was itself attacked.

Although the morning's bombing had been slight, with two soldiers injured, the airfield was scarred with bomb craters which made operations difficult.

The day's fighting had been fierce, however, with two Bf109s apiece by Sergeant Lacey and Pilot Officer Skalski near Ashford, and a further four enemy aircraft claimed as damaged. No.501Squadron's losses included Pilot Officer Rose-Price who was shot down and killed near Ashford during his first operational sortie. Sergeant Adams was also shot down near Ashford, fortunately without injury, while Pilot Officer Skalski was slightly injured in a forced-landing near Gravesend.

On the last day of Phase Three, 6th September, 1940, the squadron engaged a 100-strong formation over Rye, with Sergeants Adams, Houghton and Pearson exchanging their lives for a solitary Bf109 of 5./JG 27 near Ashford by Flight Lieutenant Gibson. The eleven squadron Hurricanes had left for an early morning patrol over Dungeness and in the confusion of the ensuing fight, No.501 Squadron split up and was bounced by the fighter escort over Westwell. While Red Leader was able to shoot down one of the attackers, Sergeant Hugh Adams was forced to bale out near Elham and was killed when his parachute failed to open. A few minutes later, Sergeant Oliver Houghton was shot down by a Bf109 and killed when his aircraft crashed at Long Beech Wood, Charing.

Newcomer, Sergeant Geoffrey Pearson found himself separated from the rest of his Section and was attacked and shot down by enemy fighters. He crashed at

Hawker Hurricane Mk.I P3208, No.501 (County of Gloucester) Squadron, Pilot Officer R.C. Dafforn, Hawkinge, August 1940.

Cowleas Farm, Hothfield, and was buried, four days later, with a unmarked headstone; it would be another forty-two years before his body would be finally identified and a proper headstone erected.

Two days later, twelve of No.501 Squadron's Hurricanes were airborne after lunch and vectored to Hawkinge in order to patrol the coastline. As the squadron neared the coast, Green Section, which was acting as the rearguard, was bounced a single Bf109. Diving into cloud to avoid the enemy fighter, Pilot Officer Duckenfield spotted the attacker in front of him and, with two short bursts, sent it crashing into the sea off Folkestone.

NEW GERMAN STRATEGY

As the timetable for the German invasion of England began to slip because of the resistance of the RAF during August, an attack on the Capital city seemed the next logical step. So, at the beginning of September, Goering switched to all-out daylight attacks on London by his bombers in the belief that Britain would be weakened, as had earlier been the case with Warsaw and Rotterdam.

To counteract this threat, the RAF quickly moved its fighter squadrons to aerodromes where they could readily defend the Capital. At mid-day on 10th September, the unit moved to Kenley, thirteen miles from the Luftwaffe's chief target.

The following day, eleven Hurricanes took off 15.20 hrs to patrol Maidstone in company with No.253 Squadron, No.501 Squadron's neighbours at Kenley. Intercepting a large force of He111s and Do17s, the Hurricanes attacked the enemy formation head-on and were met by return fire from the bombers. The engine sump of Sergeant Pickering's aircraft was immediately shot away and he was forced to bale out and come down into the Guard's Barracks at Caterham; his aircraft crashing into Happy Valley, Old Coulsdon.

Although a Bf109 was shot down during the action, together with a Do17 shared by Witorzenc and Morfill, a report in the Squadron ORB claims that one pilot damaged "three He113s" (He would later confirm, however, that he was mistaken and that his "claims" were Bf 109s!)

Fresh back from leave on 13th September, Sergeant "Ginger" Lacey volunteered for a patrol to search for a lone enemy raider that had bombed London and was returning to base above the protection of a heavy layer of cloud. At 14,000 feet, under the guidance of the Ground Controller, Lacey spotted the He111P of III./KG 27 and dived after it, firing a quick burst whe-

never the opportunity presented itself. At last his determination paid off and the Heinkel spiralled into the cloud and crashed near the Kent coast, killing all four crew members.

However, a parting burst of machine-gun fire from the bomber's rear gunner had punctured the oil tank of Lacey's Hurricane, forcing him to bale out near Leeds Castle with slight burns. Returning to Kenley, he was informed by excited colleagues that his victim had earlier bombed Buckingham Palace and later in the month he was awarded a BAR to the DFM he had received in August. A few months later, Lacey received the personal congratulations of HM the Queen for his fearless action and determination.

Sunday, 15th September 1940, now recognized as the climax of the German assault on Great Britain was an extremely busy day for units of both the Luftwaffe and the hard-pressed RAF. The heaviest raids stretched the squadrons of RAF Fighter Command to the limit, with No.11 Group - whose responsibility was the defence of south-east England and therefore bore the brunt of the Luftwaffe's air attacks - committing its entire resources.

The first attack was met by Nos.501 and 253 Squadrons over Maidstone just before lunch. A formation of 20 Do17s was intercepted and a fierce battle developed when the Hurricanes were in turn set upon by the fighter escort. Pilot Officer Van den Hove, a Belgian pilot who had transferred from No.43 Squadron the previous day, was hit in the cooling system by a Bf109 over Ashford. Wrestling with the controls of his damaged Hurricane, Van den Hove was killed when it exploded and crashed into the River Stour. Squadron Leader Hogan's Hurricane was also shot in the radiator but was able to make a successful emergency landing at Sundridge. Squadron claims amounted to three enemy aircraft shot down, one damaged and one probable.

At 14.00 hrs, with 30 RAF fighter squadrons airborne, a running fight ensued in the skies over south-east England. No.501 Squadron, together with No.605 Squadron from Croydon, intercepted a large force of Do17s and He111s, with fighter escort, at 5,000 feet over Heathfield. The enemy fighters were attacked by No.501 Squadron's Hurricanes which shot down two in the resultant melee without loss to themselves.

A third Luftwaffe attack developed at 17.00 hrs, followed by the final offensive of the day an hour later during which Sgt Lacey was able to shoot down a He111 and Bf109 before running out of ammunition. The day's fighting had seen 58 German aircraft shot down by the RAF for the loss of 26 of its own figh-

Pilots of the Squadron, probably at Colerne, October 1940.
Back row, left to right : F/Sgt P.F. Morfill, P/O S.A.H. Whitehouse, Sgt T.G. Pickering, Sgt V. Ekins, Sgt G.G. Laws.
Middle row, left to right : Sgt H.C. Grove, W.B. Holroyd, Sgt P. O'Byrne, Sgt P.C.P. Farnes, P/O E.G. Parkin, S/L H.A.V. Hogan,
F/L E. Holden, P/O R.C. Dafforn, P/O K.N.T. Lee, F/L D.A.E. Jones, P/O V.R. Snell, P/O S. Witorzenc (Polish), R.S. Don.
Front row, let to right : Sgt K. Muchowski (Polish), Sgt M. Marcinkowski (Polish), Sgt R.H. Lonsdale, P/O S. Skalski (Polish), P/O
K.W. Mackenzie, Sgt J.H. Lacey. (W/C K.W. Mackenzie)

ters. No.501 Squadron had claimed six of the enemy machines but in return had lost two Hurricanes and one pilot. At last the balance was swinging in favour of the RAF; the Luftwaffe daylight bombing offensive was drawing to a close.

High winds and cloud on 16th September brought a brief respite for RAF Fighter Command and a chance for the German High Command to rethink its invasion plans. In order to lessen their mounting losses the Luftwaffe bomber formations would have to be reduced in size - Operation *Sealion* would have to be postponed indefinitely.

The following day a section of No.501 Squadron, accompanied by another section of Hurricanes from No.253 Squadron, was attacked by 20 Bf109s over Ashford. Squadron Leader Hogan was successful in hitting one of the attackers in its radiator but it made off before further damage could be observed. However, the fighters of JG 53 inflicted a heavy toll on the squadron: Sergeant Lacey's aircraft was hit and he was forced to bale out near Ashford, while Pilot Officer Hairs suffered damage to the starboard wing from a cannon shell.

Sergeant Edward Egan was not so fortunate; posted in from No.615 Squadron in early September, he was on his third patrol of the day when, at 15.00 hrs he was mortally wounded by the fire from a Bf109 and plunged into Daniel's Wood, near Bethersden. His body and the wreckage of the Hurricane would lay undiscovered for another 37 years!

A fairly hectic day on 18th September saw Pilot Officer Hairs claiming a probable Bf109 whilst on patrol between Canterbury and Tonbridge. Chasing it out to sea, he was able to put a short burst into it and observe glycol streaming from the engine before losing it. Sergeant Cyril Saward was shot down in this action over Tonbridge when he chased a Bf109 at 24,000 feet and was attacked by another enemy fighter; after a terrific explosion, the propellor flew off and Saward baled out of his uncontrollable Hurricane and came down near Staplehurst.

In the afternoon, Red Section, led by Squadron Leader Hogan, intercepted a formation of 20 He111s with fighter escort over West Malling. The unit was bounced by the Bf109s and Squadron Leader Hogan felt the impact of bullets striking the underside of his aircraft. With oil and gycol streaming from the engine of his Hurricane, he decided to return to Kenley but was forced to bale out when the engine eventually siezed over Charing. He returned to the squadron none the worse for wear except for a black eye, gained from a confrontation with a Bramley apple!

A noticeable lull in Luftwaffe raids enabled the squadron to re-establish its pilot strength, and it was not until 27th September that No.501 Squadron was back in action when it intercepted a raid by He111s over Kent. Latching on to one of the bombers, Squadron Leader Hogan was immediately attacked by one of the Bf110 escort fighters. He was able to silence the fighter's rear gunner after a few bursts of fire and was closing in for the kill when another Hurricane flew in between them. Badly damaged, the Bf110 crashed into the garden of a house in the Sydenham/Bromley area and Squadron Leader Hogan could only submit a half-kill for the action. On his first operational flight with the squadron, Sergeant Vic Ekins was injured by cannon splinters and was forced to abandon his aircraft over Godstone and admitted to hospital.

Later in the morning, Sergeant Lacey was able to notch up his twentieth kill when he singled out a Bf109 of 6./JG 27 at 7,000 feet over Maidstone. Following a two-second burst, the enemy fighter went into a vertical dive which ripped off its wing, before exploding and falling in bits over Eccles near Aylesford. Pilot Officer Gunter was also lost when his Hurricane was badly damaged and he fell to his death when the parachute failed to open.

On the 28th, squadron new-comer, Pilot Officer Harrold was also killed after his section was mauled by Bf109s near Deal; his aircraft crashed close to College House, Ulcombe. Pilot Officer Rogers was forced to make a hurried exit from his stricken Hurricane before it crashed into the ground at East Sutton, while Pilot Officer Jones had to make an emergency landing at Kenley after his aircraft was badly shot up. There were no claims submitted by the squadron.

LAC Ben Green of Station Flight Hawkinge examines Hurricane V6799/SD-X, Pilot Officer K.W. Mackenzie crash-landed on 0710.40. That day, he attacked a Bf109 and after having damaged its glycol tank, forced it into the sea by ramming its tail with his wing tip. (501 Squadron Association)

Whilst returning from a patrol because of hood trouble on 30th September, Sergeant Paul Farnes encountered light A-A fire near Gatwick. Believing that the fire was directed at him, he saw a enemy twin-engined bomber at the same height, which was damaged and struggling to return to base. Closing for the kill, Farnes poured a quick burst of fire into the bomber which sent the Ju 88 into a steep dive and crash into the ground near the racecourse, killing one of the crew of four.

Earlier the same afternoon, Flight Lieutenant Gus Holden was able to damage a Bf109 of 4./JG 52 during a 35-minute patrol over the Thames Estuary. The German fighter eventually crashed and was written off when it overshot an attempted forced landing at Detling.

THE FINAL PHASE

The fourth phase of the Battle had come to an end without the air superiority that Goering had so badly wanted. So, on 1st October, 1940, in a fifth and final phase, he turned to "around-the-clock" bombing of London and the night bombing of other important industrial cities and towns. With the onslaught virtually over and the easing of pressure on the fighter squadrons, the unit could relax and evaluate September's critical fighting. Over 600 hours had been flown in combat, during which 22 Hurricanes had been lost with eleven pilots, either killed or wounded. A squadron record for an operational scramble of 55 1/2 seconds had been achieved and, although the crews were exhausted, morale on the unit remained high.

Flying Officer Jones and Sergeant Lacey were airborne on the afternoon of 4th October; the weather was bad with thick cloud covering most of the country, which made operational patrols to counter the enemy "sneak" raids difficult. However, the two pilots were able to glimpse a retreating Do215 in the gaps of the low cloud, which they pursued without success. Realising that their fuel state was now critical and that the visibility was not going to improve, the pilots resigned themselves to a forced-landing; Jones was fortunate to put down in a field near Cuckfield, whilst Lacey also escaped injury when he made an emergency landing at Hassocks, near Brighton.

Red Section was active on 5th October when ten Bf109s were engaged during a fighter-bomber sweep over Ashford railway workshops. Squadron Leader Hogan promptly shot down one, an action that earned the CO a DFC, while Flight Lieutnant Holden claimed another which crashed in flames. A further Bf109 was destroyed by Pilot Officer Mackenzie when it spun into the sea off Margate.

The morning of 7th October had started badly with loss of Flying Officer Nate Barry during a combat with Bf109s over Wrotham. A former Aide de Camp to AVM de Crespigny, Barry found the action he desperately wanted, only to fall at Wilmington, victim to a Bf109 of 2/JG.51.

The second scramble of the day at 12.50 hrs found Pilot Officer Mackenzie and his section chasing Bf109s over Ashford following a Jabo (fighter bomber) attack against London Docks. Intercepting them at 19,000 feet, Squadron Leader Hogan sent one of the fighters diving into cloud for safety after a quick burst of fire. Mackenzie went after the fighter as he emerged from cloud and, after a three-second burst at 150 yards, sent the Bf 109 of 2/JG.51 into the sea off Dymchurch, Hythe.

Returning to the fight, Pilot Officer Mackenzie climbed to 26,000 feet and spotted eight Bf 109s slightly above him, attacking the rearmost fighter with an accurate burst of fire, forcing it break away and turn towards the coast. Losing height and speed rapidly, Mackenzie caught up with the damaged fighter at 8,000 feet over Folkestone harbour. Now down to sea-level, Mackenzie lined up for the the *coup de grace* only to find that he was out of ammunition. Determined that the enemy fighter should not escape he positioned his Hurricane on the Bf109's port side with his starboard wing over the tailplane. Applying starboard aileron, Mackenzie slammed his wing tip on the fighter's port tailplane, which snapped off and sent the 109 into the sea.

This violent and unorthodox manoeuvre immediately severed the Hurricane's wingtip. Fortunately for Mackenzie it was clean break which still allowed him some aileron control and, although pursued by two more Bf 109s which poured machine-gun fire into his radiator and armour plate, he managed to clear the cliffs at Dover and bellyland near Fokestone. The force of the impact threw Pilot Officer Mackenzie against the gun-sight which cut through his lower lip and knocked out four of his teeth. This daring feat, plus "five in one week", earned him a DFC.

On 12th October, Squadron Leader Hogan, Flight Lieutenant Holden and Sergeant Lacey each shot down a Bf109 during a short scrap near the Kent coast, with Pilot Officer Mackenzie sharing in the destruction of an enemy bomber which later crashed in the English Channel.

Five days later, Kenley felt the impact of the Luftwaffe's night offensive when a stick of bombs fell on the airfield at about 20.00 hrs, damaging five

Hurricanes. Nuisance raids in the form of Bf109s adapted to carry bombs and attacking targets of opportunity were also not infrequent, and during the last days of October the squadron shot down several of these "hit-and-run" raiders in rapid succession. Three were destroyed on the morning of 25th October when they were intercepted over the Thames Estuary by Blue Section. In the afternoon two more Bf109s were shot down for the loss of four Hurricanes during a confused melee at 28,000 feet over Tenterden. Misjudging his attack on a fighter, Pilot Officer Vilhelm Goth collided with Pilot Officer Mackenzie, who was forced to abandon his Hurricane over Tolehurst. Goth was not so lucky when his aircraft fell into an orchard at Tolehurst. Sergeant Whitehouse also had to abandon his aircraft after being hit by cannon-fire from a Bf109 and was taken to a farm-house near Tonbridge, where he was joined by Pilot Officer Vivian Snell who was also shot down during this action. Both pilots were later returned to the squadron, much to the delight of their colleagues who presumed them to be both dead.

Snell had been shot down whilst attacking a Bf 109 and his intended victim was spotted by Flight Lieutenant Holden and Pilot Officer Mackenzie as it darted between cloud cover. Suspecting that the Bf109 would do an about turn to shake off his attackers, both Hurricanes dived on the fighter as it reappeared, simultaneously firing full deflection shots. Hit in the fuel tank, the Bf109 erupted in a ball of flame and forcing the pilot to abandon the wreckage which fell on farmland near Marden.

Another Bf109 fell to the guns of newly-arrived Czech pilot, Pilot Officer Zaoral, who managed to put a burst of fire into the fighter's radiator and forced it to make an emergency landing at Hunton. Two more enemy fighters were destroyed by Flight Lieutenant Holden and Sergeant Gent during an afternoon skirmish between Cranbrook and Tenterden. The following day, one more enemy fighter was destroyed and another damaged by Sergeant Lacey and Flight Lieutenant Holden, respectively.

A morning scramble to patrol an area from East Grinstead to Maidstone on the 27th soon developed into a major scrap near Redhill after an enemy raid was intercepted and broken up. Pilot Officer Mackenzie bounced a 109 and sent him spiralling out of control near Tonbridge after two short bursts of fire, while Sqn Ldr Hogan was forced to break off his attack because of throttle problems and could only submit a probable claim. On 29th October, Sergeant Farnes claimed a further probable, with Pilot Officer

Mackenzie sending a Bf109 into the ground near Dungeness after a short burst of his guns when it was seen attacking a Spitfire.

To complete the score-sheet, on 30th October Pilot Officer Bob Dafforn and Sergeant Ginger Lacey shot down a Bf 109 of 6./JG 53, which lost a wing and crashed in flames at Meopham, whilst Sergeant Lacey went on to claim his twenty-third and final kill of 1940 when another German fighter was caught in his gun-sights over Folkestone.

In early November, a long-overdue DFC was awarded to Flying Officer "Hawkeye" Lee before he was posted to the Special Duties Flight at Stormy Down. Next to leave the squadron was the recently-promoted Wing Commander Harry Hogan, who was posted to No.58 OTU, as Chief Instructor. The command of the Squadron was passed to Squadron Leader Gus Holden on 6th November who immediately appointed Flight Lieutenants Jones and "Spike" Morello as his Flight Commanders.

The squadron's last days at Kenley were to prove eventful: on 8th November, Sergeant Paul Farnes was separated from his section during a morning patrol and joined up with the Hurricanes of No.605 Squadron. Spotting a formation of Bf109s, Farnes singled out two fighters from the last vic which he attacked with a turning deflection shot. Hitting one of the Bf109s in the cockpit and sending it spiralling downwards, he then exhausted his ammunition on the second fighter which dived away and crashed near Cranbrook.

In an afternoon engagement with 30 Bf109s near Sevenoaks, the squadron destroyed two and damaged another for the loss of Sergeant Grove. Two days later, on 12th November, Red Section (Flight Lieutenant Morello and Pilot Officer Mackenzie) attacked a lone Ju88 at 8,000 feet over Folkestone. Taking turns to rake the enemy bomber with machine-gun fire which succeeded in setting the starboard engine on fire, the two pilots watched as the Ju88 appeared to level out above the sea, stall and slide almost vertically to a watery grave. Pilot Officer Mackenzie claimed another Bf 109 on 15th November, when he attacked it with a long burst of fire over the Thames Estuary. The enemy pilot managed to bale out before the fighter broke up and plunged into the sea.

During its last major engagement in November, the squadron was ordered up in the early afternoon of the 28th to patrol Biggin Hill with the Hurricanes of No.253 Squadron. Attacked from behind by three Bf109s, Sergeant Patterson was singled out by one of the fighters and, despite repeated warnings to take evasive action, was shot down into the sea off Hastings.

During Spring 1941, No.501 Squadron gave up its Hurricanes and was equiped with Spitfires Mk.I as interim. Here believed to be Sergeant Marsden and David S. Thomas are changing over durings patrols, at Colerne in June 1941. (501 Sqn Association)

Finally, on 17th December, after an eventful twelve months, the unit returned home to Filton. No.501 Squadron had emerged from the Battle with 93 kills between June and November, making it the second most successful Hurricane unit and the fifth highest-scoring squadron overall. Sergeant "Ginger" Lacey had also been credited among the RAF Fighter Command's top-scoring pilots during the conflict, with eighteen enemy aircraft destroyed, four probables and a further six damaged.

The cost to the squadron had been high, however, with 43 aircraft lost, 20 pilots killed and a further eight injured.

SPITFIRES AND THE OFFENSIVE

The relative tranquility of No.501 Squadron's return to Filton and the long periods of inactivity caused by bad weather gave the squadron a much-needed rest from active operations.

The Luftwaffe's change of tactics to bombing towns and cities, particularly London was principally aimed at breaking civilian morale. Plymouth, Cardiff, Bristol, Birmingham and Coventry also became targets for the German bombers' night offensive, which caused considerable loss of life and damage to property. In January 1941, to counter these attacks No.501 Squadron was detached to Charmy Down, near Bath, to join No.87 Squadron, also flying Hurricanes, for a period of night operations. The hopeless and frustrating task of trying to locate enemy bombers resulted in few contacts;

similar operations against "hit-and-run" raiders attacking factories in the Bristol, Gloucester and Yeovil areas were equally unsuccessful.

Despite frequent radar contacts, successful interceptions of lone raiders sneaking across the Bristol Channel were hampered by low cloud, mist, rain and snow. Whenever the weather permitted, the squadron mounted convoy patrols over the Bristol Channel and continued to train the replacement pilots. However, during the first three months of 1941, three Sergeant pilots were lost in as many months through flying accidents. April was to prove no better, with two more pilots killed, Pilot Officer Waine in flying accident, while Pilot Officer Lockyer was killed in an unfortunate motoring accident.

On 9th April the squadron moved to Colerne in order to take part in Winston Churchill's "Set Europe Alight" programme. For the RAF this meant that they were at last going over to the offensive, beginning by escorting daylight bombing raids on targets in France, and on 17th April, Flight Lieutenant Cam Malfroy led six Hurricanes on its first operational sortie, providing an escort cover to 18 Blenheims bombing Boulogne docks. Operating from Westhampnett with the Tangmere Wing, enemy resistance was heavy during the two-hour patrol and a concentrated hail of flak claimed several of the bombers.

The escort patrol to Boulogne was to prove the last full-scale Hurricane operation flown by the squadron; in November 1940, No.66 Squadron at Exeter had

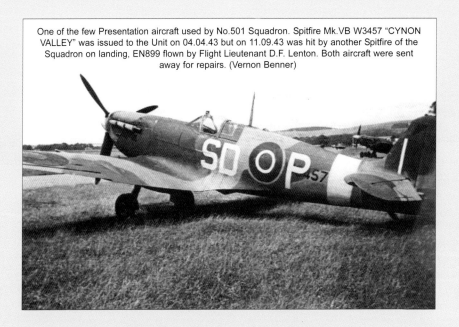

One of the few Presentation aircraft used by No.501 Squadron. Spitfire Mk.VB W3457 "CYNON VALLEY" was issued to the Unit on 04.04.43 but on 11.09.43 was hit by another Spitfire of the Squadron on landing, EN899 flown by Flight Lieutenant D.F. Lenton. Both aircraft were sent away for repairs. (Vernon Benner)

THE SUPERMARINE SPITFIRE

The Supermarine Spitfire was the main RAF fighter during World War II, and the only British fighter to remain in production throughout. It made its maiden flight on 5th March 1936 powered by a Rolls-Royce 990 hp Merlin C engine. Suitably impressed, the Air Ministry, placed an order in July and mass production of the **Spitfire Mk.I**, powered with Rolls-Royce Merlin II 1,030 hp engine, commenced.

It entered service in August 1938 and ten squadrons were operational at the outbreak of war. During the Battle of France a few Spitfires flew reconnaissance duties although its first serious test took place during the evacuation of Dunkirk.

During the Battle of Britain it proved superior to the Hurricane and was to remain the RAF's principal fighter until the end of the war. The updated **Spitfire Mk.II** powered by a 1,175 hp Merlin XII appeared in August 1940, and was, in turn replaced by the **Spitfire Mk.V**, during the Spring of 1941. This version was powered by a 1,470 hp Merlin 45, was better armed and was the first of the two dominant variants of the Spitfire. It did have serious bother though combating the FW190 that subsequently appeared.

The **Spitfire Mk.IX**, the second major variant (1,650 hp Merlin 63) arrived in July 1942, to arrest the situation for the RAF, but it was not until well into 1943 that it appeared in sufficient enough numbers.

A second generation of Spitfires appeared during 1944, when the Rolls-Royce Griffon engine, capable of delivering upwards of 2,000 hp, was developed. However these only partially replaced the Merlin-powered Marks, and the Packard Merlin Spitfire Mk. XVI (which appeared in October 1944), a virtual Mk.IX, which were largely relegated to the fighter-bomber role. From March 1942 Spitfires were sent overseas in numbers and by the end of the war were present in all RAF theatres of operation. Both generations of Spitfire were widely used in the post-war RAF until jet aircraft replaced them during the early fifties.

SERIALS OF SPITFIRE I IN USE ON 7TH MAY 1941.

R : 6837, 6979, 7141
X : 4165, 4258, 4353, 4478, 4606, 4641, 4645, 4720, 4896, 4920, 4926, 4989

Total : 15

started to re-equip with Spitfire IIAs, rendering its older Mk. Is surplus to requirements. These redundant Spitfire Is were passed to No.501 Squadron to form the basis of the squadron's re-equipment programme and it was with mixed emotions that the Hurricane was gradually withdrawn.

The first three Spitfires were collected on 24th April 1941 and the squadron pilots eagerly sought to put the type in their log books, if not without risk to themselves; the dubious honour of No.501 Squadron's first Spitfire accident rested with Sergeant Wilf Holroyd when he bellylanded his aircraft at Colerne on 15th May with undercarriage problems. Two days later, Pilot Officer Ginger Lacey collided with Colerne's OC Flying, Wing Commander Victor Beamish whilst landing after a cine-gun exercise. Fortunately both pilots escaped without injury.

In early June 1941, Squadron Leader Gus Holden was promoted and posted to West Africa as OC Despatch Flight, RAF Takoradi. His successor, Squadron Leader Adrian Boyd, DFC, arrived on 3rd June following a six-month tour as an instructor, having previously flown with No.145 Squadron during the Battle of Britain and claiming twelve aircraft as shot down or damaged.

June also saw the loss of Sergeant Barton in a flying accident and the transfer of the squadron to Chilbolton, a recently-built satellite aerodrome for Middle Wallop. The move to Chilbolton on 25th June was seen as a response to the night raids inflicted by German bombers and the squadron immediately launched itself into night flying patrols over Portsmouth.

Success eventually came in the early hours of 8 July when Squadron Leader Boyd, Flight Lieutenant Ginger Lacey, Flying Officer Bob Dafforn and Sergeant Wilf Holroyd intercepted a Ju88 during a ninety-minute patrol over Portsmouth. Squadron Leader Boyd quickly despatched the raider, thereby notching up the squadron's first kill in No.10 Group. Three days later, more claims came the squadron's way while providing

After working-up on Spitfire Mk.Is, the Squadron received a batch of Spitfire Mk.IIs with which the pilots flew during Summer 1941. Here, P8249/SD-R is warming its engine up for another operational flight. (501 Squadron Association)

This Spitfire Mk.IIA P7378 was issued to No.501 Squadron on 12.05.41. If the code "SD" has been painted on the fuselage, the individual letter "W" still remain to be. (501 Squadron Association)

a fighter escort to RAF Blenheims attacking Cherbourg. Approaching the French coast, two Bf109s were spotted diving on the bomber formation and intercepted by Squadron Leader Boyd and Flight Lieutenant Lacey; the CO sent one of the fighters down in flames after a short burst of fire, while Flight Lieutenant Lacey damaged the other.

On 24th July, Sqn Ldr Boyd took twelve of the squadron Spitfires down to Predannack in Cornwall. Taking off from Predannack at 14.40hrs, the Spitfire Wing arrived over the target some fifty minutes later. With its task almost completed, No.501 Squadron was about to leave the Brest area when an attack by a large force of Bf109s developed. In the desperate fight that followed, Flight Lieutenant Lacey exhausted his ammunition and had to depend upon his flying skills to avoid the fire from a Bf109 on his tail. Pulling his Spitfire into a steep climb he was astonished to see his attacker locked together with another German fighter and falling out of the sky; the two Luftwaffe pilots

having collided whilst trying to shoot him down. Squadron Leader Boyd surprised two more unsuspecting Bf109s at 17,000 feet and 22,000 feet, respectively, and shot them down in rapid succession.

The two Bf109s claimed by Squadron Leader Boyd was a fitting finale; in early August he was promoted to Wing Commander and posted to Middle Wallop as its Wing Leader. Boyd was replaced as CO by another Battle of Britain veteran, Squadron Leader Christopher "Bunny" Currant, DFC, a pre-war pilot with a creditable number of victories while flying with No.605 Squadron.

On 5th August 1941, No.501 Squadron moved again, this time to Ibsley in Hampshire. Opened six months previously as a forward airfield in the Middle Wallop sector, Ibsley was a widely dispersed airfield which No.501 Squadron shared with other Spitfire squadrons of the Wing, including Nos.66, 118 and 234 Squadrons. The Spitfire Wing at Ibsley was tasked with providing escort duties for RAF

SERIALS OF SPITFIRE IIA IN USE ON 1ST SEPTEMBER 1941.

P : 7354, 7378, 7382, 7432, 7433, 7498, 7563, 7599, 7627, 7672, 7677, 7681, 7990, 8074, 8075, 8141, 8196, 8209, 8249, 8256, 8208, 8664, 8741

Total : 23

Supermarine Spitfire Mk.I X4478, No.501 (County of Gloucester) Squadron, Pilot Officer R. Wheldon, Colerne, May 1941.

David Niven and Leslie Howard set up the next shot during filming "First of the Few" at Ibsley, October 1941. (W/C C.F. Currant)

Whirlwinds and Blenheims detailed to carry out anti-shipping strikes at Cherbourg. These fighter-escort daylight attacks proved extremely dangerous at times, as squadron new-comer, Sergeant Beacham was shot down over the Channel and killed just one day after the squadron's arrival at Ibsley.

It was during September that the C-in-C Fighter Command began to take a personal interest in a proposed film telling the story of the Supermarine Spitfire and its designer, R.J. Mitchell, that the crews of No.501 Squadron became "film stars". The squadron was chosen for the flying sequences because, to portray the earlier marks of the Spitfire in action, the Mark II was required because it still carried an armament of eight .303" machine guns. The film starred David Niven and Leslie Howard, who was also in charge of production. Made partly at Ibsley and the film studios at Denham, the pilots were drawn from Nos.501 and 118 Squadrons and represented a typical dispersal area on an airfield during the Battle of Britain. As well as producing the film, Leslie Howard starred in the leading role as R.J. Mitchell, David Niven played the Station Commander, and "Bunny" Currant was portrayed as the Squadron Commander - "Hunter Leader". The scenes of 'Bunny' Currant flying an aircraft were filmed in a studio, whilst the depicted Heinkel He 111 was a captured example, AW177 from the Enemy Aircraft Flight.

Despite the temporary diversion, the Squadron retained its operational commitment and on one occasion during the filming (9th October) the squadron was scrambled to intercept a Ju88 off Portland Bill. Determined that all of his pilots should share in the action, "Bunny" Currant led the eleven Spitfires into the attack and the enemy bomber eventually crashed at Cap de la Hague. Meanwhile, squadron life for the "film stars" continued and in November three pilots, were lost, Pilot Officers Shore and Greenaway with Sergeant Dean reported as missing.

THE CHANNEL DASH

January 1942 was a very cold month with very little activity apart from the untimely death of Sergeant Campbell. Hardly had the news been broken to his comrades when a signal was received informing them that Campbell's commission had been finally approved. In the middle of February 1942 the expected "Channel Dash" of the Scharnhorst and Gneisenau up the Straits of Dover from their anchorage in Brest Harbour finally materialised. The two German ships had inflicted heavy losses to Allied shipping and had for some time frustrated both the Royal Navy and the RAF's efforts to put them out of action. In an attempt to cripple them whilst they were being refitted at Brest, RAF Bomber Command had managed to hem them in with repeated attacks. However, on 12th

February, in low cloud and poor visibility the warships slipped their moorings, accompanied by the light cruiser Prinz Eugen and a heavy escort of destroyers and E-Boats, to head for the safety of the German port of Wilhelmshaven.

Heavy fog over the airfields of Southern England that morning precluded any RAF reconnaissance flights, which enabled the enemy convoy to slip through undetected. A few hours later, Group Captain Victor Beamish, Kenley's Station Commander and Wg Cdr Adrian Boyd, the Wing Leader at Kenley, caught sight of the convoy as it entered the Straits of Dover. Following a hectic evasive action with two Bf 109s, they reported their sighting to No.11 Group which immediately committed five squadrons: three for top cover and two for diversionary attacks. At 13.05 hrs, the Squadron was racing off to West Malling, where the Spitfires refuelled and took off again with orders to maintain air cover, fifteen miles off Ostend.

Although heavy formations of RAF bombers were encountered returning over the south coast, cloud and rain over the target area obscured the visibility and the enemy convoy was not spotted. Reluctantly, 501 returned to West Malling and flew back to Ibsley in the late afternoon; the Scharnhorst and Gneisnau had made good their escape.

On 18th February, a mid-morning *Rhubarb* by four Spitfires resulted in the destruction of a distillery at Baupte, which was blasted by cannon-fire and, although nine Bf 109s were encountered during the return journey, these were evaded by entering cloud and leaving the Spitfires to return to Ibsley independently.

These small-scale fighter attacks on opportunity targets (*Rhubarbs*) were sorties fraught with danger. Coupled with the possibility of attacks by FW190s and Bf109s, the seventy miles of sea separating the Isle of Wight from Cherbourg was an uncomfortable flight for a returning, flak-damaged Spitfire and Group HQ eventually decided to limit this type of operation to one every three days. Nevertheless, with its normal convoy escort duties and countering the sneak raids by Luftwaffe fighter-bombers on the south coast towns, No.501 Squadron was kept very busy.

By March 1942, the policy of the C-in-C Fighter Command, Air Marshal Sir Trafford Leigh-Mallory, to entice German fighter units into the air and to provide RAF fighter units with combat experience, had incurred a loss rate among pilots and aircraft that was considered by many as too high a price to pay for the results it achieved. Squadron Leader "Bunny" Currant was to prove this to his own cost when, on 9th March, two No.11 Group Wings, plus two squadrons of the Ibsley Wing, which totalled some 160 Spitfires, were detailed to provide *Circus* cover for six Bostons attacking Mazingarbe in the Pas de Calais.

Eleven aircraft of No.501 Squadron took off from Redhill at 14.35hrs and rendezvoued with the bombers over Rye. Close to the target, the squadron spotted twelve Bf109s and pursued them down to 4,000 feet, where Pilot Officer Robin Newberry was able to shoot one down while Squadron Leader Currant caught another in a turn, into which he poured a quick burst and watched him go down trailing smoke but could only claim as a probable. Without warning, three FW109s suddenly pounced on the CO and raked

Despite the temporary diversion with the filming, No.501 Squadron retained its operational commitment. (P. Sortehaug)

Above and below : After admonishing his pilots for poor taxiing procedures, Squadron Leader C.F. Currant jumped into his Spitfire (W3846/SD-Z) and taxied into the another aircraft, AD200/SD-W. (W/C C.F. Currant and J. Rajlich)

his Spitfire with cannon fire, smashing the instrument panel and hitting him in the back of the head. With blood pouring down his neck as he dived to avoid the enemy fighters, "Bunny" Currant headed for home and an emergency landing at Lympne, unaware that his tyres had been punctured by the attackers. The Spitfire overturned as the wheels dug into the ground, trapping the CO in the cockpit as it began to fill with petrol fumes. Fortunately, the rescue crews were quickly on the scene and dragged him from the wreckage, from where he was taken to hospital. Within a month, the CO was back flying with the squadron, complete

with seven fragments of metal in his skull to carry as a permament reminder.

For some time in early 1942, Luftwaffe night bombers had been using a radio beam as a navigational aid to attack their targets and it was suspected that the system was now being used experimentally in daylight on selected targets, usually in bad weather which ruled out a response from RAF fighters. On 4th April, in an effort to counter the German Blind Bombing System, the squadron was ordered to attack a suspected radio beam station on the Cap de la Hague peninsula. The day had started badly with the loss of Flight

CODENAMES - OFFENSIVE OPERATIONS

CIRCUS :
Bombers heavily escorted by fighters, the purpose being to bring enemy fighters into combat.

RAMROD :
Bombers escorted by fighters, the primary aim being to destroy a target.

RHUBARD :
Freelance fighter sortie against targets of opportunity.

RODEO :
A fighter sweep without bombers.

SWEEP :
An offensive flight by fighters designed to draw up and clear the enemy from the sky.

Sergeant Thomas during a convoy patrol, but at 18.59 hrs, four aircraft flown by Pilot Officers Newberry, Drossaert, Palmer-Tomkinson and Sergeant Thomas took off and made their way across the Channel. As they approached the French coast, the visibility began to deteriorate, with mist and rain over the target area which threatened the success of the operation. With a stroke of luck, Palmer-Tomkinson spotted the masts of the radio station in the murk and the four Spitfires attacked the target with cannon and machine-gun fire, which was later confirmed as being an adjoining RDF installation.

Four day's later, a long-awaited DFC was awarded to the New Zealand pilot, Flight Lieutenant Bob Yule. On the last day of April, the recently-promoted Czech pilot, Flight Sergeant Bauman was able to destroy a Bf109 without firing a shot during a twelve-aircraft sweep off Cherbourg with Nos.66 and 118 Squadrons. This claim could only slightly compensate for the loss of five aircraft and four pilots killed five days before during a furious dogfight with Bf109s.

Further success followed on 5th May when Wing Commander Gleed claimed a FW190 as a probable during a No.11 Group *Rodeo*. On 9th May, Flight Lieutenant Bob Yule was leading the squadron again on an escort sweep to Hazebrouk when a force of up to 30 FW190s were seen attacking the Spitfires of No.118 Squadron. Going to their assistance, the American pilot, Pilot Officer Gillespie became detached from the squadron during the ensuing fight and was shot down by a FW190.

The presence of the FW190 over the Pas de Calais during early 1942 was seen as a considerable threat to the RAF, which totally outclassed the Spitfire VB in every respect and provided the answer to the air superiority that, in recent months, had been slowly slipping away from the Luftwaffe. On 3rd June, 1942 No.501 Squadron encountered its new adversary again whilst escorting six Bostons to Cherbourg when three FW190s approached while the squadron was still ten miles from the target. Although the enemy fighters failed to engage, as the Wing escort returned across the Channel a running fight developed, and three Spitfires were shot down against claims of one enemy fighter destroyed, one probable and a further four as damaged.

Although several successful escort missions to RAF "Hurri-bombers" attacking shipping in Cherbourg harbour had been mounted throughout May and early June, the Squadron's first real opportunity to finally engage the FW190 came on 4th June during an attack on Maupertus aerodrome. The attack by the Hurricane bombers had caused some damage to the aerodrome and the Wing formation left the target towards Cap Levy to regain height. Whilst still climbing through the haze, No.501 Squadron was attacked by ten FW190s; a surprised Sergeant Strachan was immediately shot down and seen to crash into the sea, while the Belgian pilot, Sergeant Pottelle fortunately managed to bale out before his aircraft hit the water. Quickly recovering from the surprise attack, No.501 Squadron retaliated with Sergeant Jerabek firing a half-second burst into the exposed belly of a FW190, sending it spiralling into the Channel. Flight Lieutenant Phillip Stanbury and Pilot Officer Dicky Lynch almost collided as they fired at the same enemy fighter and frustratingly watched their intended victim skim across the waves back to the French coast.

Starboard side

Port side

Supermarine Spitfire Mk.IIA P8249, No.501 (County of Gloucester) Squadron, Flight Lieutenant R.C. Dafforn, Chilbolton, July 1941.

No.118 Squadron quickly came to No.501Squadron's rescue and joined in the action, claiming a probable and a further two as damaged.

During one of the rare free weekends at Ibsley when the squadron was released from operations, the crews took the opportunity to celebrate the award of the DFC to Flight Lieutenant Philip Newberry. Returning to the action, a diversionary sweep by the Ibsley Wing over the Pas de Calais area on 20th June was met by stiff opposition from the Luftwaffe, when a force of 25 FW190s and twelve Bf109s rose up to meet the Spitfires. The Squadron's Blue and Yellow sections were attacked by three FW190s, one of which was in turn attacked by Pilot Officer Johnny Jackson was able to fire a long burst. Although a vivid flash was seen behind the cockpit as the enemy fighter went into spiral dive and trailing smoke, Jackson could only claim it as a probable as its fate was not observed.

After becoming separated from his section, Pilot Officer Drossaert was lucky to escape from the fire of an enemy fighter by taking evasive action and returned home alone. Flight Lieutenant Philip Stanbury was also forced to make his own way back, low on fuel, and while crossing the French coast he helplessly watched as Flight Sergeant Bauman was attacked and shot down near Cap Griz Nez.

Squadron Leader "Bunny" Currant's promotion and the command of RAF Ibsley in June 1942, came as no real surprise to the squadron. Neither did Bob Yule's appointment as CO of No.66 Squadron. The Squadron's new CO, Squadron Leader John "Pancho" Villa, DFC, had barely time to settle into the squadron when it was ordered to Tangmere. Rumours that something "big" was imminent failed to materialise and despite a signal which informed everyone that "... *hopes were high that we should get cracking at last....*", after four days of waiting, the squadron returned to Ibsley.

The weeks that followed proved to be a period of mixed fortunes for the squadron: a claim of a possible Ju88 over Bournemouth on 30th July had to be set against the loss of Sergeant Bill Leitch on 5th August when he was shot down by FW190s and also the loss of the New Zealand pilot, Pilot Officer Brannigan when his flight was attacked by four FW 190s whilst returning from an early morning shipping recce on 11th August.

OPERATION "*JUBILEE*"

Little known to No.501 Squadron and the other squadrons at Ibsley, plans were being laid for an Allied return to the Continent. A site was required on the French coast where a large-scale landing could take place and briefly secured, and where AVM Leigh-Mallory's No.11 Group squadrons could readily provide the all-important fighter cover. Dieppe was eventually chosen for the raid and the assault, code-named *Jubilee*, would be undertaken by two Brigades of the 2nd Canadian Division and a Canadian tank regiment - a total, with supporting Commandos, of 6,000 men.

Originally planned for early in July 1942, the landings were cancelled because of bad weather. The go-ahead had now been given for mid-August and, as a result, No.501 Squadron returned to Tangmere on 16th August, where it was briefed by Ibsley's new wing leader, Wing Commander Pat Gibbs.

The morning of 19th August meant an early start, with the crews up at 02.30 hrs to bring the aircraft to readiness by 04.00 hrs. A thick ground mist temporarily grounded the squadron, which could hear the sounds of gunfire from the attack that already started across the Channel.

At 07.50 hrs, Squadron Leader "Pancho" Villa at last led No.501 Squadron into action when, in company with No.66 Squadron, they escorted five Blenheims of No.614 Squadron. After being airborne for just fifteen minutes all the aircraft were recalled while the formation was 20 miles south of Selsey Bill when the mission was cancelled.

Following a hurried breakfast, No.501 Squadron was airborne again at 10.24 hrs to provide an escort for No.87 Squadron's Hurricane fighter bombers while they carried out an attack on gun emplacements on East Beach. During the mid-afternoon, the Luftwaffe began attacking the main convoy in the Channel with Do217 and Ju88 bombers, escorted by Fw190s. Nos.501 and 118 Squadrons, together with the Spitfires of the Tangmere Wing, were scrambled at 14.55 hrs to go to the assistance of the ships at the rear of the flotilla. Reaching the convoy eight miles off Dieppe, No.501 Squadron was immediately involved in a furious scrap with ten FW190s, one of which was damaged by Flight Lieutenant Philip Stanbury before it disappeared in cloud.

Meanwhile, Flight Sergeant Alan Mawer chased after two Do217s and was able to damage one before his ammunition ran out. As Mawer turned for home a FW190 dived on him from the cover of cloud and, at 200 yards, opened fire on the defenceless Spitfire. A cannon shell burst above the cockpit, shattering the perspex and lacerating his head. Momentarily stunned, the Australian pilot jettisoned the canopy and prepared to abandon the aircraft. However, noticing that the FW190 had flown off after being itself attacked by another Spitfire, Mawer decided to remain with his aircraft and eventually made it back to Tangmere.

Pilot Officer Lightbourne had the luckiest escape of the day when, after deciding to abandon his badly shot-up Spitfire, he was thrown violently against the aircraft's tailplane by the slipstream. With a broken leg and entangled against the Spitfire's tail as it dived towards the sea, he struggled to free himself. After frantic efforts, Lightbourne eventually parted company with his aircraft and parachuted into the sea close to the convoy, which sent a boat to pick him up.

By mid-afternoon, the weather had deteriorated so badly that the squadron was recalled to base. With the visibility down to 600 yards as No.501 Squadron crossed the coast, four aircraft were able to land safely at Tangmere, with another six having to divert to nearby Shoreham. Segeant Lee was unable, however, to locate either aerodrome in the low cloud and was killed when he crashed in to the side of hill at Billingshurst, twelve miles north of Tangmere.

The cost of the Dieppe operation to the Allies had been enormous. The Allies had paid a tragic sacrifice, but the lessons learned at Dieppe would prove invaluable for the later invasions of North Africa, Sicily and Normandy. On 24th August, No.501 Squadron returned to Middle Wallop and settled back into its normal routine of shipping recces,

convoy patrols and bomber escorts.

In the autumn of 1942 the Luftwaffe began to operate daylight, high-altitude bombing raids over the southwest of England. The scale of these "nuisance" raids was demonstrated when, in early September, a single bomb was dropped on Bristol from 42,000 feet, causing many casualties and inflicting a great deal of damage. On 11th September, Pilot Officers Chilton and Johnny Johnson were scrambled from Warmwell at 08.25 hrs to intercept a bomber flying at altitude to the south of Bristol. The two pilots climbed to 37,000 feet where they identified the bomber as a Ju86P. Close to the Spitfire's operational ceiling the aircraft became difficult to handle: the rate of climb decayed, the controls became sloppy in the rarified atmosphere, while the pilots began to suffer from excruciating stomach pains in the intense cold. Chasing the enemy bomber down to Poole, Chilton and Jackson had to reluctantly abandon the pursuit when it began to outclimb the Spitfires to avoid the anti-aircraft fire from the coastal batteries.

The autumn of 1942 was also a period of bad luck for No.501 Squadron, when a series of unrelated incidents began to plague the squadron, no less than seven pilot being killed between 27th August and 17th September. Therefore, it was decided to rest No.501 squadron from operational flying and transfer the squadron to Ballyhalbert, an aerodrome

Spitfire Mk.VB BM312/SD-Y. In charge of the Squadron between 06.05.43 and 10.11.43, it was mainly flown in operations by Warrant Officer J.L. Lilburn during Summer that year. (Vernon Benner)

to the south of Belfast, in Northern Ireland.

With the squadron assembled at Ballyhalbert, A Flight was detached to Eglinton, near Londonderry, with the Flights being rotated on a monthly basis. Here the squadron continued to fly convoy patrols and, although the period spent in Northern Ireland was considered a rest from operations, the long hours, monotony and unpredictable Irish weather soon proved to be very tiring.

Two fatal accidents in early 1943, in some degree due to the severe Irish winter, were considered by many on No.501 Squadron as a futile waste of lives. More fortunate was Sergeant Baynton who suffered an engine failure whilst on patrol to the south-west of the Isle of Man. Unstrapping himself, he turned his Spitfire on its back and fell out, landing in the freezing water. Scrambling into his dinghy, Bayton was found half-an-hour later by the crew of the Newcastle lifeboat, who quickly revived him with copious quantities of Irish whisky!

It came as a great relief therfore when, in April 1943, the crews celebrated their return to the mainland with a tremendous farewell party. A tiring 48-hour journey to Westhampnett by boat, train and bus was completed by 30th April, by which time the squadron's Spitfires had arrived and the rear party was flown over by transport Harrows.

NEW KIND OF ACITIVITY

On 1st May 1943 Squadron Leader Robinson was posted from the squadron and replaced as CO by Squadron Leader "Bats" Barthold. One of No.501 Squadron's duties during this period was weather and reconnaissance patrols, which were usually flown from Le Havre/Dieppe to Boulogne, or from Boulogne to Cap Gris Nez and past Ostend. These regular "milk runs" were vital in that they checked the weather in both areas for future raids and reported on any shipping, E-Boats, etc., and were usually by met by heavy resistance from the German defences, which proved hazardous for the pilots.

On 21st June, No.501 Squadron flew up to its old Battle of Britain base at Hawkinge and assumed to duties of No.91 Squadron, which had been actively engaged on Jim Crow patrols, seeking enemy intruders. Four days after No.501Squadron's arrival at Hawkinge, Flight Lieutenant Tim Lenton was vectored on to a FW190, two miles from Le Treport on the French coast. Lenton went after the Luftwaffe fighter, firing two bursts before it disappeared behind some trees, apparently out of control. A claim of a probable was submitted by Lenton following his return to base. For the shipping recces

two pairs of Spitfires would fly across the Channel coast at low level, one pair turning north to inspect Calais, Dunkirk and Ostend, and the other pair going south to cover Boulogne, Le Touquet, Dieppe and Cherbourg. Radio silence was maintained at all times, and in the event of a sighting the report was not passed to Fighter Command until the Spitfires returned to Hawkinge and rocket-equipped Typhoons would be despatched to attack the target.

As the Allied day-bombing offensive was stepped up, No.501 Squadron began flying more fighter sweeps and close formation missions for the bombers attacking targets in Northern France. During an attack on railway targets at Hazebrouck on 11th July, Flight Lieutenant Bob Stockburn was attacked by a FW190 and last seen near Dunkirk. He was, however, fortunate to evade capture and return to the squadron with the help of the French Resistance, who smuggled him over the Pyrenees and into Spain.

The following month, Flying Officer Dave Davies and the American pilot, Lt Meserve, were slightly more fortunate following an attack by FW190s during a weather recce, ten miles north-west of Merville. Although sustaining considerable damage to the wings and radiators, both Spitfires were able to limp back to Hawkinge.

Before the practice was eventually discontinued, pilots could request to carry out individual *Rhubarb* missions over Northern France, attacking targets of opportunity. Ammunition trains featured high on the list of targets of Rhubarb missions and one squadron pilot who specialised in these was the Frenchman, Capt Bernard Fuchs. Before his eventual posting to the FLS in March 1944 and the award of the *Croix de Guerre* and three Bars, his tally included lorries, sailing vessels, trains, a Bf109 during a *Jim Crow* near Camaches on 11th August 1943, and a probable FW190 during a weather recce near Cayeaux on 7th October 1943. Squadron colleagues recalled Bernard Fuch's personal dislike of Frenchmen who drove French trains for the Germans and, despite a ban imposed upon him carrying out such attacks, he would invent a reason for an air-test and speed across the Channel in search of some unsuspecting train driver between the Pas de Calais and Abbeville.

In late 1943 a handful of Spitfire IXs, with their improved ceiling and increased speed were delivered to No.501 Squadron, which not only restored the balance against the superior FW190 and Bf109 but also enabled the squadron to carry out more high-level bombing raids and weather recces.

Coinciding with the delivery of the Spitfire IXs in

The Squadron at Hawkinge on 29.04.44.
Back row left to right : F/O R.C Stockburn, F/L A.J. Grottick, F/O J.M. Griffin, F/Sgt S.L. Clarke (Can), W/O F.W. Mossing (Can), P/O R.H. Bennett, P/O W.F. Polley, F/O R. Deleuze (Free French), P/O S.H. Cheeseman, F/L W.B. Peglar (Can), F/L L.P. Griffith (NZ), F/L H. Burton and F/Sgt R.E. Farrow.
Middle row, left to right : F/O G.N. Mann, F/O N.N. Galer, F/O W.B. Atkinson, S/L M.G. Barnett (NZ) - CO, F/L O.E. Willis, F/O N.T. Andrews (Can), *Capitaine* J. Vaissier (Free French).
Front row, left to right : W/O E. Twigg, Sgt A.E. Gunn, F/O Wakinson (Admin), P/O East (IO), F/L J.R. Davies.
(501 Squadron Association)

October 1943, Squadron Leader Barthold was forcibly promoted to Wing Commander and posted to Fighter Command HQ. His replacement, the New Zealand pilot Squadron Leader Gary Barnett, went into action almost immediately when, on 1st November, he damaged a Bf109 during a shipping recce off Calais.

High-altitude weather recces carried out by the squadron during this period proved extremely hazardous for some pilots and not necessarily from the Luftwaffe, as ex-Fleet Air Arm pilot, Flight Lieutenant Colin Hodgkinson, found to his cost in November. A planned *Ramrod* mission on 25th November, for which No.501 Squadron was detailed to escort Boston and Mitchell bombers attacking V-1 sites in the Pas de Calais, found Colin carrying out a weather recce to the south of Amiens, the previous morning. During the sortie his Spitfire developed a fault with the oxygen system and, barely conscious, he decided to attempt a forced-landing before the aircraft ran out of fuel. As he broke through the cloud he became aware of *flak* opening up around him, before eventually passing out and crashing at Audincthum, 40 miles from St Omer. Two local Frenchmen pulled

Colin from the blazing wreck and took him to a nearby farmhouse, from where a party of Germans took him to a military hospital. In September 1944, he was eventually repatriated to the UK.

The following month, a more serious and tragic incident occurred. On 21st December, the squadron was briefed for *Ramrod* 382. Contact with the B-26 Maurauders was lost soon after take-off and when No.501 Squadron's Spitfires arrived at the rendezvous point they were no-where to be seen. Four USAAF P-47 Thunderbolts then arrived on the scene and began to slowly circle the squadron Spitfires. Suddenly, without warning, the large American fighters dived into Blue Section, hitting Pilot Officer Tony Griffiths, who was last seen diving away and trailing glycol. Flight Lieutenant Dave Davies was also hit by a hail of fire from a Thunderbolt as it swept past him but was able to return to Hawkinge for an emergency landing.

Shocked by the whole incident, the remaining pilots were told of a similar incident the same day when two Typhoons of No.609 Squadron were also shot down by P-47s and quickly complained of the "trigger-happy" attitude of the American fighter pilots. The following day, the squadron was visited by AVM Saunders who expressed his regret over the incident and asssured the pilots that everything was being done to avoid such a repetition.

PRELUDE TO D-DAY

Most of January 1944 was taken up with armament training at 17 APC, Southend. Returning to Hawkinge on 4th February, No.501 Squadron continued to fly escort missions for Allied bombers attacking *Noball* sites in Northern France. These portable "ski-sites" for launching the German V1 weapons were well defended by the Luftwaffe. Two Spitfires flown by Pilot Officer Reg Farrow and Flight Sergeant Knight had been detached from *Ramrod* 420 to photograph the attack by Mitchells on Bois Carre, south of Abbeville, during which both aircraft were badly damaged during a surprise attack by eight FW190s. Although Pilot Officer Farrow was able to evade the fighters and return to base, Flight Sergeant Knight managed to regain control of his stricken aircraft until the engine failed and he was forced to put down at the edge of the Crecy Forest. Rescued by French farmworkers and German soldiers, he was taken prisoner. The following month, No.501 Squadron also lost Pilot Officer Cheeseman during a *Ranger* mission for American Marauders attacking Gilze-Rijen. Later in the month, Warrant Officer Lilburn was also taken prisoner and to add to the squadron losses, the Canadian pilot, Warrant Officer Frankie Vid, was shot down by flak during a high-level weather recce between Gravelines and Abbeville in March.

By the Spring of 1944 it became evident that an invasion attack by the Allied forces on the European mainland was being planned: the increasing attacks by Allied aircraft on selected targets in Northern France, mass troop movements, and large numbers of transport aircraft and gliders being deployed to aerodromes in the south of England pointed to an invasion date at Normandy in the early summer.

On 30th April, the squadron moved to Friston in Sussex, where they joined No.350 (Belgian) Squadron, also flying Spitfire VBs. Although secrecy regarding the invasion was vital to ensure its success, both squadrons were informed of their primary role of the defence of the beachhead, together with their secondary role of bomber escort duties and fighter sweeps deep into France. No.501 Squadron was designated to be the first squadron over the beachhead before dawn on the day of the invasion and was not expected to leave the area until after dusk.

The crews of No.501 Squadron had been briefed in the greatest of secrecy the previous evening (5th June) and, despite the Spitfires being fitted with anti-glare exhaust shields and painted with black and white "invasion" stripes during the night, many still believed that was still only an exercise. However, at 03.30 hrs, Nos.501 and 350 Squadrons were airborne for their first patrol of the day, patrolling the eastern end of the assault beaches and acting as low cover for the ships and landing craft. The patrol was carried out without incident, as were the other three patrols flown throughout the day, and by the time the last aircraft landed at Friston at midnight the pilots had all witnessed the massive Allied invasion.

The following day road and rail targets were attacked by Allied fighters. No.501 Squadron flew four lowcover patrols of the beaches, during which Flight

---

SERIALS OF SPITFIRE V & IX IN USE ON 1ST MAY 1944.

X : 4272 (Mk.VA)
W : 3702, 3931
AA : 945
AD : 324
AR : 519
BL : 409
BM : 256, 304, 385, 593
BS : 474*
EP : 109, 244, 277, 281, 385, 395, 398, 707
MA : 585*, 817*
MH : 333*, 362*, 855*, 909*, 939*
MJ : 129*, 311*

Total : 29

*Spitfire IX.

Lieutenant "Ollie" Willis attacked a Bf109 which was able to shake him off and make good his escape.

By 8th June, the Luftwaffe had quickly moved fighter units into the area, and during its first patrol at dawn No.501 Squadron was able to gain its first victory over the beachhead after being vectored to the scene of enemy air activity. Led by Wing Commander Johnnie Checketts of No.142 Wing, the squadron changed course and detached Yellow Section after more enemy aircraft were reported on the squadron's flank. Six Bf109s were spotted below them, heading away from Le Havre, and were attacked by the Spitfires. Flight Lieutenant "Foob" Fairbanks shot one down in flames and badly damaged another, while Flight Lieutenant Griffiths chased after another into which he poured a burst of fire before it disappeared in low cloud. Pilot Officer Ron Bennett also claimed a Bf109 as a probable, as did Wing Commander Johnnie Checketts.

On 12th June 1944, after an absence of four years, No.501 Squadron returned to France, landing at an advanced strip in the American Sector at St Pierre du Mont, flying back to Friston the following day after a patrol over the beachhead. By end of June, the bridgehead was at last secured, and although No.501 Squadron could relax the pressure slightly, the squadron still patrolled the assault area until the end of June. On 30th June, its hard work was rewarded when Friston's Wing Leader, Wing Commander Don Kingaby, and Flying Officer Bob Stockburn shared in the destruction of a Bf109 during a morning patrol near Cazelle.

On 2nd July, with the invasion underway and the Allied front moving from south to west, No.501 Squadron moved to Westhampnett to patrol the convoy routes across the Channel and to carry out deeper fighter sweeps in France. Ten days later Red Section crossed the French coast near Ouistreham during such a patrol, only to be fired upon by the Allied anti-aircraft defences. Two Spitfires flown by Flying Officer Peter Beloe and the newly-commissioned Pilot Officer Reg Farrow were hit by the concentrated naval gun fire and unfortunately killed.

The squadron suffered a similar misfortune on 14th July when a section of four Spitfires led by Flight Lieutenant Ollie Willis attacked an enemy radar

Formation of three Tempests stationned at Bradwell Bay in October 1944. The first Tempest (EJ763/SD-X) is flown by Flying Officer Gilbert Wild. (501 Squadron Association)

V-1 Flying Bomb

Incensed by Allied air attacks on Germany, Hitler ordered the development of a series of retaliatory weapons, the first of which was tested as early as December 1942. Their existence was eventually confirmed to the British in November 1943 from photographs obtained by photo-reconnaissance aircraft during a routine patrol over Peenemunde on the Baltic coast.

Powered by a ramjet engine burning low-grade fuel, the Fiesler Fi103 *Vergeltungswaffe Einz* (Reprisal Weapon No.1 or V-1) carried a 1,000lb warhead, with a maximum speed of 480 mph and a range of 200 miles. Most bombs were launched from inclined ramps constructed of prefabricated metal sections known as "ski sites" which were situated on the north coast of France between Dieppe and Calais, a mere 130 -140 miles from London.

Development of the V-1 was accelerated after D-Day, and, at 04.18 hrs on 13th June, 1944, the first "Doodle Bug" fell on Gravesend which signalled the beginning of the offensive. Successful interceptions of the flying bombs by the defending fighters depended upon accurate and timely information concerning their course and speed, and could be extremely hazardous; the fighter would fire a series of deflection bursts at maximum range, at the same time exercising extreme caution as the resultant explosion could cripple the attacker. Although these attacks were normally sufficient to destroy the V-1, another method was to topple the V-1's gyro by flying alongside and tipping it into the ground with the aircraft's wing.

By October 1944, most of the V-1 launching sites in the Pas de Calais had been captured by the advancing Allied troops, to which the Luftwaffe responded by resorting to its original intention of air-launching the weapon from specially modified He 111 bombers based in Central Holland. With a V-1 fitted under the wing, the bomber crossed the North Sea at low level to avoid detection and, after climbing to 1,000 feet, launched the bomb against its target. About 850 were launched by this method until it was abandoned in January 1945.

The V-1 offensive ended on 29th March, 1945, when a flying bomb came down at Datchworth, near Hatfield. Over 8,600 bombs had been launched towards London during the battle, of which 3,957 had been destroyed, 1,878 by the AA guns, 1,847 by the defending fighters, and 232 by balloon cables. The cost of human life and widespread damage to property was, however, enormous, with 6,139 people killed and a further 17,239 injured. The worst incident being on 20th June, 1944 when a bomb landed in the Guard's Chapel at Wellington Barracks, killing or injuring 260 people.

---

installation at Cap D' Antifer as part of *Ramrod* 1088. Although considerable damage had been inflicted on the installation by the squadron aircraft, the *flak* from the defenders was intense. Ollie Willis Spitfire was hit by the withering fire and he was fortunate to make an emergency landing at an ALG near Caen. Flying Officer Andy Anderson was not so lucky, being killed when his parachute fouled the tailplane as he attempted to abandon the aircraft.

THE V-1 OFFENSIVE

In mid-1944, a new and more frightening menace to Britain materialised in the form of the V-1 flying bomb. Launched from portable sites in the Pas de Calais, the V-1 offensive began on 13th June 1944 and required the evolvement of new tactics by the British defences to counter the threat. By the end of the month, light anti-aircraft guns, barrage balloons and fighter squadrons were arranged to form a defensive belt to the south of London; while AI radar-equipped Mosquito squadrons operated interception patrols at night, Typhoon, Tempest, Mustang and Spitfire squadrons flew anti-Diver patrols by

day ("Diver" being the code-name for the V-1). No.501 Squadron was, in fact, no stranger to the V-1, having carried out several unsuccessful interceptions soon after the first V-1 was launched against London. On 26th June, the CO, Squadron Leader Gary Barnett, claimed a first for the squadron by shooting one down near Bexhill while air-testing his Spitfire.

At the beginning of the offensive the unit was operating a mixture of Spitfire VBs, VCs and IXs, which were found to be unsuitable for catching the flying bombs and it was decided to re-equip the squadron with the more capable Hawker Tempest fighter, which had entered RAF squadron service in January 1944. On 18th July 1944, the first of the new Tempest Mk.Vs were flown into Westhampnett to an excited reception from squadron pilots and groundcrew. Sergeant Gunn was amongst the first on the squadron to fly the Tempest and he recalled that the first aircraft was delivered by a little blonde ATA girl, who informed everyone that there were nineteen more Tempests behind her!

By 29th July, No.501 Squadron had received its full complement of Tempests and was taken off operations for a period of intensive training; at the same time the crews said their fond farewells to the Spitfire as they were flown away for disposal, thereby ending a three-year acquaintanceship.

In early August the squadron moved to Manston, only to disband and immediately reform as a night-fighter squadron, designated to maintain a sector patrol from Manston to Folkestone. The crews for the "new" 501 Squadron were drawn from those with suitable night-fighter experience, including the Tempest Flight of the Fighter Interception Unit at Manston, which had developed the technique of intercepting V-1s at night. On 5th August the squadron opened its score-sheet when Flying Officer Bill Polley shot down a V-1 near Ashford, quickly followed by another which he shared with Flight Sergeant Ryman. Two days later, Flying Officer Regis "Lulu" Deleuze brought one down near Tenterden to add to the squadron's steadily increasing score. During his time with the Squadron, Flying Officer Bill Polley shot down six V-1s and shared another, and like most other pilots he shot at others but had no confirmation of success. The area of chase was very limited between the coastal batteries and the armoured balloons, and once vectored onto a contact by the Ground Controller, the pilots had minutes at the most to find the target, get into position and open fire before rapidly breaking off!

August also saw the departure of the CO, Squadron Leader Gary Barnett, who moved to the other side of the airfield to command No.274 Squadron, which was also in the process of exchanging its Spitfires for Tempests. On 11th August, 1944, No.501 Squadron officially became a Night Fighter squadron, commanded by Squadron Leader Joe Berry, DFC, from the FIU, and it marked the occasion by destroying eight of the flying bombs; Flight Lieutenant Thornton and Flying Officer Miller claiming three apiece during the same patrol. Joe Berry was already a V-1 ace by the time he took over the squadron and opened his score with the unit on 12th August when he despatched a V-1 near Sandhurst during a night patrol over the south-east of England.

Soon after taking command Joe Berry was summoned to the Air Ministry and returned with sombre news: "*I have received instructions about and received instructions about the role of 501 against the night intruders. It was said to me that these instructions came from the Prime Minister himself, to the effect that the squadron must consider itself expendable and thus will take off to try to effect interception in every weather condition in every weather condition, even though all other squadrons are grounded. This, because it is felt that*

that the threat of the V-1 is so great, the people on the ground must at least 'hear' fighters airborne whenever there is a V-1 warning. So the squadron will still get airborne even if it is quite impossible to make any interception..." even though all other squadrons are grounded. This, because it was felt that the threat of the V-1 is so great that the people on the ground must at least 'hear' fighters airborne whenever there is V-1 warning. So the squadron will still get airborne even it is quite impossible to make any interception.

The "expendability" factor was re-inforced with a visit from the Secretary of State for Air, Sir Archibald Sinclair, who informed the pilots that civilian morale was low due to the V-1 attacks and the Government had decided to treat the situation quite seriously; even to the extent that they were prepared to sacrifice the lives of several pilots for every flying bomb brought down. This scale of "expendability" was quickly realised when the squadron suffered its first fatality after re-equipping with the Tempest when, on 21 August, Flight Lieutenant Thornton flew into the ground at Woodnesborough, Kent, while descending through thick fog.

Pilot Officer Ron Bennett had joined No.501 Squadron at Ballyhalbert in February 1943 and remained with the squadron when it re-equipped with Tempests, making his first flight with the type in July 1944. He claimed his first V-1 near West Malling on 18th August 1944, with a second nine days later. His third and fourth V-1 "kills" were claimed during the last two weeks of August.

On 30th August 1944, Bennett also came to appreciate the risks involved in flying in marginal weather conditions, having being sent off in all weather conditions and the probability that the airfield would be covered in fog or thick cloud at the end of the patrol. Following a particularly long, two-hour patrol, he was diverted to Ford and whilst circling the airfield was horrified to see his port wingtip light reflecting off the wet rooftops! He was eventually able to land safely, slightly shaken by the experience.

Others were not so lucky and the weather continued to take its toll of the squadron pilots. On the night of 25th September, Flight Lieutenant "Snowy" Bonham, DFC, was scrambled out towards the sea in bad weather, only to radio back that his compass had developed a fault and that he was returning to base. His Tempest crashed at Spitfield Farm, Essex and he was killed. Four days later, Flight Lieutenant 'Paddy' Farraday was also killed when his engine failed and his aircraft crashed four miles east of Clacton.

Flying Officer Gilbert Wild was more fortunate when,

A nice shot of Tempest EJ555/SD-Y at the end of Summer 1944. The Tempest was the last piston-engined fighter to see operational service with the RAF. (Chris Thomas)

THE HAWKER TEMPEST

A development of the earlier Typhoon, the Tempest was designed as a fighter-bomber and managed to combine the power of its predecessor and the smoothness and manoeuvrability of the Spitfire.

One of the shortcomings of the Typhoon was its bad high altitude performance. Thence, Hawker decided to use a new eliptical wing, and a extended airframe in trying to improve the high altitude performance. Known at first as Typhoon Mk.II, it received the name of "Tempest" in August 1942. To equip the new British fighter, various engines were studied and the RAF ordered prototypes with the Sabre IV (Tempest Mk.I), the Centaurus IV, radial engine (Tempest Mk.II), the Griffon IIB (Tempest Mk.III), the Griffon 61 (Tempest Mk.IV) and the Sabre II (Tempest Mk.V). Of these, only the Tempest Mk.II and Mk.V were put into production, the **Tempest Mk.V** being the only variant to see active service during WW2.

The Tempest Mk.V first flew on 2nd September, 1942. It became soon clear that this version would need less time to be put into production and Hawker's efforts were soon concentrated on this version.

When the first production Tempest Mk.V made its maiden flight in June 1943, it was powered by a 2,180 hp Sabre II liquid cooled engine, and was armed with four Hispano Mk.V 20mm cannons. After intensive trials, the Tempest Mk.V was put into service in January 1944, being declared operational during the following April. The Tempest was intensively used against the V-1 offensive which started in June 1944.

With the production increasing, seven Squadrons were fully equipped with the Tempest by the end 1944, firstly with the Air Defence of Great Britain, and later with the 2nd TAF based on the Continent from end September 1944. Although the production of this variant reached 800 aircraft, the re-equipment of other squadrons were cancelled due of lack of machines.

The Tempest remained in service after the war, but by the end of the 1940s, it had been replaced by the first generation of jet fighters.

Flight Officer B.F. Miller (USAAF) is taxiing his Tempest EJ558/SD-R for another anti-diver patrol. Eight V-1 "kills" can be seen under the cockpit. (IWM FLM3111)

whilst chasing a V-1 on the night of 23rd September, the engine of his Tempest siezed and he was forced to bale out. He landed in a cherry tree at Stanway Hall, near Colchester, and was taken to a local police station, where he spent the next two hours "helping with enquiries" before being returned to base.

In September 1944 the squadron moved again, this time to Bradwell Bay in Essex, to enable night patrols to be maintained against the flying bombs coming in across the east and south-east coast. Bradwell Bay was very prone to sudden blanketing by sea fog and was fitted with a series of pipes erected by the side of the runway, in which petrol vapour was burnt. The installation called FIDO (Fog Investigation Dispersal Operation) burnt away the fog and helped many returning bombers to land safely - even if the resultant noise and flames was considered as terrifying to many on the ground!

By September 1944, the Allied advance through France resulted in a reduction in V-1 activity and the Squadron began flying Ranger sorties, attacking targets of opportunity in Germany and Holland. At 05.35 on 2nd October, a section of three Tempests flown by Sqn Ldr Joe Berry, Flight Lieutenant "Willie" Williams and Flight Lieutenant "Horry" Hansen took off to attack bomber airfields and rail yards. The flight would take them to Zwischenhan and the Luftwaffe He 111 airfields between there and the Rheine. Soon after take-off, the section encountered small arms fire from a solitary gun post at a newly-installed Jagdschloss radar site, east of Veendam, hitting the glycol tank of Joe Berry's Tempest. Struggling with the controls, he crashed in flames at Kibbelgaarn, north of Arnhem, and was killed instantly. The two remaining pilots continued with their patrol and destroyed four

---

SERIALS OF TEMPEST V IN BELIEVED IN USE ON 15TH AUGUST 1944.

EJ : 520*, 535*, 538, 551, 553*, 580, 583, 585, 589, 590, 591, 593, 594, 596, 597, 598, 600, 602, 603, 605, 607, 608

JN : 855*

Total : 23

*Former FIU machines still coded ZQ-L (EJ553), ZQ-U (JN855), ZQ-Y (EJ520) and ZQ-Z (EJ535)

trains transporting V-1s to their launch sites.

Joe Berry was succeeded by Squadron Leader Parker-Rees, DFC, an ex-Mosquito pilot from No.68 Squadron, and although the flying bombs were still coming across the English coast in some quantity, the new gun-laying radar fitted to the AA guns enabled them to take a useful toll. No.501 Squadron was therefore left to track down the "left-overs", and four days after the squadron moved to Hunsdon on 1st March, 1945, Flying Officer Johnson re-opened the score-sheet when he sent a V-1 into the ground near North Weald.

From becoming operational in August 1944, the Squadron had destroyed at least 93 flying bombs, and the monthly totals to December 1944 indicated:

August	40 V-1s
September	10 V-1s
October	25 V-1s
November	10 V-1s
December	8 V-1s

On 26th March 1945, Flight Lieutenant Jimmie Grottick shot down the last flying bomb to be claimed by a fighter aircraft during the war when, at 02.35 hrs, he was scrambled and vectored to the south west. It was a clear night and he soon saw the "jet light" of a V-1, about two miles off his port side and travelling very fast. He turned towards it and came through a 180-degree approach, throttling back to close the range and opened fire with a two to three-second burst at 200 yards. There were no immediate strikes and then the flame feathered, sending the last of the flying bombs into the ground near North Weald.

Four days later, No.501 Squadron was released from operations and at dawn on 1st April, 1945 returned to the day fighter role. Of the 6,700 V-1s that had crossed the English coast between June 1944 and March 1945, and had managed to elude the AA guns and balloons, 1,846 had been claimed by the defending fighter squadrons. As the only RAF Tempest squadron to operate at night during the offensive, No.501 Squadron had destroyed over 100 of the flying bombs.

With the war in Europe drawing to a close and the consequent decrease in enemy air activity, No.501 Squadron was disbanded at Hunsdon on 20th April 1945.

Tempest pilots at Bradwell in October 1944.
Back row, left to right : F/O K.V. Panter, F/O J. Maday (Can), F/O J.AL. Johnson (Can), F/L H. Burton, F/O R.C. Stockburn, F/O W.F. Polley, F/O R.H. Bennett.
Front row left to right : W/O E. Wojczynski (Pol), Captain Payne (Army liaison officer), F/L R.L.T Robb, F/L C.A Hansen (NZ), S/L A. Parker-Rees - CO, F/L O.E. Willis, F/L Birks (non-flying), W/O S.H. Balam, F/L A.T. Llandon-Down, F/O A.J. Grottick, F/O Harte (non-flying). The aircraft below is believed to be EJ538/SD-R stripped of paint to increase its top speed by 5mph.
(501 Squadron Association)

APPENDICES

Hurricanes at dispersal at Filton in 1939.
(501 Squadron Association)

No.501 (*County of Gloucester*) Squadron

Authorized H.M. King George VI : December 1938

DESCRIPTION
A boar's head couped

MOTTO
NIL TIME
Fear nothing

SIGNIFICANCE OF DESIGN
The boar's head is taken from the arms of Gloucester; the animal is also noted for its courage.

SQUADRON COMMANDERS 1937-1945	
S/L M.V.M. CLUBE	01.07.37 - 29.06.40
S/L H.A.V. HOGAN	29.06.40 - 06.11.40
S/L E. HOLDEN	06.11.40 - 04.06.41
S/L A.H. BOYD	04.06.41 - 14.08.41
S/L C.F. CURRANT	14.08.41 - 22.06.42
S/L J.W. VILLA	22.06.42 - 19.09.42
S/L A.I. ROBINSON	19.09.42 - 01.05.43
S/L B. BARTHOLD	01.05.43 - 07.10.43
S/L M.G. BARNETT[1]	07.10.43 - 10.08.44
S/L J. BERRY (†)	10.08.44 - 02.10.44
S/L A. PARKER-REES	13.10.44 - 20.04.45

[1] New Zealander

CODE : SD

Formed
14.06.29

Disbanded
20.04.45

When "*Gus*" Holden arrived on 05.05.40 to the Squadron, he soon became one a key-man of the unit during the Battle of France. Logically after the return of the unit, he led one of the flight for most of the Battle of Britain, before leading the unit in November 1940. (IWM C1678)

OPERATIONAL DATA

NUMBER OF SORTIES

	Hurr. I	Hurr. X	Spit. I	Spit. II	Spit. V	Spit. IX	Tempest V
First sortie	11.11.39	26.08.40	09.05.41	29.05.41	03.10.41	24.11.43	05.08.44
Last sortie	25.05.41	26.11.40	14.06.41	24.10.41	27.07.44	29.04.44	29.03.45
Total by type	3,808	232	134	620	7,883	338*	1,006

* Form 541 for the dates between 24.03.44 to 29.03.44 are misssing. This total can be a bit more.
Total for the unit : 14,140 sorties.

	Hurr. I	Hurr. X	Spit. I	Spit. II	Spit. V	Spit. IX	Tempest V
Aircraft lost	72	3	-	3	60	1	7
Claims (Conf. & Prob.)	178.$^{1/3}$	3.$^{1/6}$	-	7	12.5	-	-
V-1s	-	-	-	-	1	-	+83

Total for the unit : 146 aircraft lost, 201 claims, and over 84 V-1s destroyed.

NUMBER OF PILOTS LOST

	Hurr. I	Hurr. X	Spit. I	Spit. II	Spit. V	Spit. IX	Tempest V
Killed	29	1	-	2	28	-	4
PoW	-	-	-	-	6	1	-
Evaded	-	-	-	-	1	-	-

Total for the unit : 64 pilots killed, 7 pilots PoW, 1 evaded.

BREAKDOWN OF PILOTS KILLED BY CITIZENSHIP

Americans	:	2
Belgian	:	1
British	:	50
Canadians	:	4
Czechoslovaks	:	3
French	:	1
New Zealanders	:	2
Poles	:	2
South African	:	1

DETAILS OF THE FIRST AND LAST MISSION (SERIAL, NAME, TIME OF DEPARTURE AND RETURN)

11.11.39	29.03.45
Active operattion (interception)	Night scramble for Divers
L2055/K F/L E.S. Williams 1050 1130	EJ580/G F/L J.G. Musgrave 0245 0330

MAJOR AWARDS

DSO	DFC	DFM
1	**13**	**6**
	DFC : 12	DFM : 5
	BAR : 1	BAR : 1

HIGHER COMMANDS

<u>FIGHTER COMMAND</u>
No.11 Group
01.09.39/10.05.40

<u>AASF</u>
10.05.40/21.06.40

<u>FIGHTER COMMAND</u>
No.11 Group
21.06.40/04.07.40

No.10 Group
04.07.40/25.07.40

No.11 Group
25.07.40/10.09.40

Kenley Sector, No.11 Group
10.09.40/17.12.40

Exeter Sector, No.10 Group
17.12.40/09.04.41

Colerne Sector, No.10 Group
09.04.41/25.06.41

Middle Wallop Sector, No.10 Group
25.06.41/03.07.42

Tangmere Sector, No.11 Group
03.07.42/07.07.42

Middle Wallop Sector, No.10 Group
07.07.42/08.10.42

Biggin Sector, No.11 Group
08.10.42/10.10.42

Middle Wallop Sector, No.10 Group
10.10.42/19.10.42

RAF Northern Ireland
19.10.42/30.04.43

Tangmere Sector, No.11 Group
30.04.43/17.05.43

Debden Sector, No.11 Group
17.05.43/05.06.43

Woodvale Sector, No.9 Group
05.06.43/12.06.43

Tangmere Sector, No.11 Group
12.06.43/21.06.43

Biggin Hill Sector, No.11 Group
21.06.43/15.11.43

<u>ADGB</u>
Biggin Hill Sector, No.11 Group
15.11.43/21.01.44

Hornchurch Sector, No.11 Group
21.01.44/04.02.44

Biggin Hill Sector, No.11 Group
04.02.44/30.04.44

Kenley Sector, No.11 Group
30.04.44/02.07.44

Tangmere Sector, No.11 Group
02.07.44/02.08.44

Hornchurch Sector, No.11 Group
02.08.44/22.09.44

North Weald Sector, No.11 Group
22.09.44/15.10.44

<u>FIGHTER COMMAND</u>
North Weald Sector, No.11 Group
15.10.44/20.04.45

KNOWN INDIVIDUAL LETTERS

A : L2045, P2549, P3646, V6612, V7051, V7234, AD116*, AR274* [IR-G], BM131*, BR168*, EJ585**, EP244*, EP395*, EP570*

B : L2052, P2760, V6723, BM565*, EJ593**, EN910*, EN958*, EP522*, EP707*, EP757*

C : AB184*, AB989*, AD348*, AD378*, BL856*, EJ596**, EP570*

D : L1868, P3820, P8256*, AA917*, AR392*, BM653*, EJ597**, EN974*, MJ311*

E : L2054, P3083, P3582, R7195*, R7197*, V7498, V7614, W3606*, AA837*, AA917*, AA945*, BL564*, BL565*, EJ626**, EN963*, EP555*, EP705*, MH909*

F : L1853, V7357, V7596, W3624*, AB493*, AR429*, BM641*, EJ600**, EP281*, EP538*, MA817*

G : L2056, P2793, P2986, P3102, P8664*, R4219, V6841, AA862*, AB279*, AB374*, BL993*, BM238*, BM258*, EJ580**

H : L2124, P3349, P3397, P3803, P8075*, R4222, V6644, V7230, V7433, AD572*, AR448*, AR519*, BL688*, BM587*, EJ598**, EP133*, MH362*

I : BL615*, MA585*

J : P5194, P8741*, V6780, W3313*, X4381*, BM411*, EJ589**, EJ763**, EP128*

K : L1824, L2055, N2329, V7469, AB402*, AD129*, BL388*, BL468*, BL579*, BM158*, EJ605**, EP651*, MH939*

L : L1572, L2037, P2691, P3714, P8074*, R4223, V6646, V7402 , W3605*, AD324*, BL409*, BL520*, EJ590**, EN956*, EP120*, EP871*

M : L1949, L2053, N2617, P5189, X4990*, W3702*, BL425*, BL933*, EJ603**, EN960*, EP747*

N : L1910, P2964, P3059, P3084, P3347, P3450, V6540, V7190, V7209, V7403, AB828*, AB871*, AB961*, AD465*, AR606*, BL778*, BM157*, BR168*, EJ607**

O : L1639, L1949, P2969, P3815, P5189, P7327*, P7677*, P7681*, V7015, V7054, V7650, X4353*, W3817*, AD188*, BL579*, BL762*, MJ129*

P : L1866, L1911, P3040, P3407, P7463*, P8720*, R4101, V7540, X4645*, W3457, W3722*, AB186*, AR616*, BL541*, BM124*, EJ602**, EN899*, EP191*, EP398*, EP559*

Q : W3946*, AB452*, BL377*, BM593*, EJ584**, EP277*

R : L1624, L1865, L1867, L1991, P2959, P3816, P8249*, V6600, V6672, V6787, V6919, V7056, W3841*, BL344*, BL592*, BL962*, BM574*, EJ538**, EP109*, EP129*, EP388*

S : L1636, P3397, P7432*, P7664*, P8799*, AD465*, AR529*, BL632*, EJ551**, EP126*, MH855*

T : P3082, P3208, P3653, P7433*, V6645, V7469, AD237*, BM304*, EJ656**, EP121*, EP289*

U : L1824, AA910*, AB467*, EJ558**, EJ594**

V : L2038, N2485, P7354*, P7627*, R6979*, V6805, V7229, W3766*, AA733*, AA743*, AD353*, AD579*, AR609*, BL344*, BM256*, EJ583**, EJ672**, EN962*, EP118*

W : N2485, P3141, P3417, P5200, P7378*, R4105, R4120, V6806, V6959, V7595, X4478*, W3245*, AB518*, AD200*, AD266*, BM385*, EE680*, EJ599**

X : P3119, P3767, P7681*, P7731*, R7141*, V6799, V7497, X4258*, W3939*, AB960*, AD362*, BL965*, EJ763**, EN961*

Y : L1636, P8143*, P8196*, V6840, V7626, X4989*, W3378*, W3703*, AB183*, AB491*, AR296*, BL969*, BM312*, BP855*, EJ555**, EP120*, EP126*, EP130*

Z : P3820, P7382*, W3846*, W3931*, AB275*, AB491*, AR295*, AR372*, BL681*, EJ591**, EP300*, MH333*

2 : MJ311*

3 : MJ129*

4 : BS474*, BS538*

5 : MH855*

6 : MH909*

Spitfire*
Tempest**

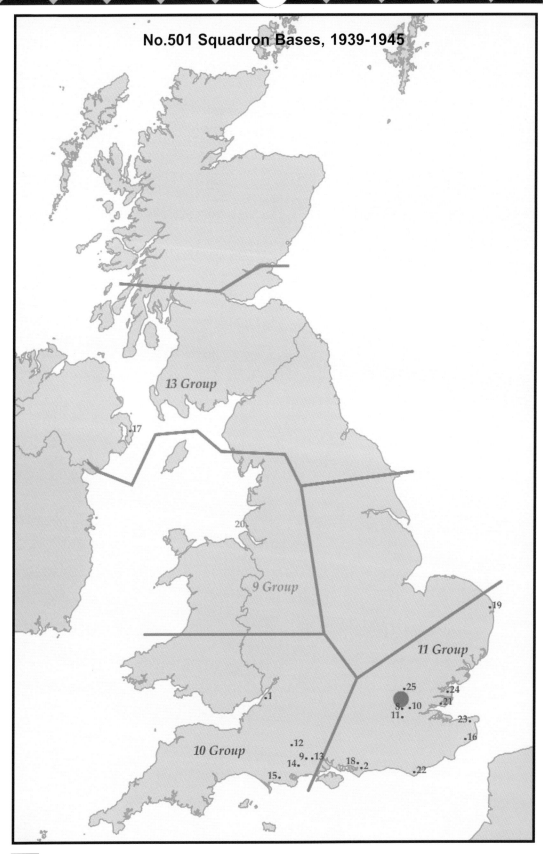

No.501 Squadron Bases, 1939-1945

13 Group

9 Group

11 Group

10 Group

Squadron Bases, France & United Kingdom

Filton* [1]	14.06.29 - 27.11.39	Ibsley [14]	07.07.42 - 24.08.42
Tangmere [2]	27.11.39 - 10.05.40	Middle Wallop [9]	24.08.42 - 08.10.42
Bétheniville [3]*	10.05.40 - 16.05.40	Hawkinge [16]	08.10.42 - 10.10.42
Anglure [4]*	23.03.42 - 02.06.40	Middle Wallop [9]	10.10.42 - 19.10.42
Le Mans [5]*	02.06.40 - 16.06.40	Ballyhalbert [17]	19.10.42 - 30.04.43
Dinart [6]*	16.06.40 - 19.06.40	Westhampnett [18]	30.04.43 - 17.05.43
St-Helier [7]*	19.06.40 - 21.06.40	Martlesham Heath [19]	17.05.43 - 05.06.43
Croydon [8]	21.06.40 - 04.07.40	Woodvale [20]	05.06.43 - 12.06.43
Middle Wallop [9]	04.07.40 - 25.07.40	Westhampnett [18]	12.06.43 - 21.06.43
Gravesend [10]	25.07.40 - 10.09.40	Hawkinge [16]	21.06.43 - 21.01.44
Kenley [11]	10.09.40 - 17.12.40	Southend [21]	21.01.44 - 04.02.44
Filton [1]	17.12.40 - 09.04.41	Hawkinge [16]	04.02.44 - 30.04.44
Colerne [12]	09.04.41 - 25.06.41	Friston [22]	30.04.44 - 02.07.44
Chilbolton [13]	25.06.41 - 05.08.41	Westhampnett [18]	02.07.44 - 02.08.44
Ibsley [14]	05.08.41 - 25.01.42	Manston [23]	02.08.44 - 22.09.44
Warmwell [15]	25.01.42 - 07.02.42	Bradwell Bay [24]	22.09.44 - 03.03.45
Ibsley [14]	07.02.42 - 03.07.42	Hunsdon [25]	03.03.45 - 20.04.45
Tangmere [2]	03.07.42 - 07.07.42		

*Filton was under No.11 Group authority until the formation of No.10 Group on 01.06.40.
*France

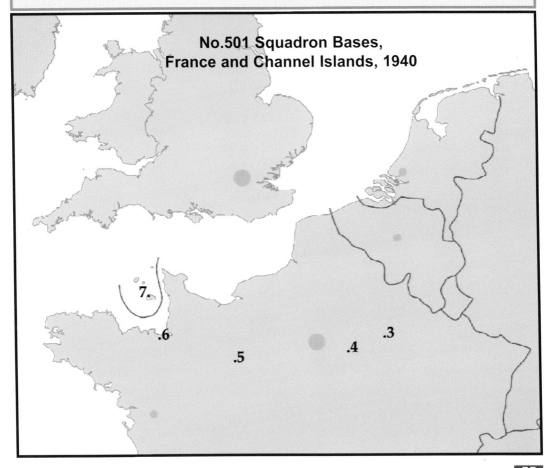

No.501 Squadron Bases,
France and Channel Islands, 1940

OPERATIONAL DIARY - NUMBER OF SORTIES

DATE	NUMBER	DATE	NUMBER	DATE	NUMBER	DATE	NUMBER
		14.05.40	13	14.07.40	9	01.09.40	30
		15.05.40	18	15.07.40	6	02.09.40	42
11.11.39	6	16.05.40	12	16.07.40	29	03.09.40	24
Total for the month : **6**		17.05.40	6	17.07.40	18	04.09.40	20
		18.05.40	6	18.07.40	7	05.09.40	40
06.12.39	6	19.05.40	11	19.07.40	15	06.09.40	33
17.12.39	3	20.05.40	15	20.07.40	26	07.09.40	32
Total for the month : **9**		21.05.40	15	21.07.40	35	08.09.40	16
		22.05.40	6	23.07.40	19	09.09.40	23
01.01.40	3	23.05.40	15	24.07.40	29	11.09.40	23
10.01.40	1	24.05.40	9	25.07.40	24	12.09.40	1
11.01.40	3	25.05.40	14	27.07.40	46	13.09.40	4
25.01.40	2	26.05.40	21	28.07.40	29	14.09.40	36
Total for the month : **9**		27.05.40	20	29.07.40	17	15.09.40	23
		28.05.40	3	30.07.40	18	16.09.40	11
03.02.40	3	29.05.40	9	*Total for the month* : **426**		17.09.40	15
07.02.40	5	*Total for the month* : **279**				18.09.40	40
09.02.40	4					19.09.40	3
20.02.40	3	01.06.40	8	01.08.40	27	20.09.40	18
21.02.40	6	02.06.40	15	02.08.40	24	21.09.40	16
26.02.40	3	03.06.40	14	03.08.40	18	22.09.40	2
Total for the month : **24**		04.06.40	6	04.08.40	3	23.09.40	24
		05.06.40	17	05.08.40	13	24.09.40	49
02.03.40	2	06.06.40	13	08.08.40	14	25.09.40	14
04.03.40	5	07.06.40	6	09.08.40	31	26.09.40	12
09.03.40	3	08.06.40	21	10.08.40	13	27.09.40	35
12.03.40	3	09.06.40	2	11.08.40	20	28.09.40	30
14.03.40	3	10.06.40	20	12.08.40	33	29.09.40	13
17.03.40	18	11.06.40	22	14.08.40	42	30.09.40	38
18.03.40	3	14.06.40	12	15.08.40	64	*Total for the month* : **667**	
21.03.40	1	15.06.40	4	16.08.40	35		
22.03.40	5	16.06.40	2	17.08.40	3		
23.03.40	3	17.06.40	1	18.08.40	58	01.10.40	13
24.03.40	2	18.06.40	1	19.08.40	9	02.10.40	22
27.03.40	8	19.06.40	3	20.08.40	19	04.10.40	9
28.03.40	9	25.06.40	3	21.08.40	12	05.10.40	34
29.03.40	3	26.06.40	1	22.08.40	17	07.10.40	25
30.03.40	3	*Total for the month* : **171**		23.08.40	18	08.10.40	16
Total for the month : **71**				24.08.40	85	09.10.40	28
		06.07.40	4	25.08.44	22	10.10.40	10
01.04.40	2	07.07.40	7	26.08.40	39	11.10.40	30
Total for the month : **2**		08.07.40	6	27.08.40	18	12.10.40	46
		09.07.40	5	28.08.40	24	15.10.40	34
10.05.40	15	10.07.40	18	29.08.40	15	16.10.40	5
11.05.40	21	11.07.40	15	30.08.40	47	17.10.40	20
12.05.40	36	12.07.40	21	31.08.40	29	19.10.40	16
13.05.40	14	13.07.40	23	*Total for the month* : **752**		20.10.40	9

Date	Value	Date	Value	Date	Value	Date	Value
21.10.40	6	23.12.40	5	20.03.41	2	27.05.41	2
22.10.40	8	25.12.40	12	21.03.41	2	29.05.41	22
24.10.40	15	27.12.40	2	23.03.41	2	31.05.41	2
25.10.40	28	28.12.40	1	26.03.41	20	*Total for the month* : **257**	
26.10.40	11	29.12.40	4	27.03.41	10		
27.10.40	27	*Total for the month* : **192**		29.03.41	2	02.06.41	10
28.10.40	16			30.03.41	23	03.06.41	2
29.10.40	44	01.01.41	4	31.03.41	6	06.06.41	2
30.10.40	25	03.01.41	14	*Total for the month* : **114**		07.06.41	2
31.10.40	2	04.01.41	8			09.06.41	6
Total for the month : **507**		05.01.41	6	01.04.41	2	10.06.41	6
		09.01.41	5	03.04.41	2	11.06.41	2
		10.01.41	4	04.04.41	9	12.06.41	20
01.11.40	24	11.01.41	2	05.04.41	2	13.06.41	7
02.11.40	21	12.01.41	2	06.04.41	7	14.06.41	6
05.11.40	32	13.01.41	1	07.04.41	11	16.06.41	6
06.11.40	15	15.01.41	1	08.04.41	8	17.06.41	6
07.11.40	12	16.01.41	10	09.04.41	11	18.06.41	8
08.11.40	20	17.01.41	11	10.04.41	21	19.06.41	12
09.11.40	5	22.01.41	2	12.04.41	9	20.06.41	2
10.11.40	10	*Total for the month* : **70**		13.04.41	15	22.06.41	2
12.11.40	4			15.04.41	7	23.06.41	6
13.11.40	1	02.02.41	5	16.04.41	12	24.06.41	2
14.11.40	25	04.02.41	12	17.04.41	1	25.06.41	2
15.11.40	22	06.02.41	6	18.04.41	2	26.06.41	10
16.11.40	16	08.02.41	1	20.04.41	24	27.06.41	2
17.11.40	36	15.02.41	5	22.04.41	20	*Total for the month* : **121**	
18.11.40	2	18.02.41	1	24.04.41	8		
20.11.40	22	19.02.41	3	28.04.41	2		
21.11.40	12	20.02.41	6	29.04.41	1	02.07.41	4
23.11.40	37	21.02.41	2	30.04.41	14	06.07.41	2
24.11.40	11	22.02.41	4	*Total for the month* : **188**		07.07.41	7
26.11.40	11	23.02.41	1			09.07.41	4
27.11.40	12	24.02.41	2			10.07.41	14
28.11.40	11	25.02.41	3	02.05.41	13	11.07.41	6
Total for the month : **361**		26.02.41	2	03.05.41	17	12.07.41	10
		27.02.41	3	05.05.41	14	14.07.41	13
		Total for the month : **56**		06.05.41	6	15.07.41	6
01.12.40	23			07.05.41	8	17.07.41	16
02.12.40	21	01.03.41	4	09.05.41	13	20.07.41	8
05.12.40	25	03.03.41	6	11.05.41	30	23.07.41	11
06.12.40	10	04.03.41	4	12.05.41	8	24.07.41	15
07.12.40	12	05.03.41	4	13.05.41	27	28.07.41	2
08.12.40	12	06.03.41	2	14.05.41	2	29.07.41	8
10.12.40	2	08.03.41	5	15.05.41	14	*Total for the month* : **126**	
11.12.40	23	09.03.41	8	17.05.41	22		
12.12.40	12	10.03.41	2	19.05.41	8		
13.12.40	3	11.03.41	4	21.05.41	14	01.08.41	4
17.12.40	5	13.03.41	1	22.05.41	1	02.08.41	4
19.12.40	11	14.03.41	1	23.05.41	18	04.08.41	2
21.12.40	6	15.03.41	3	24.05.41	2	05.08.41	15
22.12.40	3	19.03.41	3	25.05.41	14	06.08.41	21

Date		Date		Date		Date	
07.08.41	4	19.10.41	10	10.01.42	4	07.04.42	10
08.08.41	11	21.10.41	6	11.01.42	4	08.04.42	16
09.08.41	4	23.10.41	9	17.01.42	5	09.04.42	2
10.08.41	8	24.10.41	13	*Total for the month* : **39**		11.04.42	10
12.08.41	14	30.10.41	12			12.04.42	10
14.08.41	22	*Total for the month* : **137**				13.04.42	6
16.08.41	11			10.02.42	11	14.04.42	8
17.08.41	20	03.11.41	8	11.02.42	2	15.04.42	10
18.08.41	14	04.11.41	12	12.02.42	12	16.04.42	14
20.08.41	7	05.11.41	11	14.02.42	6	17.04.42	24
22.08.41	12	07.11.41	4	15.02.42	4	18.04.42	18
24.08.41	14	08.11.41	16	16.02.42	6	19.04.42	6
26.08.41	12	09.11.41	4	17.02.42	8	20.04.42	27
27.08.41	6	10.11.41	6	18.02.42	10	22.04.42	12
30.08.41	12	11.11.41	12	20.02.42	6	23.04.42	8
Total for the month : **217**		13.11.41	13	21.02.42	12	24.04.42	18
		17.11.41	4	22.02.42	8	25.04.42	30
		18.11.41	8	23.02.42	4	26.04.42	8
01.09.41	8	19.11.41	10	24.02.42	12	28.04.42	11
02.09.41	6	22.11.41	4	26.02.42	4	30.04.42	22
03.09.41	4	24.11.41	10	27.02.42	8	*Total for the month* : **336**	
04.09.41	18	25.11.41	6	28.02.42	14		
08.09.41	20	26.11.41	10	*Total for the month* : **127**			
09.09.41	8	27.11.41	12			01.05.42	20
10.09.41	6	28.11.41	12	01.03.42	11	02.05.42	16
11.09.41	2	30.11.41	6	03.03.42	11	03.05.42	6
13.09.41	2	*Total for the month* : **168**		07.03.42	8	04.05.42	10
16.09.41	8			08.03.42	18	05.05.42	23
17.09.41	2	01.12.41	4	09.03.42	13	06.05.42	2
18.09.41	4	04.12.41	2	10.03.42	4	07.05.42	14
20.09.41	11	05.12.41	4	12.03.42	4	08.05.42	11
21.09.41	10	06.12.41	8	13.03.42	13	09.05.42	11
23.09.41	2	07.12.41	4	14.03.42	13	11.05.42	2
27.09.41	6	09.12.41	8	15.03.42	12	14.05.42	2
30.09.41	20	11.12.41	4	19.03.42	8	15.05.42	22
Total for the month : **137**		12.12.41	6	20.03.42	2	16.05.42	16
		13.12.41	2	23.03.42	24	17.05.42	2
		15.12.41	12	24.03.42	6	18.05.42	14
01.10.41	6	16.12.41	6	25.03.42	10	19.05.42	16
02.10.41	2	17.12.41	2	26.03.42	22	20.05.42	6
03.10.41	14	18.12.41	12	27.03.42	2	21.05.42	2
05.10.41	2	21.12.41	2	28.03.42	16	22.05.42	2
07.10.41	11	22.12.41	4	29.03.42	19	23.05.42	12
09.10.41	16	30.12.41	12	*Total for the month* : **216**		24.05.42	25
10.10.41	6	31.12.41	1			25.05.42	4
11.10.41	6	*Total for the month* : **93**				26.05.42	4
12.10.41	23			01.04.42	6	27.05.42	11
13.10.41	14	02.01.42	4	02.04.42	18	28.05.42	4
14.10.41	5	04.01.42	4	03.04.42	9	29.05.42	12
15.10.41	12	06.01.42	10	04.04.42	16	30.05.42	11
16.10.41	8	08.01.42	4	05.04.42	10	31.05.42	14
17.10.41	12	09.01.42	4	06.04.42	7	*Total for the month* : **294**	

01.06.42	28	31.07.42	20	01.10.42	4	24.01.43	16

Date	Value	Date	Value	Date	Value	Date	Value
01.06.42	28	31.07.42	20	01.10.42	4	24.01.43	16
02.06.42	16	*Total for the month* : **322**		02.10.42	12	*Total for the month* : **32**	
03.06.42	22			03.10.42	5		
04.06.42	17	01.08.42	12	06.10.42	8	03.02.43	2
05.06.42	16	02.08.42	4	11.10.42	15	04.02.43	6
06.06.42	18	03.08.42	12	12.10.42	6	08.02.43	6
08.06.42	26	04.08.42	24	13.10.42	11	13.02.43	2
09.06.42	6	05.08.42	16	14.10.42	4	17.02.43	2
10.06.42	12	06.08.42	8	15.10.42	10	18.02.43	7
11.06.42	16	09.08.42	6	16.10.42	6	19.02.43	2
14.06.42	10	10.08.42	4	21.10.42	10	20.02.43	4
15.06.42	14	11.08.42	36	23.10.42	4	21.02.43	2
16.06.42	4	12.08.42	10	24.10.42	6	24.02.43	4
17.06.42	2	13.08.42	8	25.10.42	2	25.02.43	8
18.06.42	16	14.08.42	4	26.10.42	2	*Total for the month* : **45**	
20.06.42	18	17.08.42	12	28.10.42	2		
21.06.42	12	19.08.42	34	31.10.42	2	11.03.43	2
22.06.42	14	20.08.42	7	*Total for the month* : **109**		16.03.43	8
23.06.42	24	22.08.42	8			17.03.43	2
24.06.42	8	23.08.42	8			20.03.43	2
25.06.42	6	24.08.42	16	10.11.42	2	23.03.43	6
26.06.42	13	25.08.42	2	12.11.42	4	29.03.43	2
27.06.42	14	27.08.42	6	13.11.42	4	*Total for the month* : **22**	
28.06.42	2	28.08.42	12	15.11.42	2		
29.06.42	18	29.08.42	6	16.11.42	2	02.04.43	2
30.06.42	4	30.08.42	2	18.11.42	2	03.04.43	4
Total for the month : **356**		*Total for the month* : **257**		19.11.42	2	04.04.43	8
				22.11.42	2	09.04.43	6
				29.11.42	4	16.04.43	12
02.07.42	8	01.09.42	12	30.11.42	2	17.04.43	4
08.07.42	6	02.09.42	2	*Total for the month* : **26**		19.04.43	4
09.07.42	26	03.09.42	6			20.04.43	4
11.07.42	14	04.09.42	10	02.12.42	4	21.04.43	6
12.07.42	10	05.09.42	12	12.12.42	20	24.04.43	4
13.07.42	10	06.09.42	15	14.12.42	4	27.04.43	2
14.07.42	20	07.09.42	6	15.12.42	2	30.04.43	6
15.07.42	25	08.09.42	18	17.12.42	6	*Total for the month* : **62**	
16.07.42	12	09.09.42	8	18.12.42	4		
17.07.42	10	10.09.42	10	19.12.42	2	01.05.43	2
18.07.42	20	11.09.42	4	20.12.42	2	03.05.43	14
19.07.42	6	12.09.42	1	21.12.42	8	11.05.43	11
20.07.42	10	15.09.42	17	23.12.42	4	12.05.43	35
21.07.42	6	16.09.42	18	26.12.42	6	13.05.43	22
22.07.42	8	17.09.42	20	*Total for the month* : **62**		14.05.43	19
23.07.42	10	22.09.42	4			15.05.43	19
24.07.42	12	23.09.42	2	12.01.43	2	16.05.43	22
25.07.42	9	24.09.42	2	13.01.43	2	17.05.43	11
26.07.42	24	25.09.42	20	14.01.43	2	23.05.43	5
27.07.42	16	26.09.42	2	15.01.43	2	*Total for the month* : **160**	
28.07.42	18	27.09.42	10	18.01.43	2		
29.07.42	6	30.09.42	6	20.01.43	2	01.06.43	28
30.07.42	16	*Total for the month* : **205**		23.01.43	4	02.06.43	22

Date		Date		Date		Date	
03.06.43	12	02.08.43	24	22.09.43	16	15.11.43	6
04.06.43	12	03.08.43	22	23.09.43	10	16.11.43	10
08.06.43	2	04.08.43	26	24.09.43	16	17.11.43	2
13.06.43	4	05.08.43	16	25.09.43	6	18.11.43	6
16.06.43	20	06.08.43	6	26.09.43	24	19.11.43	12
17.06.43	14	07.08.43	18	27.09.43	18	20.11.43	12
18.06.43	2	08.08.43	12	28.09.43	2	22.11.43	2
19.06.43	4	09.08.43	14	29.09.43	8	23.11.43	22
20.06.43	28	10.08.43	10	30.09.43	10	24.11.43	7
24.06.43	12	11.08.43	20	*Total for the month* : **456**		25.11.43	10
25.06.43	10	12.08.43	20			26.11.43	5
26.06.43	20	13.08.43	5			27.11.43	6
27.06.43	18	14.08.43	10	02.10.43	14	29.11.43	17
28.06.43	18	15.08.43	16	03.10.43	22	30.11.43	12
29.06.43	16	16.08.43	24	04.10.43	20	*Total for the month* : **275**	
30.06.43	14	17.08.43	20	05.10.43	12		
Total for the month : **256**		18.08.43	8	06.10.43	12		
		19.08.43	32	07.10.43	7	01.12.43	18
		20.08.43	10	08.10.43	16	03.12.43	8
01.07.43	8	21.08.43	8	10.10.43	2	04.12.43	23
02.07.43	14	22.08.43	16	13.10.43	14	05.12.43	18
03.07.43	10	23.08.43	14	14.10.43	4	07.12.43	6
04.07.43	24	24.08.43	22	15.10.43	2	10.12.43	4
05.07.43	26	25.08.43	6	16.10.43	4	11.12.43	2
06.07.43	28	26.08.43	6	17.10.43	2	13.12.43	11
07.07.43	18	27.08.43	26	18.10.43	17	14.12.43	8
08.07.43	14	28.08.43	8	19.10.43	12	15.12.43	8
09.07.43	18	29.08.43	14	20.10.43	10	20.12.43	20
10.07.43	11	30.08.43	6	21.10.43	18	21.12.43	14
11.07.43	5	31.08.43	12	22.10.43	10	22.12.43	16
12.07.43	12	*Total for the month* : **460**		23.10.43	20	23.12.43	4
13.07.43	22			24.10.43	12	24.12.43	22
14.07.43	22			25.10.43	12	25.12.43	2
15.07.43	26	01.09.43	19	26.10.43	10	28.12.43	6
16.07.43	16	02.09.43	10	31.10.43	8	30.12.43	20
17.07.43	16	03.09.43	28	*Total for the month* : **260**		31.12.43	16
18.07.43	16	04.09.43	26			*Total for the month* : **226**	
19.07.43	16	05.09.43	16				
20.07.43	8	06.09.43	22	01.11.43	20		
22.07.43	12	07.09.43	30	02.11.43	6	01.01.44	18
23.07.43	10	08.09.43	19	03.11.43	14	02.01.44	16
24.07.43	18	09.09.43	26	04.11.43	6	03.01.44	14
25.07.43	24	10.09.43	12	05.11.43	8	04.01.44	29
26.07.43	34	13.09.43	20	06.11.43	6	05.01.44	20
27.07.43	24	14.09.43	10	07.11.43	18	06.01.44	22
28.07.43	29	15.09.43	7	08.11.43	12	07.01.44	20
29.07.43	20	16.09.43	11	09.11.43	12	08.01.44	4
30.07.43	26	17.09.43	6	10.11.43	14	10.01.44	6
31.07.43	30	18.09.43	24	11.11.43	20	11.01.44	14
Total for the month : **557**		19.09.43	14	12.11.43	2	14.01.44	21
		20.09.43	30	13.11.43	4	15.01.44	10
01.08.43	9	21.09.43	16	14.11.43	4	16.01.44	11

Date	Value	Date	Value	Date	Value	Date	Value
17.01.44	2	25.03.44	6	18.05.44	12	16.07.44	12
Total for the month : **207**		26.03.44	8	19.05.44	34	17.07.44	25
		27.03.44	6	20.05.44	13	18.07.44	22
		28.03.44	12	21.05.44	35	21.07.44	2
04.02.44	12	29.03.44	16	22.05.44	25	22.07.44	12
05.02.44	26	30.03.44	6	23.05.44	4	23.07.44	12
06.02.44	23	31.03.44	16	25.05.44	23	24.07.44	12
08.02.44	32	*Total for the month* : **362**		27.05.44	20	25.07.44	12
09.02.44	12			28.05.44	32	26.07.44	12
10.02.44	16			29.05.44	24	27.07.44	12
11.02.44	15	01.04.44	16	30.05.44	12	*Total for the month* : **277**	
12.02.44	5	02.04.44	6	31.05.44	4		
13.02.44	30	04.04.44	4	*Total for the month* : **484**			
14.02.44	14	08.04.44	11			05.08.44	34
15.02.44	32	09.04.44	4			06.08.44	22
16.02.44	4	10.04.44	8	03.06.44	6	07.08.44	39
18.02.44	4	11.04.44	10	04.06.44	6	08.08.44	24
20.02.44	4	12.04.44	6	06.06.44	50	09.08.44	33
21.02.44	30	13.04.44	19	07.06.44	46	10.08.44	42
22.02.44	15	14.04.44	28	08.06.44	24	11.08.44	18
23.02.44	12	15.04.44	18	10.06.44	38	12.08.44	7
24.02.44	14	16.04.44	2	11.06.44	20	13.08.44	10
25.02.44	14	18.04.44	23	12.06.44	32	14.08.44	8
26.02.44	8	19.04.44	18	14.06.44	12	15.08.44	8
28.02.44	10	20.04.44	16	15.06.44	40	16.08.44	13
29.02.44	16	21.04.44	6	16.06.44	38	17.08.44	11
Total for the month : **350**		22.04.44	23	17.06.44	38	18.08.44	13
		23.04.44	14	18.06.44	36	19.08.44	15
		24.04.44	18	19.06.44	19	20.08.44	16
01.03.44	6	25.04.44	14	20.06.44	23	21.08.44	3
02.03.44	28	26.04.44	16	21.06.44	12	23.08.44	4
03.03.44	22	27.04.44	28	22.06.44	24	24.08.44	8
04.03.44	14	28.04.44	16	23.06.44	21	25.08.44	14
05.03.44	8	29.04.44	10	24.06.44	40	26.08.44	11
06.03.44	10	*Total for the month* : **334**		25.06.44	12	27.08.44	17
07.03.44	8			27.06.44	36	28.08.44	16
08.03.44	10			28.06.44	12	29.08.44	23
09.03.44	10	01.05.44	17	29.06.44	26	30.08.44	11
11.03.44	10	02.05.44	16	30.06.44	20	31.08.44	4
12.03.44	4	04.05.44	24	*Total for the month* : **631**		*Total for the month* : **424**	
13.03.44	18	05.05.44	8				
14.03.44	16	06.05.44	12				
15.03.44	4	07.05.44	14	01.07.44	12	01.09.44	22
16.03.44	28	08.05.44	36	03.07.44	11	03.09.44	3
17.03.44	2	09.05.44	12	04.07.44	24	04.09.44	6
18.03.44	24	10.05.44	24	06.07.44	4	05.09.44	8
19.03.44	4	11.05.44	23	07.07.44	12	06.09.44	2
20.03.44	12	12.05.44	12	09.07.44	23	15.09.44	3
21.03.44	12	13.05.44	23	10.07.44	12	16.09.44	5
22.03.44	14	15.05.44	12	11.07.44	4	18.09.44	1
23.03.44	16	16.05.44	7	12.07.44	12	20.09.44	3
24.03.44	12	17.05.44	6	14.07.44	30	22.09.44	6

23.09.44	6	19.10.44	8	21.11.44	2	15.01.45	2
24.09.44	3	20.10.44	4	22.11.44	2	23.01.45	2
25.09.44	4	21.10.44	7	23.11.44	7	*Total for the month* : **18**	
26.09.44	10	23.10.44	6	24.11.44	3		
27.09.44	12	24.10.44	8	25.11.44	5	02.03.45	6
28.09.44	12	25.10.44	6	27.11.44	2	03.03.45	10
29.09.44	6	27.10.44	8	28.11.44	7	05.03.45	1
30.09.44	4	28.10.44	5	*Total for the month* : **125**		06.03.45	5
Total for the month : **116**		29.10.44	2			08.03.45	8
		30.10.44	8			15.03.45	2
		31.10.44	1	02.12.44	7	17.03.45	5
01.10.44	11	*Total for the month* : **201**		04.12.44	10	18.03.45	4
02.10.44	11			05.12.44	7	19.03.45	2
03.10.44	10			07.12.44	4	20.03.45	2
04.10.44	8	01.11.44	13	11.12.44	3	21.03.45	4
05.10.44	8	02.11.44	4	12.12.44	3	22.03.45	6
06.10.44	9	03.11.44	7	16.12.44	2	23.03.45	2
07.10.44	5	04.11.44	8	17.12.44	8	27.03.45	6
08.10.44	10	05.11.44	8	22.12.44	4	28.03.45	4
09.10.44	8	06.11.44	9	23.12.44	4	29.03.45	1
10.10.44	4	08.11.44	4	25.12.44	2	*Total for the month* : **68**	
11.10.44	5	09.11.44	12	*Total for the month* : **54**			
12.10.44	6	10.11.44	8				
13.10.44	5	11.12.44	9			*GRAND TOTAL* :	
14.10.44	12	13.11.44	4	03.01.45	3	**11,140**	
15.10.44	6	14.11.44	4	05.01.45	4		
16.10.44	4	15.11.44	3	12.01.45	4		
17.10.44	7	19.11.44	2	13.01.45	1	**Extrated from ORB**	
18.10.44	9	20.11.44	2	14.01.45	2	**AIR27/1948 - 1953**	

Tempest EJ558/R being prepared for another anti-diver patrol during Autumn 1944. (Chris Thomas)

CLAIM LIST OF PROBABLE (P) AND CONFIRMED (C) KILLS

Date	Pilot	Type	Serial	Number	Statute
		HURRICANE I/X			
10.05.40	F/O D. Pickup	Do17	L2037/L	1	C
11.05.40	Sgt R.C. Dafforn	Do17	L1910/N	1	C
	F/L E.S. Williams	Do17	L2055/K	1	C
	P/O C.S. Hulse	Bf110	L2053/M	1	C
	Sgt P.F. Morfill	Bf110		1	C
	F/O C.E. Malfroy	He111	L1866/P	1	C
	F/Sgt A.D. Payne	He111	L1991/R	1	C
12.05.40	F/O P.H. Rayner	He111	L2054/E	1	C
	P/O E. Holden	He111		1	C
	P/O E.J.H. Sylvester	He111		1	C
	P/O E. Holden	Do17		1	C
	F/Sgt A.D. Payne	He111		1	C
	P/O K.N.T. Lee	Do17	L1919/N	1	C
		Do17	L1919/N	1	P
	Sgt P.C.P. Farnes	Do17	L2045/A	0.5	C
	P/O E.J.H. Sylvester	Do17		0.5	C
	Sgt J.E. Proctor	Do17		1	C
		Bf110		1	C
	Sgt P.C.P. Farnes	He111		1	C
	Sgt D.A.S. McKay	He111		1	C
	Sgt P.F. Morfill	He111		1	C
	F/Sgt A.D. Payne	He111		1	C
13.05.40	Sgt J.H. Lacey	Bf109		1	C
		He111		1	C
		Bf110		1	C
	F/L C.D. Griffiths	Bf110		1	C
	P/O K.N.T. Lee	Bf110		1	C
14.05.40	Sgt J.E. Proctor	He111	L1991/R	2	C
	Sgt R.C. Dafforn	He111	L1866/P	1	C
	F/Sgt A.D. Payne	He111	L2045/A	1	C
	F/O J.R. Cridland	He111		1	C
	F/O E.J.H. Sylverster	Do17		0.5	C
	Sgt P.C.P. Farnes	Do17		0.5	C
15.05.40	F/L C.D. Griffiths	Do17		1	C
	P/O P.R. Hairs	Do17		0.5	C
	Sgt P.F. Morfill	Do17		0.5	C
	F/O J.R. Cridland	Do17		1	C
	P/O J.E. Proctor	Do17		1	C
27.05.40	P/O E. Holden	He111		1	C
	F/O J.R. Cridland	He111		1	C
	P/O K.N.T. Lee	He111	P2814	1	C
	P/O C.L. Hulse	He111		1	C
	P/O J.A.A. Gibson	He111		1	C
		He111		0.5	C
	Sgt D.A. Dafforn		L1949/M	0.5	C
	P/O D.A. Hewitt	He111		1	C

Date	Pilot	Aircraft	Serial	Score	C/P
	Sgt J.H. Lacey	He111		2	C
	Sgt D.A.S. McKay	He111		1	C
		He111		1	P
	Sgt R.C. Dafforn	He111		1	C
	P/O J.E.H. Sylvester	He111		1	P
	Sgt P.C.P. Farnes	He111		0.5	P
	Unknown			0.5	P
05.06.40	Sgt J.E. Proctor	Bf110		1	C
	F/Sgt A.D. Payne	Bf110		1	C
	P/O D.A. Hewitt	Bf110		1	P
	P/O J.A.A. Gibson	He111		1	C
	F/O J.R. Cridland	He111		1	C
	P/O C.L. Hulse	He111	L1949/M	1	C
06.06.40	P/O K.N.T. Lee	Do17		1	C
08.06.40	F/O J.A.A. Gibson	Bf109	L1864/K	1	C
	Unknown	Bf109		1	P
	Unknown	Bf109		1	P
10.06.40	F/O J.A.A. Gibson	Bf109		1	C
11.07.40	P/O D.A. Hewitt	E/A [1]	P3040	1	C
12.07.40	S/L E. Holden	Do17	P3646/A	1	P
13.07.40	P/O J.A.A. Gibson	Do17	P2986	1	C
20.07.40	Sgt J.H. Lacey	Bf109	P3349	1	C
		Bf109	P3349	0.5	C
	F/L P.A.N. Cox		L1865/R	0.5	C
	S/L H.A.V. Hogan	Bf109	P3803/H	1	C
27.07.40	P/O K.N.T. Lee	Bf109	P3059/N	1	P
29.07.40	P/O J.A.A. Gibson	Ju87	P3083/E	1	C
		Ju87	P3083/E	1	P
	P/O J.W. Bland	Ju87	P3141/W	1	C
	P/O B.L. Duckenfield	Ju87	P3646/A	0.5	C
	F/L G.E.B. Stoney		P3803/H	0.5	C
	Sgt D.N.E. McKay	Ju87	P3041	1	P
	F/Sgt P.F. Morfill	Bf109	P3397/S	1	C
12.08.40	Sgt J.H. Lacey	Ju87	P3815/O	1	C
		Ju87	P3815/O	1	P
		Bf110	P3815/O	1	P
	P/O J.A.A. Gibson	Ju87	R4101/P	2	C
		Bf109	P2986	1	C
	P/O K.N.T. Lee	Ju87	P3059/N	1	C
	P/O R.C. Dafforn	Ju87	P3820/D	1	C
	Sgt P.C.P. Farnes	Ju87	P2760/B	1	C
	P/O P. Zenker	Ju87	P3397/S	1	P
	S/L A.L. Holland	Bf109	P3816/R	1	P
15.08.40	Sgt A. Glowacki	Ju87	V7234/A	1	C
	P/O J.A.A. Gibson	Ju87	P3582	1	C
	F/O S. Witorzenc	Ju87	V7230	2	C
	F/L G.E.B. Stoney	Ju87	R4101/P	2	C
		Ju87	R4101/P	1	P
	Sgt P.C.P. Farnes	Ju87	P2760/B	2	C
	Sgt D.N.E. McKay	Ju87	P3141/W	2	C
	P/O R.C. Dafforn	Bf110	P3208/P	1	C
16.08.40	Sgt J.H. Lacey	Bf109	N2617/M	1	P
18.08.40	P/O P. Zenker	Bf109	R4105/W	1	C
	F/O S. Witorzenc	Bf109	L1868/D	1	C
	Sgt A. Glowacki	Bf109	P3820/Z	1	C

[1] Enemy Aircraft, identified as "Enemy Hurricane"

Date	Pilot	Aircraft	Serial	Score	C/P
24.08.40	Sgt A. Glowacki	Bf109	V7234/A	3	C
		Ju88	V7234/A	2	C
	Sgt J.H. Lacey	Ju88	P8816	1	C
	P/O J.A.A. Gibson	Ju88	R4222/H	2	C
	P/O K.R. Aldridge	Ju88	L1865/R	2	C
27.08.40	S/L H.A.V. Hogan	Do215 [2]	R4222/H	0.33	C
28.08.40	F/Sgt P.C.P. Farnes	Bf109	P2760/B	1	C
	P/O B.L. Duckenfireld	Bf109	R4105/W	1	C
	Sgt A. Glowacki	Bf109	P5193/O [Mk.X]	1	C
29.08.40	F/L J.A.A. Gibson	Bf109	P3102/G	1	C
	Sgt J.H. Lacey	Bf109	L1578	1	C
30.08.40	Sgt W.B. Henn	He111	L1868/D	1	C
	Sgt J.H. Lacey	He111	P8816	1	C
		Bf110	P8816	1	P
	P/O S. Skalski	He111	P3820	1	C
	F/Sgt P.F. Morfill	He111	R4105/W	1	C
31.08.40	Sgt J.H. Lacey	Bf109	P2760/B	1	C
	P/O S. Skalski	Bf109	P5194/J [Mk.X]	1	C
	Sgt A. Glowacki	Bf109	V6540/N	1	C
02.09.40	Sgt J.H. Lacey	Bf109	V7357/F	1	C
		Bf109	V7404	1	C
	P/O S. Skalski	Bf109	V7230/H	2	C
	P/O H.C. Adams	Bf109	V7234/A	1	C
	F/O S. Witorzenc	Do17	L1868/D	1	C
05.09.40	P/O P.R. Hairs	Bf109	V6645/T	1	C
	Unknown	Bf109		1	P
	Sgt J.H. Lacey	Bf109	V7404	2	C
	Sgt R.J.K. Gent	Bf109	P2760/B	1	P
06.09.40	F/L J.A.A. Gibson	Bf109	V7357/F	1	C
08.09.40	P/O B.L. Duckenfield	Bf110	R4105/W	1	C
11.09.40	F/O R.C. Dafforn	Do215	V6670	0.16	C
	F/Sgt P.F. Morfill		P3397	0.16	C
	F/O S. Witorzenc		P5194 [Mk.X]	0.16	C
	Unknown			0.16	C
	Unknown			0.16	C
	Unknown			0.16	C
13.09.40	Sgt L.H. Lacey	He111	P2793	1	C
15.09.40	F/Sgt P.F. Morfill	Do17	P5193/O [Mk.X]	1	C
	P/O E.B. Rogers	Do17	P3397	1	C
	Sgt J.H. Lacey	Bf109	V7357/F	2	C
		He111	V7357/F	1	C
	Sgt E.J. Egan	Bf109	P3820/Z	1	C
17.09.40	S/L H.A.V. Hogan	Bf109	V6645/T	1	P
	P/O P.R. Hairs	Bf109	V6645/T	1	P
18.09.40	Sgt W.J. Glowacki	Bf109	L1572/Y	1	P
27.09.40	S/L H.A.V. Hogan	Bf110 [3]	V6703	0.5	C
	Unknown	Bf110		1	C
	Sgt J.H. Lacey	Bf109		1	C
	Unknown	Bf109	V7498/E	1	C
30.09.40	F/L E. Holden	Bf109	V6799/X	1	P
	Sgt P.C.P. Farnes	Ju88	V7229	1	C
05.10.40	P/O K.W. Mackenzie	Bf109	V6799/X	1	C
	S/L H.A.V. Hogan	Bf110	V7229	1	C

[2] Shared with two pilots of No.56 Sqn
[3] Shared with a pilot of No.303 (Polish) Sqn

James Harry Lacey in 1940, the top scorer of the Battle of Britain with 18 confirmed victories. He is also one of 56 RAF member to have been awarded a BAR to his DFM.
(501 Squadron Association)

07.10.40	F/L E. Holden	Bf109	V6806/W	1	C
	P/O K.W. Mackenzie	Bf109	V6799/X	1.5	C
	S/L H.A.V. Hogan		V7229	0.5	C
	Sgt J.H. Lacey	Bf109	V6840/Y	1	P
12.10.40	Sgt J.H. Lacey	Bf109	V6840/Y	1	C
	S/L H.A.V. Hogan	Bf109	V7229	1	C
	F/L E. Holden	Bf109	V6805/V	1	C
15.10.40	S/L H.A.V. Hogan	Bf109	V7229	1	C
25.10.40	P/O V. Zaoral	Bf109	R4101/P	1	C
	P/O V.R. Snell	Bf109	P3119/X	0.5	C
	F/L E. Holden		V6805/V	1.5	C
	Sgt R.J.K. Gent	Bf109	V6841/G	1	C
26.10.40	Sgt J.H. Lacey	Bf109	V7614/E	1	C
27.10.40	P/O K.W. Mackenzie	Bf109	P3119/X	1	C
	S/L H.A.V. Hogan	Bf109	V6723	1	P
29.10.40	Sgt T.G. Pickering	Bf109	R4101/P	1	C
	P/O K.W. Mackenzie	Bf109	P3119/X	1	C
	Sgt P.C.P. Farnes	Bf109	V7614/E	1	P
30.10.40	P/O R.C. Dafforn	Bf109	P3397	1	C
	Sgt J.H. Lacey	Bf109	V7614/E	1	C
	Sgt J.H. Lacey	Bf109	V7614/E	1	P
08.11.40	F/Sgt P.C.P. Farnes	Bf109	V7469/K	1	P
	F/L D.A.E. Jones	Bf109	V7469/K	1	C
	P/O K.W. Mackenzie	Bf109	V7650/O	1	C
15.11.40	P/O K.W. Mackenzie	Bf109	V7650/O	1	C
24.11.40	*Unknown*	Bf109 **[4]**		0.20	C
	Unknown			0.20	C
	Unknown			0.20	C
	Unknown			0.20	C

SPITFIRE II

07.07.41	S/L A.H. Boyd	Ju88	P8256/D	1	C*
10.07.41	F/L J.H. Lacey	Bf109	P7990	1	C
17.07.41	F/L J.H. Lacey	He59	P7408	1	C
24.07.41	S/L A.H. Boyd	Bf109	P7448	2	C
	F/L J.H. Lacey	Bf109	P7902	2	C

*At night

SPITFIRE V

09.10.41	*Squadron*	Ju88	-	1	C
09.03.42	P/O R.A. Newberry	Bf109	P8741/J	1	C
13.03.42	P/O R.C. Lynch	Ju88 **[5]**	AD538	0.5	P
17.04.42	S/L C.F. Currant	Bf109	AR372/Z	1	P
04.06.42	Sgt J.K. Jerabek	FW190	AB491	1	C
20.06.42	P/O J.A.G. Jackson	FW190	AB452	1	P
19.08.42	F/L P.J. Stanbury	Do217	EP538/A	1	C
27.07.43	F/O A.J. Grottick	Bf109	W3457/B	1	C
09.08.43	*Capitaine* B. Fuchs	Bf109	EN899/P **[6]**	1	C
07.10.43	*Capitaine* B. Fuchs	Bf109	BL962/R	1	P

08.06.44	F/L D.C. Fairbanks	Bf109	X4272/J	1	C
	F/L L.P. Griffith	Bf109	AA945/E	1	P
26.06.44	S/L M.G. Barnett	V-1	W3702/M [7]	1	C
30.06.44	F/O R.C. Stockburn	Bf109	BL632/S	0.5	C
	W/C D.E. Kingaby		D.E.K.	0.5	C

[4] Shared with a pilot of No.421 Flt.
[5] Shared with W/C I.R. Gleed, Iblsey Wing Leader.]
[6] date unclear, the the ORB dates the combat on 11.08.43.
[7] During a non operational flight.
At least one further claim was not administred : F/L D.F. Lenton (BM411/J) , 25.06.43, a FW190 probably destroyed.

TEMPEST V

05.08.44	F/Sgt R.W. Ryman	V-1	EJ585/A	1	C
	F/O W.F. Polley	V-1	EJ598/H	1	C
07.08.44	F/O R.C. Deleuze	V-1	EJ599/W	1	C
11.08.44	F/L C.B. Thornton	V-1	JN855/U [8]	3	C*
	F/O E.L. Williams	V-1	EJ520/Y [9]	1	C*
	F/O R.G. Lucas	V-1	EJ590/L	1	C*
	Ff.Of B.F. Miller	V-1	EJ584/Q	3	C*
13.08.44	S/L J. Berry	V-1	EJ590/L	3	C*
	F/L L.R.T. Robb	V-1	EJ598/H	1	C*
14.08.44	F/L R.T Robb	V-1	JN855/U [8]	1	C*
16.08.44	S/L J. Berry	V-1	EJ590/L	2	C*
19.08.44	F/O W.F. Polley	V-1	EJ591/Z	1	C*
	P/O R.H. Bennett	V-1	EJ553/L [10]	1	C*
	F/L H. Burton	V-1	EJ603/M	1	C*
20.08.44	S/L J. Berry	V-1	EJ584/Q	1	C
24.08.44	F/O R.C. Deleuze	V-1	EJ607/N	1	C
	F/O R.C. Stockburn	V-1	EJ599/W	1	C
27.08.44	F/O R.G. Lucas	V-1	EJ590/L	1	C*
	F/L G.L. Bonham	V-1	EJ597/D	4	C
	F/O W.F. Polley	V-1	EJ598/M	1	C
	P/O R.H. Bennett	V-1	EJ593/B	1	C
28.08.44	F/O A.J. Grottick	V-1	EJ607/N	1	C
31.08.44	F/O E.L. Williams	V-1	EJ585/A	1	C*
	S/L J. Berry	V-1	EJ596/C	1	C
05.09.44	F/O K.V. Panter	V-1	EJ551/S	1	C
	F/O R.C. Deleuze	V-1	EJ591/Z	1	C
16.09.44	Flt.O B.F. Miller	V-1	?/M	2	C
05.10.44	F/O J.A.L. Johnson	V-1	EJ605/K	1	C*
06.10.44	F/O R.C. Deleuze	V-1	EJ584/Q	1	C*
07.10.44	F/L E.L. Williams	V-1	EJ590/L	2	C*
11.10.44	F/L E.L. Williams	V-1	EJ590/L	1	C*
12.10.44	F/L A.T. Langdon-Down	V-1	EJ593/B	1	C*
	F/L C.R. Birbeck	V-1	EJ598/H	1	C*
13.10.44	F/L E.L. Williams	V-1	EJ605/K	1	C*
	F/L R. Bradwell	V-1	EJ589/J	1	C*
14.10.44	W/O E.Wojozynski	V-1	EJ763/X	1	C*
15.10.44	F/O R.C. Deleuze	V-1	EJ589/J	2	C*
16.10.44	F/O R.H. Bennett	V-1	EJ580/G	1	C
17.10.44	W/O E.Wojozynski	V-1	EJ763/X	1	C*
20.10.44	F/O K.V. Panter	V-1	EJ599/W	2	C*

[8] Still coded ZQ-L, former FIU aircraft.
[9] Still coded ZQ-Y, former FIU aircraft.
[10] Still coded ZQ-L, former FIU aircraft.

21.10.44	F/O R.C. Deleuze	V-1	EJ584/Q	1	C*
	F/O J.A.L. Johnson	V-1	EJ593/B	2	C*
24.10.44	F/O D.A. Porter	V-1	EJ589/J	1	C*
	F/O R.H. Bennett	V-1	EJ608/P	1	C*
	F/L C.R. Birbeck	V-1	?/H	1	C*
25.10.44	F/O R.C. Stockburn	V-1	EJ594/U	1	C
	F/L R.L.T. Robb	V-1	EJ555/Y	1	C
29.10.44	F/L E.L. Williams	V-1	EJ590/L	1	C
31.10.44	F/O A.J. Grottick	V-1	EJ555/Y	1	C
03.11.44	F/L E.L. Williams	V-1	EJ590/L	1	C*
	F/O D.A. Porter	V-1	EJ605/K	1	C*
08.11.44	F/O D.A. Porter	V-1	EJ605/K	1	C*
	F/L R. Bradwell	V-1	EJ589/J	1	C*
09.11.44	F/L R. Bradwell	V-1	EJ589/J	1	C*
10.11.44	F/L H. Burton	V-1	EJ591/Z	1	C*
	F/O J. Maday	V-1	EJ763/X	1	C*
11.11.44	F/L H. Burton	V-1	EJ591/Z	1	C*
23.11.44	F/L H. Burton	V-1	EJ591/Z	1	C*
24.11.44	F/L H. Burton	V-1	EJ591/Z	1	C*
05.12.44	F/L H. Burton	V-1	EJ607/N	1	C*
	S/L A. Parker-Rees	V-1	EJ608/P	1	C*
07.12.44	F/L D.A. Porter	V-1	EJ605/K	1	C*
18.12.44	W/O S.H. Balam	V-1	EJ607/N	1	C*
	F/O R.C. Deleuze	V-1	EJ607/V	1	C*
	W/O E. Wojozynski	V-1	EJ580/G	1	C*
	F/L R.J. Lilwall	V-1	EJ608/P	1	C
06.03.45	F/O J.A.L. Johnson	V-1	EJ580/G	1	C*
27.03.45	F/L A.J. Grottick	V-1	EJ599/W	1	C*

*At night

Total : 201 aircraft
(four being shared with other units)
84 V-1s [11]

Aircraft damaged : 69

[11] It is generally accepted that the total V-1 'Kills' were over 100 - the final total will never be known because some pilots failed to claim the incident. By December alone, the total was 93 (see page 47).

The V-1. In the last months of the war, the destruction of this deadly machine became the main task of any pilot of No.501 Squadron. (via P. Sortehaug)

AIRCRAFT LOST ON OPERATIONS

Date	Pilot	Cause	Serial	Mark	Fate
		HURRICANE			
12.05.40	P/O M.F.C. Smith	1	L2053/M	I	†
	F/O P.H. Rayner	1	L2054/E	I	†
14.05.40	Sgt R.C. Dafforn	?	L1866/P	I	-
03.06.40	Sgt P.R. Hairs	1	P2867	I	-
05.06.40	P/O J.A. Claydon	1	P3450/N	I	†
06.06.40	F/O D.A. Hewitt	?	L1911/P	I	-
08.06.40	P/O C.L. Hulse	1	P3542	I	†
11.07.40	Sgt F.J. Dixon	1	N2485/W	I	†
12.07.40	P/O D.A. Hewitt	1	P3084/E	I	†
20.07.40	P/O E.J.H. Sylvester	1	P3082/T	I	†
26.07.40	F/O P.A.H. Cox	1	P3808	I	†
30.07.40	P/O R.S. Don	3	P3646/A	I	-
12.08.40	F/O K. Lukaszewicz	1	P3803/H	I	†
15.08.40	F/L A.R. Putt	1	P3040/P	I	-
	F/L J.A.A. Gibson	1	P3582/E	I	-
18.08.40	Sgt D.A.S. McKay	1	N2617/M	I	-
	Sgt G.E.B. Stoney	1	P2549/A	I	†
	P/O K.N.T. Lee	1	P3059/N	I	-
	P/O J.W. Bland	1	P3208/T	I	†
	P/O F. Kozlowski	1	P3815/O	I	-
	F/O R.C. Dafforn	1	R4219/G	I	-
24.08.40	P/O K.R. Aldridge	1	L1865/R	I	-
	P/O P. Zenker	1	P3141/W	I	†
29.08.40	F/L J.A.A. Gibson	1	P3102/G	I	-
	Sgt W.J. Green	1	R4223/L	I	-
31.08.40	Sgt A. Glowacki	1	V6540/N	I	-
02.09.40	P/O A.T. Rose-Price	1	L1578	I	†
06.09.40	Sgt G.W. Pearson	1	P3516	I	†
	P/O H.C. Adams	1	V6612/A	I	†
	Sgt O.V. Houghton	1	V6646/L	I	†
11.09.40	Sgt T.G. Pickering	1	P5200/W	X	-
13.09.40	Sgt J.H. Lacey	1	P2793	I	-
15.09.40	P/O A.E. van den Hove	1	P2760/B	I	†
	P/O S. Skalski	1	V6644/H	I	-
17.09.40	Sgt E.J. Egan	1	P3820/Z	I	†
	Sgt J.H. Lacey	1	V7357/F	I	-
18.09.40	Sgt C.J. Saward	1	V6600/R	I	-
	S/L H.A.V. Hogan	1	V6620	I	-
27.09.40	P/O M.E. Gunter	1	V6645/T	I	†
	Sgt V.H. Ekins	1	V6672/R	I	-
28.09.40	P/O F.C. Harrold	1	P3417/W	I	†
	P/O E.B. Rogers	1	V7497/X	I	-
30.09.40	F/O N.J.M. Barry	1	L1657	I	-
07.10.40	F/O N.J.M. Barry	1	V6800	I	†
15.10.40	Sgt S.A. Fenemore	1	V6722	I	†

25.10.40	P/O V.R. Snell	1	N2438	I	-
	P/O V. Göth	3	P2903	I	†
	P/O K.W. Mackenzie	3	V6806/W	I	-
	Sgt S.A.H. Whitehouse	1	P5193/O	X	-
01.11.40	Sgt M. Marcinkowski	3	V7405	I	†
08.11.40	Sgt H.C. Groves	1	V6805/V	I	†
28.11.40	Sgt L.J. Patterson	1	P5189/M	X	†
02.12.40	P/O R.C. Dafforn	1	V6919/R	I	-
11.05.41	Sgt R.A. Smithers	3	V7056/R	I	†

Aircraft lost in France with no date more details : L1624/R, L1949/M, L1953/F, L1991/R, L2037/L, L2050, L2056, P2959, P2964/N, P2969/P, P3270, P3347/N, P3407, P3453, P3491, P3604, P3651.

SPITFIRE

10.06.41	Sgt C.J. Barton	3	P8143/Y	IIA	†
06.08.41	Sgt A. Beacham	3	P7731/X	IIA	†
04.11.41	P/O E.H.L. Shore	1	AA837/E	VB	PoW

Pilot Officer E.H. Shore's Spitfire AA837/SD-E being inspected by German soldiers after his emergency landing on a French beach on 04.11.41. (RAF Museum P.9888)

08.11.41	P/O W.J.H. Greenaway	1	AD188/O	VB	PoW
17.11.41	Sgt R.F.C. Dean	3	AD129	VB	†
04.04.42	F/Sgt D.S. Thomas	3	BL789	VB	†
25.04.42	Sgt M. Rocovsky	1	W3840	VB	†
	P/O A. Palmer-Tomkinson	1	W3894	VB	†
	Sgt J. Blair	1	AB179	VB	-
	Sgt K. Vrtis	1	AB251	VB	†
	F/Sgt V. Bauman	2	AB538	VB	-
	F/O R. Wheldon	1	BL974	VB	†
09.05.42	P/O E.W. Gillespie	1	W3845	VB	†
04.06.42	Sgt B. Strachan	1	W3842	VB	†
	Sgt J.E.A. Potelle	1	AB381	VC	PoW
20.06.42	F/Sgt V. Bauman	1	AB497	VC	PoW
05.08.42	Sgt W.R. Leicht	1	BP855/Y	VB	†

Flight Sergeant V. Bauman in front of a Spitfire Mk.V coded SD-J, a few days before being shot down and made PoW.
(Jiri Rajlich)

11.08.42	P/O S.G. Brannigan	1	EP128/J	VB	†
19.08.42	P/O W.R. Lightbourne	1	AB402/K	VB	-
	Sgt A. Lee	3	EN963/E	VB	†
27.08.42	F/Sgt A.R. McDonald	3	EN958/B	VB	†
	F/Sgt E.H. Shabolt	3	EN956/L	VB	†
07.09.42	Sgt L.H. Foxwell	3	BR168/N	VB	†
	P/O H.G. Harwood	3	EP705/E	VB	†
16.09.42	Sgt W. Strang	3	EP118/V	VB	†
17.09.42	P/O J.M.B. Scott	1	AB491/Y	VB	†
	P/O R.C. Lynch	1	EP871/L	VB	†
23.03.43	Sgt C.H.P. Bayntun	3	AB493/F	VC	-
11.07.43	P/O R.C. Stockburn	1	AA917/E	VB	Eva.
24.11.43	F/O C.G.S. Hodgkinson	3	MJ117	IX	PoW
21.12.43	P/O A.A. Griffiths	1*	EP559/P	VB	PoW
04.01.44	P/O L.R. Knight	1	AA733/V	VB	PoW
22.12.43	F/O R.C. Deleuze	3	BL681/Z	VB	-
22.02.44	P/O S.H. Cheeseman	3	BL311/V	VB	†
25.02.44	*Capitaine* P.G. Delange	3	BL344/R	VB	†
24.03.44	P/O F.J. Vid	3	R7195/E	VB	†
12.07.44	F/O P.C. Beloe	3	W3702/M	VB	†
	P/O R.E. Farrow	3	AD353/V	VB	†
14.07.44	F/O T.N. Andrews	2	EP398/P	VB	†

*Shot down by mistake by USAAF P-47s.

TEMPEST

21.08.44	F/L C.B. Thornton	3	EJ602/P	V	†
23.09.44	F/O G.D. Wild	3	EJ603/M	V	-
25.09.44	F/L G.L. Bonham	3	EJ590/L	V	†
29.09.44	F/L O.P. Faraday	3	EJ626/E	V	†
02.10.44	S/L J. Berry	2	EJ600/F	V	†
14.11.44	F/O J.A.L. Johnson	3	EJ551/S	V	-

Total : 115

1 Enemy aircraft
2 Flak
3 Other causes

Aircraft Lost by Accident

Date	Pilot	Duty	Serial	Mark	Fate
		Hurricane			
21.02.41	Sgt D.G. Grimmett	Practice	P3653/T	I	†
28.03.41	Sgt G.G.S. Laws	Practice	V6841/G	I	†
14.04.41	P/O R.W. Waine	Training	V7190/N	I	†
30.04.41	Sgt D.S. Thomas	Ferry	R4120/W	I	-
		Spitfire			
01.08.41	Sgt A. Beacham	Mid-air collision	P7664/S	IIA	-
10.01.42	Sgt E.J. Campbell	Training	BL568	VB	†
27.03.42	Sgt S.A. Childs	Training	AB965	VB	-
26.04.42	F/Sgt S.P. Jenkins	Local flying	AD200/W	VB	-
06.11.42	P/O C. Mroczyk	Training	AD378/C	VB	-
26.11.42	P/O R.B. Kingsford	Cross-country	AD116/A	VB	Int.[1]
17.01.43	F/O P.K. Woodsend	Training	BL615/I	VB	†
17.02.43	Sgt H.W. Stanley	Night cross-country	AB960/X	VB	†
26.02.43	Sgt J.A. Scott	Training	P8720/P	VB	-
12.04.43	Sgt P. Rogerson	Mid-air collision	P8741/J	VB	†
25.05.43	W/O J.L. Lilburn	Training	BL388/K	VB	-
02.04.44	F/O G.G.G. Walkinson	Training	AA743/V	VB	-
		Tempest			
18.03.45	W/O E. Wojczynski	Training	EJ591/Z	V	-
		Hind Trainer			
24.02.41	P/O E.G. Parkin	*n/a*	L7226	-	-
		Tiger Moth			
20.03.42	Sgt E.J.H. Parr	Comm. flight	T8204	II	-
27.04.43	F/Sgt H.C. Henderson	Comm. flight	DE508	II	-
06.10.44	F/O R.H. Bennett	Comm. flight	R5252	II	-
		Miles Magister			
12.01.41	Sgt R.J. Gent	Ferry flight	V1028	I	†

Total : 22

[1] Crash-landed in Eire at Ballybofey county of Donegal. Pilot released across the border that evening.

Roll of Honour-Aircrew

Name	Service No	Rank	Age	Origin	Date	Serial
ADAMS, H.C.	RAF No.85645	P/O	22	RAF	06.09.40	V6612
ANDREWS, N.T.	CAN./J.23893	F/O	24	RCAF	14.07.44	EP398
BARRY, N.J.M.	RAF No.72514	F/O	22	(SA)/RAF	07.10.40	V6800
BARTON, C.J.	RAF No.979855	Sgt	29	RAF	10.06.41	P8143
BEACHAM, A.	RAF No.1053425	Sgt	20	RAF	06.08.41	P7731
BELOE, P.C.	RAF No.150172	P/O	21	RAF	12.07.44	W3702
BERRY, J.	RAF No.118435	S/L	24	RAF	02.10.44	EJ600
BLAND, J.W.	AAF No.90895	P/O	30	RAF	18.08.40	P3208
BONHAM, G.L.	NZ402434	F/L	23	RNZAF	25.09.44	EJ590
BRANNIGAN, S.G.	NZ404885	P/O	23	RNZAF	11.08.42	EP128
CAMPBELL, E.J.	RAF No.115589	P/O	23	RAF	10.01.42	BL568
CHEESEMAN, S.H.	RAF No.152360	P/O	21	RAF	22.02.44	BL311
CLAYDON, A.J.	RAF No.72984	P/O	28	RAF	05.06.40	P3450
COX, P.A.N.	RAF No.33184	F/O	25	RAF	27.07.40	P3808
DEAN, R.F.C.	RAF No.1167919	Sgt	n/a	RAF	17.11.41	AD129
DELANGE, P.G.	RAF F.30582	Capitaine	26	FFAF	25.02.44	BL344
DIXON, F.J.P.	RAF No.742124	Sgt	21	RAF	11.07.40	N2485
EGAN, E.J.	RAF No.742787	Sgt	19	RAF	17.09.40	P3820
FARADAY, O.P.	RAF No.128067	F/L	31	RAF	29.09.44	EJ626
FARROW, R.E.	RAF No.175712	P/O	24	RAF	12.07.44	AD353
FENEMORE, S.A.	RAF No.745110	Sgt	20	RAF	15.10.40	V6722
FOXWELL, L.R.C.	RAF No.1269041	Sgt	20	RAF	07.09.42	BR168
GENT, R.J.K.	RAF No.754361	Sgt	24	RAF	12.01.41	V1028
GILLEPSIE, E.W.	CAN./J.7764	P/O	20	(US)/RCAF	09.05.42	W3845
GÖTH, V.	RAF No.81945	P/O	25	(CZ)/RAF	25.10.40	P2903
GRIMMETT, D.G.	RAF No.903560	Sgt	26	RAF	21.02.41	P3653
GROVE, H.C.	RAF No.580202	Sgt	29	RAF	08.11.40	V6805
GUNTER, E.M.	RAF No.83988	P/O	20	RAF	27.09.40	V6645
HARROLD, F.C.	RAF No.42707	P/O	23	RAF	28.09.40	P3417
HARWOOD, H.G.	CAN./J.15402	P/O	22	(US)/RCAF	07.09.42	EP705
HEWITT, D.A.	RAF No.76579	P/O	20	(CAN)/RAF	12.07.40	P3084
HOUGHTON, O.V.	RAF No.745437	Sgt	19	RAF	06.09.40	V6646
HULSE, C.L.	RAF No.70860	P/O	22	RAF	04.06.40	P3542
LAWS, G.G.S.	RAF No.745649	Sgt	21	RAF	28.03.41	V6841
LEE, A.	RAF No.934095	Sgt	21	RAF	19.08.42	EN963
LEITCH, W.R.	RAF No.657352	Sgt	26	RAF	05.08.42	BP855
LOCKYER, N.J.	RAF No.61292	P/O	19	RAF	22.04.41	-
LUKASZEWICZ, K.	RAF No.76761	P/O	27	(POL)/RAF	12.08.40	P3803
LYNCH, R.C.	RAF No.115146	P/O	21	RAF	17.09.42	EP871
MARCINKOWSKI, M.S.	RAF No.P.780491	Sgt	21	PAF	01.11.40	V7405
McDONALD, A.R.	CAN./R.2535	F/Sgt	22	RCAF	27.08.42	EN958
PALMER-TOMKINSON, A.	RAF No.62286	P/O	21	RAF	25.04.42	W3894
PATTERSON, L.J.	RAF No.741219	Sgt	23	RAF	28.11.40	P5189
PEARSON, G.W.	RAF No.742740	Sgt	21	RAF	06.09.40	P3516
RAYNER, P.H.	AAF No.90022	F/O	27	RAF	12.05.40	L2054
ROCOVSKY, M.	RAF No.787490	Sgt	23	(CZ)/RAF	25.04.42	W3840
ROGERSON, P.M.	RAF No.1217612	Sgt	20	RAF	12.04.43	P8741

ROSE-PRICE, A.T.	RAF No.39762	F/O	21	RAF	02.09.40	L1578
SCOTT, J.M.B.	RAF No.119229	P/O	n/a	RAF	17.09.42	AB491
SHADBOLT, E.W.	RAF No.915324	F/Sgt	21	RAF	27.08.42	EN956
SMITH, M.F.C.	AAF No.90026	F/O	27	RAF	12.05.40	L2053
SMITHERS, R.A.	RAF No.922853	Sgt	21	RAF	11.05.41	V7056
STANLEY, H.W.	RAF No.1330743	Sgt	20	RAF	17.02.43	AB960
STONEY, G.E.B.	RAF No.28119	F/L	29	RAF	18.08.40	P2549
STRACHAN, B.	CAN./R.85734	Sgt	28	RCAF	04.06.42	W3842
STRANG, W.N.	RAF No.1370081	Sgt	21	RAF	16.09.42	EP118
SYVELSTER, E.J.H.	AAF No.90556	P/O	n/a	RAF	20.07.40	P3082
THOMAS, D.S.	RAF No.904947	Sgt	20	RAF	04.04.42	BL789
THORNTON, C.B.	RAF No.117692	F/L	n/a	RAF	21.08.44	EJ602
van den HOVE d'ERTENRIJCK, A.E.A.D.J.	RAF No.83699	P/O	32	(BEL)/RAF	15.09.40	P2760
VID, F.J.	CAN./J.86521	P/O	25	RCAF	24.03.44	R7195
VRTIS, K.	RAF No.787447	Sgt	23	(CZ)/RAF	25.04.42	AB251
WAINE, R.W.	RAF No.61489	P/O	20	RAF	14.04.41	V7190
WHELDON, R.	RAF No.62289	P/O	25	RAF	25.04.42	BL974
WHITFIELD, W.H.	RAF No.740692	Sgt	22	RAF	11.05.40	L5813
WOODSEND, P.K.	RAF No.62692	F/O	21	RAF	17.01.43	BL615
ZENKER, P.	RAF No.76714	P/O	25	(POL)/RAF	24.08.40	P3141

21 years old Sergeant Geoffrey Wilberforce Pearson of East End, Oxfordshire, one of 544 pilots of Fighter Command who lost their life between 10th July and 31st October, 1940. He failed to return from combat over Ashford. Crashed near Hothfield and buried at Lympne under headstone marked, "Unknown Airman". His grave was identified and proper headstone erected, 42 years later!

Supermarine Spitfire Mk.VB W3846, No.501 (County of Gloucester) Squadron, Squadron Leader C.F. Currant, Iblsey, December 1941. The Squadron Leader pennant was also painted on the starboard side (see photo p34)

PRISONERS OF WAR

Name	Service No	Rank	Origin	Camp/No.PoW	Date	Serial
BAUMAN, V.	RAF No.787651	F/Sgt	(CZ)/RAF	-*	20.06.42	AB497
GREENAWAY, W.J.H.	RAF No.101024	P/O	RAF	L3/697	08.11.41	AD188
GRIFFITHS, A.A.	RAF No.156932	P/O	RAF	L3/3253	21.12.43	EP559
HODGKINSON, C.G.S.	RAF No.129361	F/O	RAF	-*	24.11.43	MJ117
KNIGHT, L.R.	RAF No.170140	P/O	RAF	L3/?	04.01.44	AA733
POTELLE, J.E.A.	RAF No.1506870	Sgt	(BEL)/RAF	357/349	04.06.42	AB381
SHORE, E.H.L.	RAF No.64926	P/O	RAF	L3/684	04.11.41	AA837

Stalag Luft 3 (L3) : Sagan and Belaria
Camp 357 : Kopernicus
*Hospitalised, later repatriated.

Ibsley, Autumn 1941. Pilots of No.501 Squadron posing for the photograph :
Top, left to right : Sgt Wilson, Sgt Allan, Sgt Cummings, F/L Dafforn, Sgt Thomas II, Sgt Lynch.
Centre, left to right : P/O Dennehey, P/O Shore, P/O Stnabury, P/O Newberry, F/L Ekins, P/O Greenaway.
Front, left to right : F/Sgt Dvorak, Sgt Rocovski, S/L Currant, F/L Graham, P/O Wheldon and Sgt Dean.
Soon after this photo was taken, Pilot Officers Shores and Greenaway will be shot down within four days
and taken prisoners. (Len Parker)

No.501 Squadron's pilots at Ibsley on the first day of August 1942 :
Back row : F/Sgt E.W. Shadbolt, Sgt Henderson, F/Sgt Carmody, Sgt Collis.
Middle row : P/O Brannigan, Sgt Kelly, F/Sgt MacDonald, Sgt Moore, Sgt Leitch, P/O Jackson, P/O De Merode, P/O Smith, P/O Mawer.
Front row : F/O Turbill, F/O Drossaert, S/L Sing, S/L Villa, F/L Stanbury, P/O Lynch, P/O Lightbourn. (501 Sqn Association)

SQUADRON ROSTER

Name	Rank[1]	Status

*Flight Leader, ** Squadron Leader, ***Flight Leader/Squadron Leader*

§ *Pilots with the Squadron at the outbreak of war.*
(†) *Pilots killed serving with squadron.*

ADAMS, Hugh C. Sgt RAF
9-39/9-40 § (†) RAF No.741254[3]
  RAF No.85645

At the squadron when the war broke out. Injured in Bombay crash, France in May 1940 and hospitalised. Returned to squadron in July. His commission was gazetted the day of his death. One confirmed victory, No.501 Sqn, Battle of Britain, 1940.
P/O : 9-40

AITKEN, Douglas S. P/O RCAF
12-41/1-42 CAN./J.7013

Posted from OTU. Native of British Columbia, Canada. Posted to No.403 (RCAF) Sqn.
†*08.03.42, Spitfire VB BL661, No.403 (RCAF) Sqn, France. (Was Wing Leader's aircraft of North Weald)*

ALDRIDGE, Keith R. P/O RAF
9-39/5-40, 7-40/8-40 § AAF No.91039

Prewar Auxiliary Air Force pilot, with the Unit since 1937. Sent out to complete his training when the Squadron was in France. Shot down and wounded in

[1] When first posted.
[2] Time passed with the Squadron (Month-Year). Unless stated, every pilot is presumed to have survived the War.
[3] When a pilot has two service numbers, the first refers to Non-Commissioned Officers (NCO), the second to Officers.

action on 24.08.40 and hospitalised. Returned to operations in 1942 and served in North Africa with No.33 Sqn in 1942. Three confirmed confirmed victories, Nos.501 and 33 Sqns, Battle of Britain and North Africa, 1940 and 1942.

ALLEN, ? Sgt ?
9-41/9-41
Posted from No.57 OTU. No details were available to help to identify this pilot.

ANDREWS, Newark T. F/O RCAF
4-44/7-44 (†) CAN./J.23893
Known as "*Andy*". Native of Ontario. Hit by flak during attack on radar installation and killed when his Spitfire crashed in Seine Estuary.

ATKINSON, William B.* Sgt RAF
9-42/7-44 RAF No.1373817
 RAF No.146881
Known as "*Jock*". No more details available. Flight Lieutenant in February 1945. Temporary A flight leader between 03.04.44 and 24.04.44 replacing D.H. Seaton. LP. Griffith took over on 24.04.44.
P/O : 7-43, F/O : 11-43

BALAM, S.H. W/O ?
8-44/4-45 ?
No details available. One V-1 with No.501 Sqn, 1944.

BARNETT, Matthew G.* S/L RNZAF
10-43/8-44 NZ391338
Known as "*Gary*". Posted from No.234 Sqn. Previously served with No.485 (NZ) Sqn in May 1942. Shot down on 31.05.42 and evaded capture returning to the unit in October. Posted to No.274 Squadron in August 1944 as CO. In September withdrawn from operations. One V-1 destroyed with No.501 Sqn.

DFC : LG 03.10.44

BARRY, Nanthaniel J.M. F/O (SA)/RAF
9-40/10-40 (†) RAF No.72514
Known as "*Nate*". Posted from No.3 Sqn, serving with it since July 1940. Former ADC (*Aide de Camp*) to Air Chief Marshall H. de Crespigny up to June 1940. Shot down and killed by Bf109s over Wrotham.

BARTHOLD, Bertram* S/L RAF
5-43/10-43 RAF No.33218
Known as "*Bats*". Posted from No.611 Sqn where he was posted as supernumerary Squadron Leader pending appointment in April 1943. Promoted as Wing Commander and posted to HQ, Fighter Command. He continued to fly for a while as Wing Commander at the head of the Squadron. Previously became first CO No.146 Sqn in India between October 1941 and March 1942. Repatriated to the UK and later posted as supernumerary Squadron Leader to No.616 Sqn between November 1942 and January 1943. One confirmed victory, No.611 Sqn, Europe, 1943.
W/C : 7-43

H.C.ADAMS

M.G.BARNETT

Joseph BERRY
RAF No.1177137 (NCO)
& RAF No.118435 (Officer)

Regarded as the RAF's top-scoring pilot, Joe Berry was born in Cassop, near Ferryhill, Co. Durham, and moved to Nottingham when he was sixteen to work as a civil servant. He joined the RAFVR on 8th August, 1940 and was posted to No.256 Squadron at Squires Gate, flying Defiant nightfighters, as a Sergeant Pilot on 22nd August, 1941.

Three months later his aircraft suffered an engine failure during a routine night fighter practice and he was forced to bale out over Skippool, Lancs; his gunner, Flight Sergeant Williams, also baled out but was blown into the Irish Sea and drowned.

Joe Berry was commissioned in March 1942 and later served as a night fighter pilot with Nos.153 and 255 Squadrons in North Africa and Italy. Flying Beaufighter Mk.VIFs during the operations at Salerno, he shot down a Ju88 on 8th September, 1943 and a Me210 on 10 September 1943. His third victory in the Mediterranean was on 23rd October, 1943 when he claimed a Ju88 over the Naples area.

Despite having to abandon his aircraft twice, he survived and returned to the UK in December 1943. Joe Berry served with the Telecommunications Flying Unit at Defford until February 1944, when he joined the Fighter Interception Unit (FIU) at Ford and was awarded the DFC the following month.

The FIU had been earlier formed at Wittering to develop the technique of intercepting the V-1 flying bombs at night and also operated a special flight of Tempests at Ford. In August 1944 the flight moved to Manston to become No.501 Squadron, of which Joe Berry was appointed as CO on 11th August.

By the time he assumed command of the Squadron, Squadron Leader Joe Berry was already a V-1 "ace" having destroyed 52.5 over the south-east of England between late June and early August 1944 while serving with the FIU; all but three of the flying bombs had been shot down at night with the half-share credited to a Mosquito. On 23rd July he had also set a record with seven shot down in one night.

With the nucleus of members drawn from the FIU, No.501 Squadron became the only squadron to operate at night during the V-1 offensive and Joe Berry re-opened his score on 12th August when he destroyed a flying bomb near Sandhurst. By the end of the month, Berry had shot down seven of the 40 V-1s claimed by the squadron and was awarded a BAR to his DFC on 1st September, 1944.

The decrease in flying bomb activity during late September and October 1944 found Joe Berry leading the squadron Tempests on Ranger sorties over Holland in support of the Allied advance into Europe. On the morning of 2nd October, 1944, he led a section of three Tempests on a Ranger to attack trains and Luftwaffe bomber airfields between Zwischenhan and the Rheine. While flying over Northern Holland the section encountered small-arms fire from a solitary gun post two miles to the east of Veendam, hitting Joe Berry's aircraft. He crashed in flames at Kibbelgaarn, a small hamlet close to Schmeeda, and was killed.

His total of recorded V-1 claims is put at 59.5. He was awarded a 2ND BAR to his DFC on 1st October, 1944, gazetted on 12th February, 1946.

B. BARTHOLD

V. BAUMAN

BARTON, Clarence J.   Sgt   RAF
3-41/6-41 (†)   RAF No.979255
Posted from OTU. Killed when his aircraft collided
with balloon cable, Weston-Super-Mare.

BAUMANN, Vaclav   Sgt   (CZ)/RAF
1-42/6-42   RAF No.787651
Posted from No.245 Sqn. Prewar CzAF NCO. Posted
to No.245 Sqn between November 1940 and January
1942. Shot down by enemy fighters and made PoW.
Repatriated to the UK in September 1944. In 1948, he
was released from the Czechoslovak Air Force due to
political reasons, being rehabilitated in 1964.
F/Sgt : 5-42

BAYNTUN, Charles H.P.   Sgt   RAF
3-43/5-43   RAF No.1317093
Posted from OTU. Posted overseas. No more details
available. With No.118 Sqn (February - November
1944). Commissioned in October 1944.

BEACHAM, Alan   Sgt   RAF
7-41/8-41 (†)   RAF No.1053425
Posted from No.61 OTU. Reported missing during
escort patrol over Channel.

BELOE, Peter C.   P/O   RAF
8-43/7-44 (†)   RAF No.150172

Posted from No.53 OTU. Shot down and killed by
own Anti-Aircraft fire over Ouistreham.

BENNER, Vernon A.T.   Sgt   RNZAF
3-43/12-43   NZ414231
Posted from No.58 OTU. Known as "*Vern*". Posted to
No.1 ADF, Croydon. No more details available.

BENNETT, Ronald H.   Sgt   RAF
2-43/4-45   RAF No.1587735
                                RAF No.154884
Posted from No.61 OTU. Posted to No.165 Sqn in
April 1945 until the end of war. Claimed four V-1s as
shot down with No.501 Sqn.
F/Sgt : 10-43, W/O : 3-44, P/O : 4-44, F/O : 9-44

BERRY, Joseph**   S/L   RAF
8-44/10-44 (†)   RAF No.118435
See biography.
2ND BAR : LG 12.02.46

BIRBECK, Clive R.   F/L   RAF
7-44/12-44   RAF No.108990
Know as "*Joe*" sometimes "*Jumbo*", born in Ceylon.
Posted from No.41 Sqn, with it since February 1943.
Posted to No.127 Sqn. Two confirmed victories,

No.41 Sqn, Europe, 1943 and three V-1s one being shared, with Nos.41 and 501 Sqns, 1944.

BLACK, Lindsay S.*   F/L   RNZAF
5-43/10-43   NZ40965
Posted from No.485 (NZ) Sqn, serving the unit since May 1942. Posted back to No.485 (NZ) Sqn in October 1943, remaining with it until October 1944. A flight leader between 18.05.43 and 05.10.43 succeeding L.M. Ralph being replaced by D.H. Seaton. One confirmed victory, No.485 Sqn, Europe, 1942. DFC [No.485 (NZ) Sqn].
†05.03.45, Spitfire IX LZ924, Day Fighter Leader School, United Kingdom.

BLACKSHAW, Herbert J.   Sgt   RAF
3-41/3-41   RAF No.1152371
Posted from OTU. Posted to No.263 Sqn remaining with the unit until his death, having received his commission in November 1941. DFC [No.263 Sqn].
†15.05.43, Whirlwind I P7094, No.263 Sqn, United Kingdom.

BLADES, Robert W.   Sgt   RAF
7-41/9-41   RAF No.1056405
Posted from OTU. Posted out, later serving with No.92 Sqn.
†09.11.42, Spitfire VB EP397, No.92 Sqn, Egypt.

BLAIR, John   Sgt   RAF
3-42/4-42   RAF No.550006
Known as "*Ian*". Former Observer, serving with Blenheims in Middle East with No.113 Sqn in 1940. Awarded the DFM when he managed to fly the Blenheim back after its pilot had been killed by enemy action. Retrained as pilot and posted to No.501 Sqn. On 25.04.42, his Spitfire was damaged by *flak* and force-landed near Worth Maltravers, Dorset. Hospitalised. Later posted to No.602 Sqn in March 1943. Commissioned in October 1943 and completed his tour in May 1944. One confirmed victory, No.602 Sqn, Europe. 1944. DFM [No.113 Sqn].

BLAND, John W.   P/O   RAF
9-39/10-39 §, 7-40/8-40 (†)   AAF No.90895
Member of AuxAF, called up for full-time service on 24.08.39. Sent to No.5 FTS to complete his training, returning to Squadron in July. Shot down and killed in combat over Canterbury. One confirmed victory, No.501 Sqn, Battle of Britain, 1940.

BLOWER, F.A.   Sgt   ?
4-43/5-43   ?
No details available.

BONHAM, Gordon L.*   F/L   RNZAF
4-44/9-44 (†)   NZ402434

L.S. BLACK

G. L. BOYD

Known as "*Snowy*". His first operational postings were in FE with No.21 Sqn, RAAF (July - September 1941), then with No.243 Sqn in September 1941 in Singapore, flying Buffaloes. Wounded in action on 19.01.42 and repatriated to New Zealand. Embarked for the UK in October 1943. Crashed and killed in Tempest, Spitfield Farm, Essex. Four confirmed V-1s, No.501 Sqn, Europe, 1944. A Flight leader from 11.08.44 until his death succeeding L.P. Griffith. Replaced by C.A. Hansen. DFC [No.243 Sqn].

BOYD, Adrian H.*   S/L   RAF
6-41/8-41   RAF No.39101
Known as "*Ginger*", born in India, prewar fighter pilot serving with No.66 Sqn. Served with No.145 Sqn October 1939 - December 1940, becoming its CO in October 1940 then sent for rest. Second tour of operations with No.501 Sqn as CO. Posted out two months later to become leader of the Middle Wallop fighter Wing. No more operational posting until the end of the war. Fifteen confirmed and three shared confirmed victories, Nos.145 and 501 Sqns, 1940, Dunkirk, Battle of Britain and Europe. DSO [Middle Wallop Wing], DFC & BAR [both No.145 Sqn].

BRADWELL, Richard   F/L   RAF
9-44/11-44   RAF No.60522
Commissioned in December 1940, he served with No.108 Sqn, a night fighter squadron in 1943, later with No.46 Sqn before returning to the UK. Remained with the RAF after being killed in a Canberra crash (WD960) on 30.04.52. Four confirmed victories, with No.108 Sqn, North Africa and Sicily, 1943 and three V-1s with No.501 Sqn, 1944. DFC [No.108 Sqn].

BRADY, Bernard J.R.   P/O   RAF
5-40/5-40   AAF No.90403
Prewar Auxiliary Air Force officer, commissioned in March 1938 within No.615 Sqn. Injured in Bombay crash in France 11.05.40 and admitted to hospital. Posted to No.21 Aircraft Park 22.05.40. No further details available.
F/O : 5-40

BRANNIGAN, Stewart G.   P/O   RNZAF
6-42/8-42 (†)   NZ404855
Posted from No.118 Sqn. Previously served with No.263 Sqn in January - February 1942 then, No.286 Sqn in March and April 1942, and No.118 Sqn in May and June 1942. Shot down and killed off Cherbourg (France).

BRECKON, Graham F.   Sgt   RNZAF
7-41/7-41   NZ402162
Known as "*Red*". Posted from No.609 Sqn. Posted to No.72 Sqn. Shot down in flames over France 20.07.41 and badly burned. After a month's hospitalisation sent off to PoW camp.

BROCKLEHURST, Derrik   P/O   RAF
3-41/6-41   RAF No.60101
Posted from OTU, commissioned in January 1941, posted from OTU. Known as "*Brock*". Posted to No.247 Sqn. Remained with it until the end of his tour, beginning of 1943. Flight Lieutenant in January 1943.

BUCKLAND, John C.   F/L   RAF
12-44/3-45   RAF No.122369
Few details available except that he was commissioned in April 1942. Remained with the RAFVR after the war.

BURTON, Horace F/O RAF
8-43/4-45 RAF No.111522
Posted from No.61 OTU. Known as "*Monty*". Posted to No.126 Sqn. Claimed six V-1s as shot down.
F/L : 8-43

BUSBRIDGE, John A. P/O RAF
7-41/8-41 RAF No.67055
Posted from No.61 OTU. Posted to No.602 Sqn remaining until December and posted to No.79 Sqn moving to India-Burma with this unit in March 1942. Later becoming CO No.34 Sqn between June 1944 and May 1945.

BUTTERWORTH, J. Sgt ?
2-43/5-43 ?
Posted overseas. No details were available to help to identify this pilot.

CAMPBELL, Eric J. Sgt RAF
3-41/1-42 (†) RAF No.919123
RAF No.115589
Posted from OTU. Killed when his Spitfire broke up in mid-air.
P/O : 1-42

CAMPBELL, Peter C.* F/L RAF
6-42/2-43 RAF No.88433
Posted to the Squadron on 21.06.42 to take command of B Flight after Y.D. Yule. Posted to No.57 OTU on

L.J.E.CLAERT

19.02.43, being temporary replaced by D.J. Smith.

CARMODY, Cornelius J. Sgt RCAF
6-42/10-42 CAN./R.51795
Background unknown. Posted overseas in October 1942 to Malta, serving with No.185 sqn.
F/Sgt : 8-42
†*08.02.43, Spitfire VB EP473, No.185 Sqn, Malta.*

CHALMERS, Hugh M.M. P/O RAF
2-43/5-43 RAF No.133261
Posted from OTU. Posted to No.277 (ASR) Sqn where he completed his tour mid-1944. Flight Lieutenant in October 1944.

CHEESEMAN, Sydney H. P/O RAF
2-44/2-44 (†) RAF No.152360
Posted from OTU. Spitfire damaged by own drop tank. Baled out and drowned, 10m SW Walcheren.

CHILDS, Sydney A. Sgt RAF
3-42/3-42 RAF No.655277
Posted from OTU. Commissioned January 1944. No more details available.

CHILTON, Stanley N. P/O RAF
9-42/9-42 RAF No.120927
Few details except that he received his commission in June 1942, ended the war as Flight Lieutetnant. Served in India-Burma toward the end of war with No.113 Sqn. DFC [No.113 Sqn].

CLAERT, Lucien J.E. P/O (BEL)/RAF
12-41/7-42 RAF No.107940
Prewar Belgian fighter pilot. Escaped from Belgium in February 1941, arriving in the UK in July 1941. Posted out in July 1942, then posted as reconnaissance pilot to No.1 PRU in September 1942. Shot down over France on 06.11.42 and bailed out. He tried to evade capture, but was finally interned in Switzerland a few weeks later in trying to reach the UK. He was repatriated to the UK in October 1944.

CLAPIN, Basil P.W. F/L RAF
8-42/8-42 RAF No.43541

A.J.CLAYDON

M.V.M.CLUBE

Reconnaissance pilot who served with No.268 Sqn between November 1940 and December 1942. Attached to gain experience on new Fighter Command tactics. With No.65 Sqn in May 1944, but shot down on 24.06.44, evading capture. DFC [No.34 Wing].

serving with No.501 Sqn since June 1936. Granted AAF commission as Squadron Leader in July 1937 and appointed Sqn CO. Posting to HQ, No.10 Group. No more operational posting until the end of war. In May 1941, he flew a couple of times with the Squadron. *W/C : 6-40*

CLARK, Norman   F/Sgt   RAF
3-44/8-44   RAF No.1315083
Posted from No.2 TEU. Posted to No.274 Sqn, remaining with this unit until the end of his tour in April 1945. Commissioned in February 1945.

CLARKE, Leslie S.   F/Sgt   RAF
3-44/8-44   RAF No.1390697
Posted from No.2 TEU. Posted to No.274 Sqn, remaining with this unit until the end of his tour in April 1945. Commissioned in July 1945.

CLAYDON, Anthony J.   P/O   RAF
9-39/6-40 (†)   RAF No.72984
Posted from ATS Hamble on 07.09.39. Shot down and killed near Rouen, France.

CLUBE, Montagu V.M.**   S/L   RAF
9-39/6-40 §   AAF No.90015
Known as "*Monty*". Prewar Auxiliary Air Force officer,

COLLIS, John A.   Sgt   RAF
7-42/10-42   RAF No.1238685
Posted from OTU. Posted overseas serving in Mediterranean with No.229 Sqn January - June 1943. Commissioned in January 1943. No more details available. One shared victory with No.229 Sqn, Malta, 1943.

COLLINS, D.G.   F/Sgt   RAF
12-44/4-45   RAF No.1387765
No details available.

CONNER, Hal C.   Captain   USAAF
7-43/7-43   O-429610
American pilot posted in to gain combat experience. Pilot of 107th TRS / 67th RG.

COUNTER, Cyril F.   P/O   RAF
11-40/1-41   RAF No.85689
Posted from No.43 Sqn. Posted to No.261 Sqn in

P.A.N.Cox

D.B.Crabtbee

January 1941, becoming its CO in December 1943 until the end of his tour in May 1944. At least one confirmed victory, No.261 Sqn, Ceylon, 1942. DFC [No.261 Sqn].

Cox, Graham J.   F/L   RAF
9-42/10-42   RAF No.41668
Posted for a second tour of operations to No.501 Sqn pending overseas posting. First tour with No.152 Sqn between June 1940 and December 1941. Later serving with No.43 Sqn in May 1943, then CO No.229 Sqn between July and October 1943. Third tour with No.72 Sqn, then as CO No.92 Sqn between February and August 1944. Eleven confirmed victories, three being shared with No.152 Sqn, Battle of Britain, 1940, Nos.43, 229 and 92 Sqns, Sicily and Italy, 1943 and 1944. DFC [No.152 Sqn].

Cox, Philip A.N.   F/O   RAF
6-40/7-40 (†)   RAF No.33184
Posted from No.43 Sqn. Known as *"Pan"*. Prewar regular officer serving with No.43 Sqn since 1937. Shot down and killed 27.07.40. One confirmed victory with No.501 Sqn, Battle of Britain, 1940.

Crabtree, Douglas B.   Sgt   RAF
9-39/10-40   RAF No.740434

Joined Squadron on 21.09.39. Injured in Bombay crash in May 1940. Hospitalised, but returned to unit until posted to No.7 OTU in October 1940. Served with No.616 Sqn in 1941 for another tour, being shot down on 03.07.41 over France but evaded capture, returning to the UK after several months, bringing back with him detailed drawings of an arms factory on cigarette papers. Commissioned in June 1942, he did not return to operations.

Cridland, John R.*   P/O   RAF
9-39/6-40, 2-41/6-41§   AAF No.90459
Member of Squadron since March 1938. Posted to No.5 OTU as instructor in June 1940. Posted back as Flight Lieutenant on 17.02.41 from No.7 OTU as A Flight commander replacing D.A.E Jones. Posted to RAF Colerne for Controller duties as Squadron Leader on 23.06.41. Replaced by J.H. Lacey. Later served in Middle East as Squadron Leader within the Northwest African Air Forces, being killed in a flying accident while doing aerobatics. Four confirmed victories, No.501 Sqn, France, 1940.
F/O : 2-40
†31.05.43, Hurricane IIC HW185, Northwest African Air Forces CF, Algeria.

Crozier, Ivor D.   Sgt   RAF
3-41/6-41   RAF No.926454

Commissioned in July 1942. Flight Lieutenant in July 1944. No further details.

CUMMINGS, Michael P.S.   Sgt   RAF
8-41/9-41   RAF No.1168519
Posted from OTU. Posted overseas and served with No.238 Sqn in Middle East.
†28.06.42, Hurricane IIB BG965, No.238 Sqn, Lybia.

CUNNINGHAM, Robert L.   Sgt   RAAF
9-42/9-42   Aus.402493
Known as *"Gig"*, native of New South Wales, Australia. Previously served with No.72 Sqn in January 1942 and No.65 Sqn between January and July 1942 being with No.501 Sqn a few days only before being repatriated to Australia. Posted to No.457 (RAAF) Sqn in March 1943 at Darwin, Australia, completing his tour in January 1944. Commissioned in May 1943. No more operational postings until the end of war. One confirmed victory, No.457 Sqn, Darwin, 1943.

CURRANT, Christopher F.   S/L   RAF
8-41/6-42   RAF No.43367
Known as *"Bunny"*. See biography.

DSO : LG 07.07.42

```
Acting Squadron Leader Christopher
Frederick CURRANT, D.F.C. (43367),
No.501 Squadron.


Squadron Leader Currant is a most
courageous pilot and a brilliant
leader. His untiring efforts and
outstanding ability have been
reflected in the splendid work
accomplished by the squadron which
he commands. One day in March,
1942, he was wounded in the head
during a sortie. Despite this, he
flew his aircraft safely back to
base. Following a short enforced
rest, he returned to operational
flying with renewed vigour.
Squadron Leader Currant has des-
troyed at least 14 and damaged many
more enemy aircraft.
```

DAFFORN, Robert C.*   Sgt   RAF
9-39/11-41   RAF No.740804
                                     RAF No.81674
Known as *"Bob"* or *"Lofty"*. Joined the Squadron on 17.09.39 as NCO from No.11(F) Group Pool, St Athan. B flight leader between 20.04.41 and 04.11.41, replacing C.E Malfroy and being replaced later by R.D Yule. Posted to No.56 OTU in November 1941, later serving overseas in Middle East with No.229 Sqn in Malta in April 1942, but shot down and wounded on his second sortie. Rapatriated to the UK for medical reasons in August 1942. No more operational posting. Six confirmed and two shared confirmed victories, No.501 Sqn France and Battle of Britain, 1940.
P/O : 5-40, F/L : 4-41
†09.09.43, Spitfire IIA P7289, Central Gunnery School, United Kingdom.

DFC : LG 17.01.41

DAVIES, John R.   F/O   RAF
6-43/7-44   RAF No.60107
Commissioned on January 1941. Posted to No.274 Sqn, remaining with it until November 1944 in completion of his tour.
F/L : 9-43

R.C.DAFFORN

Christopher Frederick CURRANT
RAF No.43367

During the Battle of Britain, "Bunny" Currant was officially credited with destroying nine and five shared enemy aircraft, one probable and a further eleven machines as damaged, and was also twice awarded the DFC. A modest and generous man, Currant was also an enthusiastic and efficient leader, and commanded No.501 Squadron at Ibsley between August 1941 and July 1942.

Born in Luton in December 1911, Currant joined the RAF as a Direct Entry Pilot in 1936 and subsequently served as a Sergeant Pilot with Nos.46 and 151 Squadrons. In April 1940 he was commissioned as a Pilot Officer and transferred to No.605 Squadron at Wick, where he flew Hurricane fighters. While operating from Hawkinge on 22nd May, 1940, his Hurricane was badly damaged by Bf109s during a patrol near Arras and he was forced to make an emergency landing, breaking his nose in the process. Currant made his way to Calais and was fortunate to board a ship and return to England.

He achieved his first success on 15th August, 1940 when the Luftwaffe launched its greatest effort of the battle. No.605 Squadron engaged the force over Tyneside, resulting in heavy Luftwaffe losses, including two He111s destroyed and a further bomber claimed as a probable by Currant over Newcastle. The squadron moved south on 7th September, operating from Croydon during the latter stages of the Battle and he re-opened his score the following day by damaging a Do17 and a Bf109 over Maidstone. On 11th September Currant damaged three Heinkels and shot down another during raids over south-east London, followed by claims of a Bf109 shot down and damage to three Do17s and a He111, three days later. His last victory during the Battle of Britain was a Bf109 shot down near Rochester on 15th October.

Currant received the DFC on 8th October, 1940, and a BAR to this on 15th November, and was made temporary squadron commander on 1st November, 1940, following the death of its CO. Currant completed his tour with No.605 Squadron with the destruction of a Bf109 over Dover on 1st December, 1940. In February 1941 he was posted to No.52 OTU at Debden and appointed as CFI in July.

On 14th August, 1941, Squadron Leader Currant arrived at Ibsley to command No.501 Squadron. He appeared as himself in the film *First of the Few*, which was made at Ibsley in the autumn of 1941 and starred Leslie Howard and David Niven, with whom he subsequently became great friends. Leading the squadron on a combined *Circus* operation to attack Mazingarbe airfield in March 1942, he was attacked by enemy fighters which badly damaged his Spitfire and wounded him in the head. He managed to make an emergency landing at Lympne but was trapped in the cockpit when the aircraft overturned. He was dragged from the wreckage and taken to Hospital for treatment, where seven fragments of metal were found in his skull and which he carried as a permament reminder. Returning to the Squadron at the end of March, he claimed a possible Bf109 during a sweep over the Cherbourg Peninsula on 17th April.

On 21st June, 1942 he was promoted to Acting Wing Commander and appointed to command the Ibsley Spitfire Wing; he was also awarded the DSO on 7th July for his work with No.501 Squadron and the Belgian *Croix de Guerre* in April 1943. From August 1943 untill July 1944, Currant led the newly-formed No.122 Wing, and led the Wing during the D-Day landings in June 1944 before departing on a four-month lecture tour of the USA. Returning to England, he went to the Operations Centre of No.84 Group Control Centre in Holland, where he was responsible for coordinating ground attack operations for the Army. He was twice mentioned in dispatches.

After the war, Currant remained with the RAF and retired from the RAF as a Wing Commander in 1960 to undertake research and development work for the RAF. He finally retired in 1976. He died on 12th March, 2006.

DEAN, Raymond F.C.   Sgt   RAF
11-41/11-41(†)   RAF No.1167919
Posted from OTU. Failed to return from a *Rhubarb* operation over France.

DEEKS, Philip V.   P/O   RAF
12-41/1-42   RAF No.108131
Posted from OTU. Posted to No.1 Flying Instructor School. Flight Lieutenant in September 1943. No further details available.

DELANGE, Pierre G.   *Capitaine*   FFAF
12-43/2-44 (†)   RAF No.F.30582
Recalled for active service when the war broke out, as reserve officer in armoured division, his *chef de corps* being Colonel de Gaulle. In January elected for an Observer course with the *Armée de l'Air*, still under training in June 1940 escaped to England the same month. Posted to No.154 Sqn November 1941 - February 1942, then No.610 Sqn February - May 1942 and No.19 Sqn May - June 1942. Second tour of operations with No.501 Sqn. Drowned in the Channel following an emergency landing.

DELEUZE, Regis   F/O   (FR)/RAF
10-43/2-45   RAF No.135504

R. DELEUZE

Known as "*Lulu*". French born in Cairo, (Egypt). Posted from No.57 OTU. Joined the UK in June 1940 but could not enlist in the FFAF because of his age, 18 years old, enlisting in the RAF instead. Posted to No.274 Sqn in February 1945. Eight confirmed V-1s with No.501 Sqn, 1944.
†*25.02.45, Tempest V EJ775, No.274 Sqn, Netherlands.*

DE MERODE, Werner (Prince)
    P/O   (BEL)/RAF
3-42/9-42, 7-43/2-44   RAF No.116473
Posted from OTU. Former regular Belgian Air Force officer serving in Air Regiment 2 (3/II/2Aé) in 1940 flying Fiat CR.42 withdrawing to France in June 1940, shooting down on Do17 on 10.05.40. Returning to Belgium during Summer 1940, he evaded from Belgium one year later reaching the UK in November 1941. Posted to No.350 (Belgian) Sqn. Shot down and evaded capture, he was posted to No.91 Sqn in May 1943, then to No.501 Sqn again. No more operational postings until the end of war.

DENNEHEY, John R.D.   P/O   RAF
8-41/9-41   RAF No.102538
Fresh graduate, commissioned in May 1941. Posted to No.602 Sqn remaining with it until August 1942.

W. DE MERODE

F.J.P. DIXON

Posted to No.164 Sqn between August 1942 and December 1943. CO No.137 Sqn December 1943 - April 1944. DFC [No.164 Sqn].

DILON, Francis J.　　　1ˢᵗ Lt　　　USAAF
10-43/10-43　　　　　　　　　　　O-439713
American pilot posted to gain combat experience. Pilot of 153ʳᵈ TRS / 67ᵗʰ RG.

J. DOUCHA

DIXON, Frederick J.P.　　　Sgt　　　RAF
6-40/7-40 (†)　　　　　　　　RAF No.742124
Posted from OTU. Shot down and killed off Portland Bill.

DON, Ralph S.　　　P/O　　　RAF
6-40/11-40　　　　　　　　RAF No.81348
Posted from OTU. Shot down and baled out after combat with Bf109 over Dover, 31.07.40, and returned from hospital on 10.10.40. Posted to Central Flying School in November. In October 1944, took command of the reformed No.142 Sqn of Bomber Command. DFC [No.142 Sqn].
†22.01.45, Mosquito B.XXV KB463, CO No.142 Sqn, Germany.

DONALDSON, George M.　　　P/O　　　RAF
10-42/2-43　　　　　　　　RAF No.49277
Known as "*Paddy*". Prewar NCO pilot serving with No.6 Sqn in Palestine at the outbreak of war. Posted to No.112 Sqn in May 1940 until June 1941. Returned to the UK in July 1942, being commissioned in the same time. Posted to No.1493 Flight in February 1943. No more operational postings until the end of war. Six confirmed victories, all against the Italians, North Africa and Greece, No.112 Sqn, 1940 and 1941.

DOUCHA, Jan　　　Sgt　　　(CZ)/RAF
4-41/5-41　　　　　　　　RAF No.788013
Posted from No.52 OTU. Czech, born in Austria. Prewar CzAF fighter pilot. Served with the FAF in 1940 with *Escadrille Légère de Défense* Chateaudun (Defense flight) and GC II/2 on Moranes. One confirmed victory with the French. Evacuated to the UK in Summer 1940, flight instructor in the RAF in 1940, before being posted to No.501 Sqn. Posted back to No.52 OTU before being posted to No.310 (Czech) Sqn in June 1942 until his death, being commissioned at the time of his posting.
†07.11.42, Spitfire VB AR502, No.310 (Czech) Sqn, France.

DROSSAERT, Albert E.　　　P/O　　　(BEL)/RAF
10-41/9-42　　　　　　　　RAF No.103480
Posted from No.53 OTU. Former prewar Belgian military pilot, serving in Air Regiment 2 in 1940. Seriously wounded on 11.05.40 and he spent a lot of time in hospital. Escaped from Belgium in February

A.E.DROSSAERT

A.DVORAK

1941 arriving in the UK via Gibraltar in July 1941. After a refresher course posted to No.501 Sqn. Posted to No.350 (Belgian) Sqn in September 1942. Then No.171 Sqn December 1942 - January 1943 and No.349 (Belgian) Sqn January 1943 - July 1944. During his postings he had many stays in hosptals because of his wounds. No more operationals postings after July 1944. Died as pilot in an accident of a SABENA Douglas DC.4, the Belgian national airlines at Gander (Canada) in September 1946.

Posted from No.52 OTU. Prewar CzAF NCO under training. Posted out, tour expired. Second tour of operations with No.312 (Czech) Sqn September 1942 - May 1944, then a third with the same unit between November 1944 and May 1945. In 1946 he joined Czechoslovak State Airlines as pilot and in 1949 he escaped to Austria after the Communist Coup. Between 1949 and 1954 served again with RAF, flying jets.
F/Sgt : 7-41, P/O : 1-42

DUCKENFIELD, Byron L.   P/O   RAF
5-40/9-40   RAF No.43368
Posted from No.74 Sqn, serving this unit unit since April 1940. Injured in Bombay accident in France in May 1940 and hospitalised. Returned to Squadron in July 1940. Posted to AFDU in September. In October 1941 became CO No.66 Sqn for another tour, then posted to No.615 Sqn in FE in February 1942. Shot down and made PoW by the Japanese on 27.12.42. Released in May 1945. Three confirmed victories, one being shared, No.501 Sqn, Battle of Britain, 1940. AFC [27.09.41].

DVORAK, Antonin   Sgt   (CZ)/RAF
4-41/2-42   RAF No.787517
                                   RAF No.115864

EASBY, Richard S.   F/L   RAF
5-43/5-43   RAF No.82670
Briefly attached from No.91 Squadron as supernumarary Flight Lieutenant, returning to his unit the same month. Served with No.91 Sqn at the end 1942 and will remain with it until February 1944. Another tour as CO No.66 Sqn between October 1944 and March 1945. DFC [No.66 Sqn].

EDMISTON, John McL.   F/O   RAF
3-43/5-43   RAF No.65580
Few details available. Commissioned in May 1941 and promoted Squadron Leader in December 1943. Posted to No.277 (ASR) Sqn serving with it until November 1943 before being posted overseas to

serve with No.292 (ASR) Sqn in India from February 1944 onwards.

EGAN, Edward J.   Sgt   RAF
9-40/9-40 (†)   RAF No.742787
Posted from No.615 Sqn. Prewar fighter pilot, with No.600 Sqn in June 1940, then serving with No.615 Sqn in August - September 1940.

EID, Andre E.   Sgt   (BEL)/RAF
12-41/9-42   RAF No.1383977
Belgian born in Cairo (Egypt), with Lebanese parentage. Posted from No.58 OTU. Living in Egypt, he volunteered for Belgian Army at the outbreak of war but could not sail to Europe before the fall of France. Arrived to the UK in January 1941 and enlisted to RAF. Posted overseas in September 1942, but returning to the UK for a brief period. No.130 Sqn in February and March 1943 before to be posted overseas again with No.349 (Belgian) Sqn in Nigeria (Western Africa) between March and June 1943. Then No.272 Sqn in ME June - August 1943 and No.601 Sqn from August 1943 onwards. Two confirmed victories with No.601 Sqn, Italy, 1943 - 1944.
F/Sgt : 8-42
†15.05.44, Spitfire VIII JG258, No.601 Sqn, Italy.

E.A.EID

EKINS, Victor H.*   Sgt   RAF
9-40/4-42   RAF No.745414
                             RAF No.63073
Posted from No.111 Sqn. With No.111 Sqn July - September 1940. Injured in combat 27.09.40, hospitalised, returning to the unit in November. Became A flight leader on 20.08.41 suceeding J.H. Lacey. Posted to No.10 Group HQ on 26.04.42. Replaced by V. Raba. To No.286 Sqn May - September 1942, then No.66 Sqn September - November 1942. CO No.19 Sqn, November 1942 - December 1943. No more operational postings until the War's end. One confirmed victory, No.111 Sqn, Battle of Britain, 1940. MBE [01.01.46]. *P/O : 4-41, F/L : 8-41*
DFC : LG 23.06.42

FAIRBANKS, David C.   F/L   (US)/RCAF
1-44/7-44   CAN./J.9096
Known as *"Foob"*, from New York. First operational posting after near two years as instructor in Canada. Posted to No.274 Sqn in July 1944 then posted to No.3 Sqn in January 1945. Returned to No.274 Sqn in February 1945 as CO. Shot down by FW190s on 28.02.45 and made PoW. Twelve confirmed and one shared confirmed victories, with Nos.3, 274 and 501 Sqns, Europe, 1944 - 1945 and one V-1, No.274 Sqn, 1944. DFC [No.274 Sqn], 1ST BAR [No.3 Sqn] and 2ND BAR [No.274 Sqn].

FARADAY, Owen P.   F/L   RAF
9-44/9-44 (†)   RAF No.128067
Known as *"Paddy"*. Crashed 4 m E of Clacton following engine failure and killed. No more details available.

FARNES, Paul C.P.   Sgt.   RAF
9-39/2-41   RAF No.741447
                             RAF No.88437
Prewar fighter pilot, posted to No.501 Sqn shortly after the war broke out, on 17.09.39, posted from No.11 (F) Group Pool. Posted to No.57 OTU at the end of his tour. Posted overseas and started a new tour of operations with No.229 Sqn in Malta in February 1942, becoming CO the following month. Posted out at the end of May 1942. No more operational posting returning to the UK in March 1945 and posted to No.124 Sqn the following month. Seven confirmed

D.C. FAIRBANKS

P.C.P. FARNES

victories and two shared confirmed victories with No.501 Sqn France and Battle of Britain, 1940.
P/O : 11.40

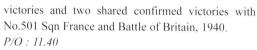

DFM : LG 22.10.40

FARROW, Reginald E.   Sgt   RAF
3-43/7-44 (†)   RAF No.956529
                                  RAF No.175712
Known as "*Reg*". Shot down by own AA fire near Ouistreham.
F/Sgt : 9-43, P/O : 4-44

FENEMORE, Stanley A.   Sgt   RAF
9-40/10-40 (†)   RAF No.745110
Posted from No.245 Sqn, being with this unit since July 1940.

FORD, J. D.   F/Sgt   ?
8-43/11-43   ?
Posted to No.222 Sqn, remaining with it until January 1945. No more details available.

FOTHERGILL, Charles   F/L   RAF
9-39/11-39 §   RAF No.34221
Posted on 12.08.39 from No.6 FTS for Adjutant and Flying Instructor duties. No further details.

FOXWELL, Leslie R.C.   Sgt   RAF
5-42/9-42 (†)   RAF No.1269041
Posted from OTU. Killed when collided H.G. Harwood's aircraft during a convoy patrol.

FRIENDSHIP, Alfred H.B.*   F/L   RAF
9-42/12-42   RAF No.81637
Posted from sick leave and took command of A flight from P.J. Stanbury on 30.09.42. First tour of operations started with No.3 Sqn between December 1939 and December 1940, being commisioned meanwhile in June 1940, then posted to No.605 Sqn, remaining with until May 1941, and posted out for recovery after a car accident. Returned to operations for another tour with No.66 Sqn in February 1942 and posted to Malta in June 1942, serving with No.126 Sqn and No.1435 Sqn before being sent back to the UK in August 1942 for medical reasons. On 16.12.42, was posted to No.65 Sqn until the end of his tour, being replaced by L. Scorer in command of A Flight two days later.

B.FUCHS

November 1941 - March 1942, then No.610 Sqn March - April 1942 and No.19 Sqn April - September 1942. Became B flight leader on 03.01.44 succeeding D.H. Hone. Posted to FLS in March 1944 at the end of his tour, being replaced by O.E. Willis at the head of B flight on 31.03.44. No more operational posting until the end of war. Remained with the *Armée de l'Air* after the war retiring in 1964 with the rank of *Général de brigade* (AVM).
Capitaine (F/L): 6-43

DFC : 05.04.44

Later in the year, he served briefly with No.604 Sqn between December 1943 and August 1944, after a night fighter conversion course. Eight confirmed victories, four being shared, No.3 Sqn, France, 1940. DFM & BAR [both No.3 Sqn].

FUCHS, Bernard M.*   *Lieutenant*   FFAF
9-42/3-44   RAF No.F.30087
At the outbreak of war was a French reserve officer in armoured divisions. Elected for an Observer course in January 1940, still under training when France collapsed. Escaped to the UK in June 1940. Switched for a pilot course, his first posting being No.154 Sqn

GADUS, Romuald   Sgt   PAF
11-40/2-41   RAF No.783651
Posted from No.607 Sqn, serving with this unit between October and November 1940. Former Air Cadet in the PAF in 1939. Reached France and in March 1940 posted to the group as staff pilot at the gunners' school at Caen. There, he joined the ad hoc fighter section. Arrived in Britain in June 1940. Posted to No.316 (Polish) Sqn as founder member, until his death.
†*01.10.41, Hurricane IIA Z2962, No.316 (Polish) Sqn, United Kingdom.*

GALER, Nyles N.   Sgt   (CAN)/RAF
2-43/5-44   RAF No.1338283
                                  RAF No.148904
Known as "*Chick*". Believed to be a Canadian in the RAF. Posted out, tour expired.
P/O : 6-43, F/O : 2-44

J.A.A.GIBSON

GENT, Raymond J.K.   Sgt   RAF
8-40/1-41 (†)   RAF No.754361
Posted from No.32 Sqn. Served briefly with No.32 Sqn in July 1940 before being sent back to No.6 OTU as found inadequately trained by his commanding officer. Killed while ferrying a squadron Magister in low cloud near Wells. One confimred victory, No.501 Sqn, Battle of Britain, 1940.

GIBSON, John A.A.*   P/O   (NZ)/RAF
5-40/10-40   RAF No.40969
Posted from Farnborough on 21.05.40 and served with No.501 Sqn in France and during Battle of Britain. B Flight leader from 25.08.40 onwards. Hospitalised with peptic ulcer 02.10.40 and, following convalescence, was assigned light flying duties at Cambridge. He was replaced by E. Holden. Posted to No.53 OTU as instructor, May 1941, then served with No.457 (RAAF) Sqn between December 1941 and March 1942. Repatriated to New Zealand, was posted to No.15 Sqn, RNZAF between June and December 1942, and December 1943 and July 1944 as CO this time. Returned to the UK, he flew with No.80 Sqn from March 1945 onwards. Fifteen confirmed victories, one being shared, with No.501 Sqn, Battle of France and Battle of Britain, 1940, and No.15 Sqn, RNZAF, Rabaul, 1944. DSO [No.15 Sqn, RNZAF].
F/L : 8-40

GILLESPIE, Edward W.   P/O   (US)/RCAF
4-42/5-42 (†)   CAN./J.7764
American, native of Missouri. Posted missing during *Circus* 160.

GLOWACKI, Antoni   Sgt   PAF
7-40/2-41   RAF No.780408
Posted from No.6 OTU. Former Polish Air Force pilot joining the UK in January 1940. Posted to No.55 OTU in February 1941. Commissioned and returned to operations in October with No.611 Sqn, but soon posted to No.303 (Polish) Sqn between November 1941 - February 1943, then posted to No.308 (Polish) Sqn February 1943 - March 1944. Another tour of operations in September 1944 as CO No.309 (Polish) Sqn until the end of war. Eight confirmed and one shared confirmed with No.501 Sqn, Battle of Britain, 1940 and No.303 Sqn, France, 1942. After the war, served the RAF until 1954 before emigrating to NZ

A. GLOWACKI

serving with the RNZAF until 1958. DFC [No.303 (Polish) Sqn].

GODFREY, I.P.   Lt   USAAF
5-43/5-43   ?
American pilot posted to gain combat experience. No further details available.

V. GÖTH

GÖTH, Vilem   P/O   (CZ)/RAF
10-40/10-40 (†)   RAF No.81945
Posted from No.310 (Czechoslovak) Sqn. Prewar Czech fighter pilot in Air Regiment 3. Served with the French Air Force in 1939-1940 in Chartres (SW of Paris). Collided with K.W. Mackenzie's Hurricane during combat with Bf109s, being killed in the process.

GRACEY, William B.W.   F/O   RAF
9-39/3-40 §   AAF No.90020
Known as "*Bill*". Pre-war Auxiliary Air Force officer. Commissioned in July 1936. Posted to No.6 FTS. Later serving with No.144 Sqn in 1942 - 1943. DFC [No.144 Sqn].

GRAHAM, Derek I.   F/O   RAF
5-41/8-41   RAF No.72023
Prewar RAFVR pilot. Posted to No.247 Sqn as Flight Commander in August 1941.
†24.10.41, Hurricane IIC BD934, No.247 Sqn, United Kingdom.

GRANT, Ian A.C.   P/O   RNZAF
10-42/12-42   NZ391351
Posted from No.52 OTU for another tour of operations. First tour with No.151 Sqn September - November 1940. Commissioned in October 1941. Posted to No.485 (NZ) Sqn in December 1942.
†13.02.43, Spitfire VB BM482, No.485 (NZ) Sqn, France.

GREEN, J.W.   Sgt   ?
9-42/1-43   ?
Posted overseas in January 1943. No more details available.

GREEN, William J.   Sgt   RAF
7-40/11-40   RAF No.813076
Prewar Auxiliary as Engine Fitter. Learnt to fly and officially joined No.501 Sqn as pilot in August 1940. Shot down twice during Battle and posted to No.504 Sqn in November 1940. No.504 Sqn November 1940 - March 1941. Commissioned in October 1942. Another tour of operations with No.56 Sqn from November 1944 until to be shot down and made PoW on 22.02.45.

GREENAWAY, William J.H.   P/O   RAF
8-41/11-41   RAF No.101024
Posted from OTU, commissioned in June 1941. Reported as "missing" following a *Rhubarb* operation and became PoW.

GRIFFIN, J.M.   F/O   ?
3-44/8-44   ?
Posted from No.13 OTU. Known as "*Sad Sack*". Further details of this pilot has not proved possible.

GRIFFITH, Lyndon P.*   F/L   RNZAF
2-44/8-44   NZ40968

W.J. GREEN

A.J.GROTTICK

Known as "*Griff*", posted from No.41 Sqn. First tour of operations completed with No.616 Sqn in 1941, then No.485 (NZ) Sqn March 1941 - August 1942 and No.122 Sqn May - September 1942. Returned to No.485 Sqn for his second tour (August - October 1943), then posted to No.41 Sqn in November before being posted to No.501 Sqn. Led A Flight from

L.P.GRIFFITH

24.04.44, replacing W.B. Atkinson. Replaced by G.L. Bonham on 11.08.44. Posted to No.274 Sqn remaining with it until November 1944. One confirmed victory, No.485 Sqn, Dieppe, 1942, and two confirmed V-1s destroyed, No.274 Sqn, 1944. DFC [No.485 (NZ) Sqn].

GRIFFITHS, Anthony A. Sgt RAF
7-43/12-43 RAF No.1316307
RAF No.156932
Posted from OTU. Shot down by mistake by USAAF Thunderbolts during *Ramrod* 385, baled out to become a PoW.
P/O : 10-43

GRIFFITHS, Charles D.* F/O RAF
9-39/6-40 § AAF No.90234
Prewar Auxiliary Air Force officer in SR from March 1933 till September 1935. Became A flight commander on 19.03.40 suceeding B.A. Hewett. Posted HQ, No.12 Group. Two confirmed victorires, one being shared, with No.501 Sqn, France, 1940.
F/L : 3-40

`DFC : LG 16.08.40`

GRIMMETT, David G. Sgt RAF
2-41/2-41 (†) RAF No.903560
Posted from OTU. Flew into balloon cable and killed in flying accident near Patchway.

GROTTICK, Albert J. F/O RAF
7-43/3-45 RAF No.136572
Known as "*Jimmie*", commissioned in October 1942. Posted to No.611 Sqn in March 1945. One confirmed victory with No.501 Sqn, Europe, 1943 and two V-1s, No.501 Sqn, 1944 - 1945.
F/L : 11-44

GROVE, Harry C. Sgt RAF
9-40/11-40 (†) RAF No.580202
Posted from No.3 Sqn, being with this unit since previous August. Shot down by Bf109 and killed when his parachute failed to open.

GUNN, Alexander E. Sgt RAF
2-44/8-44 RAF No.1560608
Known as "*Ben*". Posted from OTU. Posted to No.274

P.R.HAIRS

"*Hairy*". Posted To No.15 FTS in October 1940. Later posted to No.276 (ASR) Sqn December 1943 - May 1944. No more operational postings until the end of war. One confirmed victory, No.501 Sqn, Battle of Britain, 1940. MBE [01.01.46].

HAMMOND HUNT, Arthur P. P/O   RAF
10-42/12-42   RAF No.122123
Known as "*Peter*" his second christian name. Not much details on this pilot commissioned in March 1942. May to have been posted to No.332 Sqn, a Norwegian Sqn, but no trace of this pilot with this unit. Flight Lieutenant in March 1944 and later served with No.164 Sqn from October 1944 until April 1945. *F/O : 12-42*

HANNAH, James S.   Sgt   RCAF
9-42/9-42   CAN./J.99388
Native of New Brunswick, Canada. To RAF overseas in March 1942. First operational posting since his arrival in England. Subsequent postings unknown except that he served with No.131 Sqn in 1944 but did not follow the unit to the Far East. Commissioned in August 1944. Repatriated to Canada in January 1945 but returned to the United Kingdom in March 1945. Repatriated again, in March 1946. Rejoined RCAF between 1951 and 1958.

Sqn until the end of war. Commissioned in April 1945. One V-1 destroyed with No.274 Sqn, 1944.

GUNTER, Edward M.   P/O   RAF
9-40/9-40 (†)   RAF No.83988
Posted from No.43 Sqn, being with it less than two weeks. Shot down and killed by Bf109 five days later when his parachute failed to open.

GUERIN, James J.   P/O   RAAF
10-41/2-42   Aus.403136
Posted from No.57 OTU. Native of New South Wales, Australia. Posted out in February 1942, sailing on board HMS *Eagle* for Malta. Posted to No.249 Sqn on arrival.
†21.03.42, during air raid, Malta.

HANSEN, Claude A.*   F/L   (NZ)/RAF
                                           & RNZAF
8-44/3-45   RAF No.40386
                              NZ2216
Posted from No.68 Sqn. Known as "*Horry*". Joined RAF on a SSC 1937. Qualified as a Flying Instructor December 1938. Loaned to RNZAF as Instructor mid-war. Returned to the UK serving with No.68 Sqn (night fighters) before transferring to No.501 Sqn during August 1944. Last known A flight leader after G.L. Bonham's death on 25.09.44 onwards. Transferred RNZAF November 1944. Posted to Central Gunnery School, Catfoss in March 1945.

HAGGAS, Haydn   Sgt   RAF
7-41/10-41   RAF No.1282139
Posted from No.56 OTU. Known as "*Vic*". Posted out for service overseas, arriving at Malta with No.603 Sqn in May 1942, being attached to No.126 Sqn then posted to No.185 Sqn at the end of May. Two confirmed victories, one being shared, No.185 Sqn, Malta, 1942.
†07.07.42, Spitfire VC BR283, No.185 Sqn, Malta.

HARGREAVES, Harold L.   Sgt   RAAF
10-41/11-41   Aus.402937
Posted from No.53 OTU. Native of Queensland, Australia. Posted out and sent to Far East as member of No.266 (Fighter) Wing, being reported PoW on Japanese hands on 10.03.42. Released on 01.10.45.

HAIRS, Peter R.   P/O   RAF
1-40/10-40   RAF No.76316
Posted from No.11 (F) Group Pool. Known as

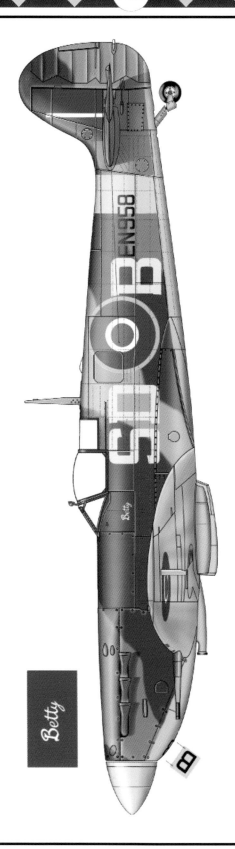

Supermarine Spitfire Mk.VB EN958, No.501 (County of Gloucester) Squadron, Pilot Officer J.A. Turbill (RAAF), Iblsey, July 1942.

C.A.HANSEN

the war, being accepted for a SSC as Flight Lieutenant in April 1952.

HENDERSON, H.C.   Sgt   RAF
7-42/5-43   RAF No.1395572
Posted from OTU. Posted out on 19.05.43. No details were available to help identify this pilot.
F/Sgt : 5-43

HENN, William B.   Sgt   RAF
8-40/12-40   RAF No.906097
Little is known except that he received his commission in September 1942 and ended the war as Flight Lieutenant. One confirmed victory, No.501 Sqn, Battle of Britain, 1940. AFC [01.01.45].

HARRISON, James C.   P/O   RAAF
1-42/4-42   Aus.401067
Posted from OTU, native of Victoria, Australia. Posted out and repatriated to Australia. Later served with No.76 Sqn, RAAF between March and September 1943. Discharged RAAF as Flight Lieutenant in March 1945. DFC [No.76 Sqn, RAAF].

HESSELYN, Raymond B.   F/O   RNZAF
2-43/7-43   NZ404362
Posted from No.61 OTU. Former NZ Territorial Army soldier transferred to RNZAF in 1940. First operational posting with No.234 Sqn in the UK from end 1941 until February 1942 when he sailed to Malta. Posted to No.249 Sqn until July 1942, being commissioned in the meantime. In July 1943 posted to No.222 Sqn, remaining with it until to be shot down and made PoW on 03.10.43. Eighteen confirmed and one shared confirmed victories, No.249 Sqn, Malta, 1942, and No.222 Sqn, Europe, 1943. DFM & BAR [both No.249 Sqn], DFC [No.222 Sqn].

HARROLD, Frederick C.   P/O   RAF
7-40/8-40, 9-40/9-40 (†)   RAF No.42707
Posted to No.151 Sqn for a month before returning to No.501 Sqn. Shot down and killed during combat with Bf 109s.

HEWETT, Brian A.*   F/L   RAF
9-39/3-40 §   AAF No.90016
Prewar Auxiliary officer, in command of A Flight at the outbreak of war. Posted to RAF Tangmere for Operations Room (Controller) duties, being replaced by C.D. Griffiths on 19.03.40. No more details traced on subsequent postings during the war. Squadron Leader by March 1941.

HARWOOD, Horace G.   Sgt   (US)/RCAF
4-42/9-42 (†)   CAN./R.79188
                                                CAN./J.15402
Posted from OTU. American, native of Vermont. To RAF overseas in December 1941. Killed when collided LR.C. Foxwell's aircraft during a convoy patrol.
P/O : 5-42

HEWITT, Duncan A.   P/O   (CAN)/RAF
5-40/7-40 (†)   RAF No.76579
Canadian, native of Ontario, in SSC with the RAF. Joined squadron on 21.05.40 while still based in France. One confirmed victory, France, 1940. He also reportedly shot down a Hurricane in "German markings" on 11.07.40.

HASTINGS, Iain   Sgt   RAF
6-43/8-43   RAF No.1349770
Posted from OTU. Posted to No.616 Sqn, serving with this unit until the end of his tour in May 1944. Commissioned in August 1944, ending the war as Flying Officer. Known to have served RAF after

D.A.HEWITT

HICKS, John L. Sgt RAF
7-41/9-41 RAF No.968502
Posted from No.247 Sqn, with it since January 1941. Commissioned in March 1942 and posted overseas, serving with No.126 Sqn from Spring 1942 until his death. One confirmed victory, with No.126 Sqn, Malta, 1942.
†09.07.42, Spitfire VC BR355, No.126 Sqn, Malta.

A.HOCHMAL

HIGGS, Sgt ?
7-41/8-41 ?
Posted from No.56 OTU. No details were available to help identify this pilot.

HOCHMAL, Alois P/O (CZ)/RAF
4-41/5-41 RAF No.82548
Posted from No.247 Sqn, with which he served for only two weeks. Prewar CzAF officer. Posted to No.313 (Czech) Sqn, remaining with it until October 1942. Second tour of operations again with No.313 Sqn in May 1943, becoming its CO in May 1944 until the end of his tour in September 1944. In 1948, after the Communist Coup, escaped from Czechoslovakia joining the RAF again.

HOCKEY, William F. Sgt RCAF
9-42/9-42 CAN./R.88364
Briefly served with the Squadron from 16.09.42 until 19.09.42. Posted out and sent overseas completing a tour with at least No.93 Sqn in North Africa and Sicily - Italy, being commissioned in May 1943. Repatriated to Canada in December 1944, being released in February 1945.

HODGKINSON, Colin G.S. P/O RAF
5-43/6-43, 10-43/11-43 RAF No.129361

Known as "*Hoppy*" posted from No.610 Sqn. Ex-FAA pilot who lost his legs due to flying accident in June 1939. Transferred to RAF in January 1942. Served with No.131 Sqn in December 1942 - January 1943 and No.610 Sqn between February and May 1943 before being posted to No.501 Sqn and then posted to No.611 Sqn. Returned as Flying Officer to No.501 Sqn in October 1943. Crashed near St Omer, becoming a PoW. Repatriated to the UK in September 1944 serving as a ferry pilot until the end of the war. Two confirmed victories with No.611 Sqn, Europe, 1943.

HOGAN, Henry A.V.**   S/L   RAF
6-40/11-40   RAF No.26181
See biography.

HOLDEN, Eustace***   F/O   RAF
5-40/6-41   RAF No.37970
Known as "*Gus*", Posted from No.56 Sqn, which he originally joined in April 1937. An all-round sportsman, he represented the RAF in the inter-services tennis championship and won the Singles Championship at Wimbledon in 1938. Arrived on the unit just before being sent to France. Returning to England, he was appointed as B flight commander but was admitted to hospital on 23.07.40 relinquishing command G.E.B. Stoney on 28.07.40. Following his return to the squadron he took command command again of B flight between 02.10.40 and 06.11.40, replacing J.A.A. Gibson. The B flight was given to F.V. Morello on 08.11.40. Posted to Accra, MEAF. Seven confirmed victories, No.501 Sqn, Battle of France and Battle of Britain, 1940.

DFC : LG 16.08.40

HOLLAND, Arthur H.   S/L   RAF
8-40/8-40   RAF No.05204
Prewar regular RAF officer. Posted to gain operational experience. Posted to No.65 Sqn as CO remaining with it until November. Transferred to the Technical Branch following medical problems. Remained with the RAF after the war retiring with the rank of Group Captain in 1960.

HOLMES, Joseph W.E.   Sgt   RAF
3-41/3-41   RAF No.938843
Posted from OTU. Posted to No.263 Sqn, remaining with the unit until June 1943. Commissioned in October 1941. DFC [No.263 Sqn].

E. HOLDEN

Henry Algenorn Vickers HOGAN
RAF No.26181

As the squadron CO during the Battle of Britain, Harry Hogan was a man of quiet calm and determination who rapidly blended a mixed bag of RAF, Auxiliary, VR and foreign pilots into a dedicated and deadly team of fighter pilots. An excellent pilot and marksman himself, he used his leadership and experience to sharpen the enthusiasm of the young squadron pilots under his command.

Hogan was born in October 1909, the son of an Indian Army colonel, and educated at Malvern College and the RAF College Cranwell. Commissioned in December 1930, he joined No.54 Squadron at Hornchurch, equipped with Siskins and Bulldogs. In March 1930 Hogan was posted to the FAA at Leuchars and subsequently flew with No.404 (Fleet Fighter) Flight and No.800 Squadron at Netheravon and HMS *Courageous*. He then qualified as an instructor at the CFS and was posted to No.1 FTS at Leuchars. In August 1936 he returned to the CFS as a staff instructor, where he remained for two years. His next move was to No.1 Bomber Group Long Range Development Unit at Upper Heyford, flying one of the three Vickers Wellesleys of the RAF Long Distance Flight from Ismalia to Darwin in November 1938. In December 1938 Hogan was promoted to Squadron Leader and, following successive posts at the Air Ministry and as an instructor, converted to Hurricanes at No.6 OTU and was given the command of No.501 Squadron. Following his arrival at Croydon on 25th June, 1940, Hogan's immediate task was to reform, re-equip and re-train the squadron following its withdrawal from France and continue operations against the impending assault on Britain by the Luftwaffe. He claimed his first victory on 20th July when he shot down a Bf109 off Portland Bill. Between

12th and 18th August he damaged two Do17s and a Bf110, followed by the destruction of a solitary Do215 on 27th August and probable Bf109 on 17th September. During the afternoon of 18 September, the squadron engaged a mixed force of He111s and Bf109s over West Malling and Hogan was attacked by an enemy fighter which badly damaged the engine of his Hurricane. Although he made an attempt to return to base, he was forced to bale out when the engine failed and his aircraft crashed into a wood at Charing; he landed safely in a nearby apple orchard.

On 27th September he shared in the destruction of a Bf110 with a pilot from No.303 Squadron, shot down another near Ashford on 5th October, shared a Bf109 with Pilot Officer Mackenzie on 7th October and shot down two more Bf109s on 12th and 15th October. His final claim was a probable Bf109 near Redhill on 27th October. Hogan was awarded the DFC on 25th October and posted to No.58 OTU at Grangemouth on 6th November, 1940.

Harry Hogan spent the rest of the war in numerous positions and posts concerned with RAF pilot training; in 1941 he was a member of the RAF Delegation in Washington and also supervised the Arnold Scheme for training RAF pilots in the USA between 1941 and 1943. The following year he was appointed as assistant commandant of the ECFS at Hullavington and later commanded No.19 FTS at Cranwell.

After the war Hogan was posted to various Staff postings retiring from the RAF in April 1962 as an Air Vice-Marshal, serving as Regional Director, Civil Defence. He was also President of the 501 Squadron Association for twenty-one years, from 1972 until his death on 28th June 1993.

C.L.HULSE

HOLROYD, Wilfred B.   Sgt   RAF
10-40/12-41   RAF No.740201
    RAF No.101040
Posted from No.151 Sqn. Posted to RAF Takoradi. Ended the war as Flight Lieutenant. No more details available.
P/O : 7-41

HONE, Douglas H.*   F/L   RAF
9-43/1-44   RAF No.80816
Posted from No.41 Sqn. B flight commander between 07.10.43 and 03.01.44, replacing D.H. Lenton, relinquishing command to B. Fuchs. Battle of Britain veteran with No.615 Sqn between July and July 1941, being shot down three times and injured twice. Second tour of operations with No.41 Sqn between May 1942 and August 1943. Posted out to become a Controller. No more operational postings until the war. Two confirmed victories, one being shared with No.615 Sqn, Battle of Britain, 1940.

HOUGHTON, Oliver V.   Sgt   RAF
8-40/9-40 (†)   RAF No.745437
Posted from No. 32 Sqn. Served previously with No.615 Sqn June - July 1940 and No.32 sqn July - August 1940. Shot down and killed in combat.

HOWARTH, Eric F.   Sgt   RAF
7-40/8-40   RAF No.741519
Injured on approach to Gravesend, 07.08.40. Later posted to No.48 Sqn of Coastal Command. Posted missing with his crew during a convoy patrol.
†05.09.41, Anson I W1769, No.48 Sqn, North Atlantic.

HULBERT, Donald J.   Sgt   RAF
10-40/10-40   RAF No.745041
Posted from No.257 Sqn, with which had served since June 1940. No more details available except that he was commissioned in April 1944. One shared confirmed victory, No.257 Sqn, Battle of Britain, 1940.

HULSE, Cecil L.   P/O   RAF
5-40/6-40 (†)   RAF No.70860
Known as *"Dickie"*. Posted shortly before the Squadron moved to France. Shot down and killed while operating from Boos, near Rouen (France). Three confirmed victories, with No.501Sqn, France, 1940.

JACKSON, John A.G.   Sgt   RAF
4-42/10-42   RAF No.1181410
    RAF No.122763
Posted from OTU. Posted out no further details. Second tour of operations with No.66 sqn between September 1943 and July 1944. Later CO No.122 Sqn for another tour of operations between February and August 1945. Two confirmed victories, with No.66 Sqn, Europe, 1943 - 1944. Remaining with the RAF, he retired with the rank of Air Commodore in 1972. DFC [No.66 Sqn].
P/O : 5-42

JAMES, Adrien C.   P/O   RAF
8-39/10-39 §   AAF No.90894
Auxiliary Air Force officer recalled on active duty on 24.08.39 Posted to No.5 FTS.
†28.04.41, Battle I K9230, No.1 AACU, United Kingdom.

JARRETT, Raymond W.E.   Sgt   RAF
9-40/10-40   RAF No.561763
Posted from No.245 Sqn. Prewar RAF aircraft apprentice who volunteered for a pilot course and posted to No.245 Sqn in May 1940 and fought in

J. JERABEK

France wounded in action when his Hurricane was attacked by Bf109s, 15.10.40. No further details except that he was commissioned in April 1945.

JEMMETT, Frank J. Sgt RAF
6-41/8-41 RAF No.928057
Posted from No.57 OTU. Posted out, and commissioned in February 1942. Later served over Malta with No.126 Sqn until his death.
†22.04.42, Spitfire VC BR180, No.126 Sqn, Malta.

JENKINS, Stanley P. F/Sgt RAF
4-42/6-42 RAF No.918081
No details available.
†25.04.43, Spitfire IX EN119, No.81 Sqn, Tunisia.

JERABEK, Jan Sgt (CZ)/RAF
4-42/6-42 RAF No.787676
Posted from No.52 OTU. Prewar CzAF NCO under training during the Munich crisis. Posted to No.313 (Czech) Sqn in June 1942 until his death. AFM [20.08.42].
†15.07.42, Spitfire VB AD372, No.313 (Czech) Sqn, France.

JOHNSON, Joseph A.L. F/O RCAF
9-44/4-45 CAN./J.18070
Canadian native of Alberta, posted for a second tour of operations. First tour in Middle East with No.108 Sqn night fighter squadron between June 1943 and April 1944 and sent back to the UK. Three confirmed victories with No.108 Sqn, Sicily, 1943, and four V-1s destroyed, No.501 Sqn, 1944 - 1945. DFC [No.108 Sqn].

JONES, Denys A.E.* F/O RAF
9-40/2-41 RAF No.40119
Posted from No.3 Sqn, in which he was serving since July 1940. Took over A Flight from 26.09.40 succeeding A.R. Putt. Force-landed twice due to enemy action in next few weeks. Posted to No.57 OTU on 17.02.41, being replaced by C.R. Cridland. Two confirmed victories, one being shared, with Nos.3 & 501 Sqns, Battle of Britain, 1940. No further details.
F/L : 10-40

KARASINSKI, Henrik Sgt PAF
10-42/3-43 RAF No.793862
Posted from No.303 (Polish) Sqn, being with it since July as first operational posting. Posted to No.308 (Polish) Sqn in March 1943 until the end of his tour in November the same year. No more operational postings until the end of war. Later with No.317 (Polish) Sqn from June 1945 onwards.

KELLY, Harold R. Sgt RAF
6-42/10-42 RAF No.657192
Posted from OTU. Posted overseas and served in Mediterranean with No.242 Sqn up to October 1943. Commissioned in April 1945.

KELMAN, A.V. Sgt ?
9-42/9-42 ?
No details available.

KINNELL, George T. F/O RNZAF
8-44/8-44 NZ413090
Previous postings unknown, having embarked for the Uk in December 1941. Briefly served with No.501 Sqn in August, before being posted to No.274 Sqn, serving the unit before being shot down and made PoW on 05.10.44.

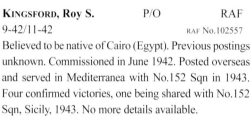

F.KOZLOWSKI

A.KRAKOWSKI

KINGSFORD, Roy S. P/O RAF
9-42/11-42 RAF No.102557
Believed to be native of Cairo (Egypt). Previous postings
unknown. Commissioned in June 1942. Posted overseas
and served in Mediterranea with No.152 Sqn in 1943.
Four confirmed victories, one being shared with No.152
Sqn, Sicily, 1943. No more details available.
F/O : 10-42

KJELDBAECH, Jorgen K. F/Sgt (DAN)/RAF
10-43/8-44 RAF No.?
RAF No.168693
Posted from No.222 Squadron, with which he had served for about two weeks in October. He was a Dane
who was working in Burma at the time of the
Japanese attack. Evacuated to the UK, and enlisting in
the RAF in May 1942. Posted to No.274 Sqn until the
end of his tour in November 1944.
P/O : 1-44, F/O : 5-44

KNIGHT, Leonard R. Sgt RAF
11-42/1-44 RAF No.1338910
RAF No.170140
Posted from OTU. Shot down by FW190, and forced
landing near Abbeville.
F/Sgt : 10-43, P/O : 12-43

KOZLOWSKI, Franciszek P/O (POL)/RAF
8-40/2-41 RAF No.76729
Prewar Polish pilot serving with 122nd Fighter Flight
in September 1939. Reached the UK in December
1939 and enlisted in the RAF. Posted to No.501 Sqn
as first operational posting. Seriously injured when
shot down over Canterbury, 18.08.40 and hospitalised
returning to Unit on 22.10.40. Posted to No.316
(Polish) Sqn in February 1941. Two shared confirmed
victories, with PAF in 1939.
*†13.03.43, Spitfire IX EN171, No.316 (Polish) Sqn,
France.*

KRAKOWSKI, Antoni F/O PAF
11-42/2-43 RAF No.P.0698
Posted from No.164 Sqn, in which he served for one
week only. Previously with No.303 (Polish) Sqn between February and October 1942. Posted out at the end
of his tour in February 1943. Second tour of operations
with No.309 (Polish) Sqn between June 1943 and
September 1944. No more operational postings until
the end of war. Killed in car accident on 26.08.45.

KUCERA, Jiri V. Sgt (CZ)/RAF
5-41/5-41 RAF No.787658
Prewar CzAF fighter pilot in Air Regiment 4. With FAF

J.V.KUCERA

1939-1940 serving in GC I/6 on Moranes then went to GB. Posted to No.310 Sqn in August 1940 but after few days posted to No.6 OTU for retraining on Hurricanes. Then posted to No.238 Sqn in September. Badly injured in accident in November 1940, returning to operations in May 1941 with No.501 Sqn before to be posted to the newly created No.313 (Czech) Sqn where he completed his tour in June 1943. He then completed courses at the SFTS College, Nos.9 and 8 OTUs, ending the war with No.544 Sqn (Photo Reconnaissance) from August 1944. After the war he flying Mosquito FB.VIs as flight commander with 24th Fighter-Bomber Air Regiment in Pilsen-Bory, but in 1949 he was released from the Czechoslovak Air Force due to political reasons. In 1949-1950 he was imprisoned by communists, being rehabilitated in 1965. Two confirmed victories with No.238 Sqn, Battle of Britain, 1940.

LACEY, James H.*   Sgt   RAF
11-39/8-41   RAF No.740042
    RAF No.60321
See biography. A flight leader between 23.06.41 and 15.08.41, replacing C.R. Cridland and being replaced by V.H. Ekins on 20.08.41.
P/O : 1-41, F/L : 6-41

DFM : LG 23.08.40   BAR : LG 26.11.40

LANGDON-DOWN, Anthony T.   F/L   RAF
8-44/12-44   RAF No 109001
Little details available. Commissioned in October 1941 and Flight Lieutenant in October 1943. One V-1 destroyed with No.501 Sqn.

LAWS, George G.L.   Sgt.   RAF
9-40/3-41 (†)   RAF No.745649
Posted from No.151 Sqn. Killed when his Hurricane crashed on approach at Stoke Gifford.

LAWSON, Geoffrey S.   P/O   (SA)/RAF
7-43/10-43   RAF No.151779
The ORB suggests probable connections with South Africa. Posted to No.41 OTU at the end of his tour. No more details on his postings available.
F/O : 10-43

LEE, Kenneth N. T.   P/O   RAF
9-39/11-40   RAF No.72998
Known as *"Hawkeye"*. Prewar fighter pilot serving with No.111 Sqn, then with No.43 Sqn. Posted to No.501 Sqn on 04.09.39. Shot down on 18.08.40, he spent almost two months at hospital, returning to squadron in October. Posted to SD Flight, Rolls-Royce in November, but reposted to No.52 OTU as instructor instead. Another tour of duty with No.79 Sqn December 1941, but sent overseas as ferry pilot soon afterwards. No.112 Sqn May - July 1942, but posted sick until September and posted to No.260 (Sudan) Sqn until March 1943 when he became CO No.123 Sqn until 23.07.43 when he was shot down and made PoW. Seven confirmed victories, No.501 Sqn, France and Battle of Britain, 1940 and No.260 Sqn, North Africa, 1942.
F/O : 12-40

DFC : LG 22.10.40

LEE, Allan   Sgt   RAF
6-42/8-42 (†)   RAF No.934095
Posted from OTU. Crashed in bad visibility on return to Tangmere.

LEICESTER, Wilfred C.F.   Sgt   RNZAF
7-41/8-41   NZ401395
Known as *"Wilf"*. Posted from No.609 Sqn in July to No.501 Sqn. Posted to Eastleigh to test contra-revol-

James Harry LACEY
RAF No.740062 (NCO)
& RAF No.60321 (Officer)

Popularly known as "Ginger" because of his mop of red hair, the likeable Yorkshireman's natural ability as a pilot, his strong sense of humour and casual attitude to life made him enormously popular with his squadron colleagues. His youthful appearance also belied a natural aggression in the air and a reputation as a keen marksman, which placed him among the ranks of top-scoring fighter pilots during the Battle of Britain with 17 confirmed, six damaged and five probable enemy aircraft to his credit.

Born in Wetherby in February 1917, Lacey joined the RAFVR in 1937 through a passion for aircraft and trained at No.11 E&RFTS, Scone, as a Sergeant u/t pilot, where he was graded as "Above Average". The following year he took an instructor's course and joined the Yorkshire Aeroplane Club at Yeadon, and in January 1939 was attached for a six week period of duty with No.1 Squadron at Tangmere. Lacey remained at Yeadon until he was called up on 3rd September, 1939 and ordered to report to No.501 Squadron at Filton as a Sergeant Pilot.

Impatient to see action, Lacey moved with the squadron to France on 10th May, 1940 following the German invasion of the Low Countries and opened his score-sheet three days later when he shot down a Bf109 and He111 of KG53 during a dawn patrol near Sedan; later the same morning he destroyed a Bf110C of 3./ZG26 at La Chesne, north-east of Vouziers and was awarded the Croix de Guerre. On 27th May two more He111s were claimed in the Blangy-Albancourt area while operating from Boos and the following month was slightly injured following a forced-landing in a boggy field near Le Mans. During the British withdrawal from France, Lacey was able to board a ship at St Malo on 19th June and sail for the Channel Islands.

On 20th July 1940 he re-opened his score with a Bf109.

During the Battle of Britain, his score continued to increase, and between 12th August and 2nd September he claimed seven enemy aircraft as destroyed, with four more as probables and three as damaged, and was awarded the DFM on 23rd August. On 13th September, Lacey shot down a He111 near Maidstone but suffered a damaged radiator by the return fire from one of its gunners, forcing him to abandon the aircraft near Leeds Castle. He was again shot down on 17th September, by Bf109s this time. For his actions, he was awarded a BAR to his DFM on 26th November 1940. He was commissioned in January 1941 and continued to fly operational patrols with the squadron. In June 1941 he was given command of A Flight, and he continued to increase his score, shooting down four more German aircraft during the Summer. Lacey's last two kills with No.501 Squadron were claimed on 24th July 1941. On 15th August, 1941 he was posted to No.57 OTU, where he remained for six months until joining No.602 Squadron at Kenley, remaining with it unitl May 1942. In June 1943, he was posted to India, assuming various commands, until November 1944, when Lacey assumed command of No.17 Squadron at Palel, equipped with Spitfire VIIIs. On 19th February 1945 Lacey engaged a force of Nakajima *Oscars* near Mandalay, shooting one down after a short burst of fire. Lacey remained with No.17 Squadron until April 1946 and partcipated to the occupation of Japan and returned to the UK. Granted a Permament Commission in December 1948, he subsequently became a Fighter Controller. Lacey retired a Squadron Leader in March 1967 and ran an air freight company before becoming a flying instructor at an airfield near Bridlington. He died on 30 May 1989. His official list of claims is 28 destroyed, 5 probables, and 9 damaged.

ving propellor Spitfire. Injured during testing. Returned to New Zealand when Japan entered the war. Operation's Officer 15 Squadron, RNZAF, and NZ Fighter Wing Operation's Officer, Tonga and Solomons.

LEITCH, William R.　　Sgt　　RAF
5-42/8-42 (†)　　RAF No.657352
Posted from OTU. Last seen chasing two FW190s.

LELLIOTT, E.R.L.　　F/Sgt　　?
?-45/4-45　　?
No details were available to help to identify this pilot. His date of arrival to Squadron is also unknown.

LENNARD, Paul L.　　Midshipman　FAA
7-40/7-40
Served with Squadron two weeks only, then posted to No.760 Sqn, RN. Completed eight sorties with the Squadron. Later received his commision and served with No.757 Sqn, RN in 1941 and Royal Navy shore base HMS *Kestrel*.
†26.03.42, Albacore I X9228, HMS **Kestrel,** *United Kingdom.*

LENTON, Douglas F.*　　F/L　　(NZ)/RAF
6-43/10-43　　RAF No.42239
The ORB suggests that he may originate from New Zealand. With No.124 Sqn during February and March 1943, and served briefly with No.222 Sqn before joining 501. B Flight commander between 31.05.43 and 07.10.43, succeeding L. Scorer. Replaced by D.H. Hone. Posted back to No.222 sqn until the end of his tour in March 1944.

LEWIS, A.A.　　Sgt　　?
5-40/6-40?　　?
This name appears only once in the ORB, on 27.05.40. No trace has been found on this pilot after that date although one Sgt A.A. Lewis was found on Equipment Branch (No.195363) in 1940.

LIGHTBOURN, Warren M.　　P/O　　RAF
5-42/8-42　　RAF No.119573
Posted from OTU, commissioned in February 1942.

D.F.LENTON

Posted to No.286 Sqn and later served with No.610 Sqn from June 1943 onwards.
†14.02.45, Spitfire XIV RM677, No.610 Sqn, Germany

LILBURN, Joseph L.　　W/O　　RAF
12-42/12-43　　RAF No.745459
　　RAF No.156634
Not much details available on this pilot. Flight Lieutenant by the end of war. Seems to have been posted to No.131 Sqn in Far East in 1945.
P/O : 7-43

LILLEYMAN, Donald　　F/O　　RAF
3-45/4-45　　RAF No.164015
Not much details available, being commissioned in February 1944 as fresh graduate. Remained with the RAFVR after war until November 1947.

LILWALL, Raymond J.　　F/L　　RAF
9-44/4-45　　RAF No.122962
Not much details available. Received his commission in March 1942 and Flight Lieutenant in March 1944.

LOCKYER, Norman J.　　P/O　　RAF
4-41/4-41 (†)　　RAF No.61292
Posted from No.56 OTU. Killed in road accident.

K. LUKASZEWICZ

LONG, Richard J.   Sgt   RAAF
5-42/10-42   Aus.401071
Posted from No.245 Sqn, in which he served since October 1941. English-born Australian. Posted to No.453 (RAAF) Sqn in October 1942, remaining with it until the end of his tour in August 1943. Repatriated to Australia. Second tour of operations with No.79 Sqn, RAAF, between February and December 1944. No more operational postings.
F/Sgt : 7-42, P/O : 9-42

LONSDALE, Robert H.   Sgt   RAF
10-40/1-41   RAF No.919410
Posted from No.242 Sqn. Prewar RAF pilot in SSC (service number 37506) who resigned his commission in November 1939 rejoining the RAFVR as NCO in January 1940. Posted to No.46 Sqn between April and July 1940, then posted to No.242 (Canadian) Sqn 1940. Posted out and served as an instructor in Canada until 1943 and returned to the UK and served with Bomber Command in a Lancaster Squadron. Two confirmed victories with No.242 Sqn, Battle of Britain, 1940.

LOVERSEED, John E.   Sgt   RAF
7-40/8-40   RAF No.907964
No details available. AFC [01.01.43]

LUCAS, Ronald G.   F/O   RAF
8-44/9-44   RAF No.156691
Known as *"Lucky"*. Posted from FIU, in which he was serving since July 1944. Believed to have six confirmed V-1s, FIU and No.501 Sqn. Posted sick and did not return to the Squadron.

LUCK, Leslie   Sgt   RAF
3-41/4-41   RAF No.917180
Posted to No.229 Sqn. Later posted out as ferry pilot.
†04.10.41, Hurricane IIB BD819, Takoradi Base, Nigeria.

LUFFMAN, William J.   Sgt   RAF
3-43/5-43   RAF No.1317567
Posted from OTU. Posted overseas in May 1943, serving with No.126 Sqn over Italy, then over occupied Europe from the UK in Spring 1944.
†07.02.45, Mustang III FZ182, No.126 Sqn, Belgium.

LUKASZEWICZ, Kazimierz   P/O   (POL)/RAF
8-40/8-40 (†)   RAF No.76761
Pre-war Polish pilot, fighting in an *ad hoc* defence flight formed by instructors in September 1939. Posted from No.303 (Polish) Sqn, he served just a couple of days in July 1940. Reported as "Missing" following combat with Bf109s near Ramsgate.

LYNCH, Richard C.   P/O   RAF
9-41/9-42 (†)   RAF No.115146
Known as *"Dickie"*. Posted from No.57 OTU. Reported as "Missing" following convoy patrol.

LYNE, John W.   Sgt   RAF
3-43/8-44   RAF No.1333471
    RAF No.161787
Posted to No.274 Sqn until the end of his tour in November 1944. Three V-1s destroyed with No.274 Sqn.
F/Sgt : 9-43, P/O : 11-43

DFC : LG 25.10.40

Kenneth William MACKENZIE
RAF No.84017

"Mac" Mackenzie was born in Belfast, Northern Ireland, in June 1916 and studied engineering at Queen's University, Belfast. He obtained a civil "A" licence with the North of Ireland Aero Club at the age of 16 and joined the RAFVR in 1939. Called up for service in December 1939, "Mac" completed his training and was posted to No.43 Squadron at Usworth on 21st September, 1940 as a Pilot Officer. A week later he transferred to No.501 Squadron at Kenley and shared in the shooting down of a Ju88 on 4th October. The following day, "Mac" shot down a Bf109 off Margate. On 7th October, he again shared in the destruction of a Bf109 with Squadron Leader Hogan, which ditched in the sea off Sandgate. A further Bf109 was damaged during the same action, which "Mac" pursued at sea level until he ran out of ammunition. Determined that the enemy fighter would not get away, he formated on the aircraft and struck its tailplane with his starboard wing, following which it crashed into the sea. Fortunately "Mac" was able to maintain control of his Hurricane, and despite being chased by further Bf 109s, carried out a successful forced-landing near Folkestone. He suffered facial injuries in the landing and did not return to the squadron until 17th October. On the 25th October "Mac" was awarded the DFC, which was celebrated with a further Bf109 as destroyed and a share of another with Pilot Officer Vivian Snell during the same action. Later that same day, he collided with Pilot Officer Vilem Göth as he led his section during an attack on a formation of Bf 109s and was forced to bale out, coming down in a hay field near Staplehurst. In the following weeks, he added six confirmed claimed and three other damaged before the Squadron returned to Filton in December 1940. He was appointed as Deputy Flight Commander in the same time. On 19th June, 1941 he was transferred to No.247 Squadron at Predannack as Flight Commander, where he continued fly Hurricanes in the night fighter role. He destroyed a Ju88 on 7th July 1941, which was repeated on 13th September, 1941 when he shot down a He111 off Land's End. On 29th September 1941 "Mac" Mackenzie was shot down by *flak* whilst leading an attack on Lannion airfield and had to paddle ashore in his dinghy. He was captured and imprisoned Warburg and Schubin PoW camps, before being transferred to Stalag Luft III at Sagan in April 1942. During his time as a PoW, "Mac" devised many ingenious escape plans, but in October 1944 was repatriated after convincing the German authorities that he was suffering from a mental illness.

A return to flying as an instructor at No.53 OTU, Kirton in Lindsey in December 1944, "Mac" was promoted to Squadron Leader in August 1947. Awarded the AFC in January 1953, his subsequent appointments included No.226 OCU at Stradishall as Chief Instructor, HQ MEAF, HQ Persian Gulf, and HQ Maintenance Command. "Mac" retired from the RAF in 1967 as a Wing Commander to become Deputy Commander of the Zambian Air Force, following which he was Managing Director of Air Kenya Ltd until his eventual retirement in 1973. A keen sportsman, he was successful in Rugby, Athletics, Motor Racing and Polo. He was also Hon. Secretary of the Battle of Britain Fighter Association, Chairman RAF Motor Sport Association, the RAF Officers Association, East Africa, and President of the 501 Squadron Association. His autobiography, "*Hurricane Combat*" was first published in 1987.

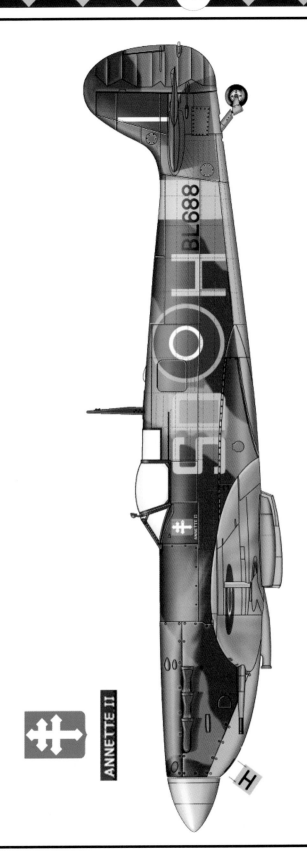

Supermarine Spitfire Mk.VB BL688, No.501 (County of Gloucester) Squadron, *Capitaine* B. Fuchs (FFAF), Hawkinge, June 1943.

C.E.MALFROY

B.MALINOWSKI

MACKENZIE, Kenneth W. P/O RAF
9-40/6-41 RAF No.84017
See biography.

MACLACHLAN, Gordon B. P/O RAF
7-41/8-41 RAF No.101490
Posted from No.56 OTU. Posted to No.616 Sqn in August, serving with it until his death.
†*16.04.43, Spitfire VI BS245, No.616 Sqn, France.*

MADAY, Josef F/O RCAF
9-44/3-45 CAN./J.23780
Canadian of Czechoslovak origins. His first name was also spelled "*Jozef*", posted to RAF overseas in May 1943. Posted from No.410 (RCAF) Sqn. Posted out, tour expired. Repatriated to Canada in August 1945 Rejoined RCAF between 1951 and 1957. One confirmed victory, No.410 Sqn, Europe, 1944, and one V-1 destroyed, No.501 Sqn, 1944.

MALFROY, Camille E.* F/O (NZ)/RAF
9-39/6-40, 2-41/12-41§ AAF No.90019
Known as "*Cam*". Pre-war Auxiliary pilot. Posted as instructor with No.7 OTU on return to England in June 1940. Rejoined the unit as Flight Lieutenant on as B Flight Commander replacing F.V. Morello and

relinquished command to R.C.Dafforn on 20.04.41. Posted to Air Ministry. Later posted to No.417 (RCAF) Sqn as its first CO between December 1941 and March 1942, then CO No.66 Sqn March - June 1942. No more operational postings. One confirmed victory, No.501 Sqn, France 1940. DFC [No.66 Sqn].

MALINOWSKI, Bronislaw Sgt PAF
12-40/4-41 RAF No.782059
Posted from No.43 Sqn. Prewar Polish Air Force pilot, being an instructor in September 1939. After the campaign of 1939 arrived in France. Following training he was posted to the 1st Polish Army Co-operation Squadron being formed there. Arrived in Britain in July 1940. First postings with No.307 (Polish) Sqn between September and October 1940, and No.43 Sqn between October and December 1940. Posted No.302 (Polish) Sqn in April 1941 before being rested from operations in May. Second tour of operations in November 1942 with No.302 Sqn again until February 1943, then being part of the "Skalski's circus" (attached to No.145 Sqn) in North Africa until July 1943 when he returned to the UK with No.302 Sqn, shot down in September but evaded capture, returning to his unit in December 1943 until March 1944. Commissioned at the end of war. Three confirmed victories, with No.145 Sqn and No.302 Sqn, ME and Europe, 1943. DFC [No.302 (Polish) Sqn].

MALLOY, John A. F/O RCAF
1-44/8-44 CAN./J.11008
Native of Ontario, Canada. Known as "*Doc*". Posted from No.1 TEU. Commissioned in March 1942 arriving in England in May 1943. Posted to No.274 Sqn.
F/L : 4-44
†13.01.45, Tempest V EJ639, No.274 Sqn, Germany.

MANN, Geoffrey N. F/O RAF
2-44/8-44 RAF No.139582
Known as "*Ace Hole*". Posted to No.274 Sqn, remaining with this unit until the end of his tour in February 1945. Three confirmed victories, one being shared, No.274 Sqn, Europe, 1944 - 1945.

MARCINKOWSKI, Mieczyslaw S.
Sgt PAF
10-40/11-40 (†) RAF No.780491
Posted from No.151 Sqn. Reported as "Missing" following combat over the Channel.

MARKHAM, L. Captain USAAF
8-43/8-43
American pilot posted to gain combat experience. No more details available.

D.A.S.McKAY

MARSDEN, Sgt ?
1-41/6-41 ?
No details were available to help to identify this pilot.

MAWER, Granville A. Sgt RAAF
5-42/10-42 Aus.403112
Posted from No.245 Sqn, being with this unit since October 1941. Native of New South Wales. Rapatriated to Australia in October 1942. Posted to "Churchill Wing" to defend Darwin, with No.54 Sqn, RAF in March 1943, then with No.452 (RAAF) Sqn from April 1943 until his death. Three confirmed victories, with Nos.54 and 452 Sqns, Darwin, 1943.
P/O : 7-42
†26.09.43, Spitfire VC A58-201, No.452 (RAAF) Sqn, Australia.

McDONALD, Alexander R. Sgt RCAF
5-42/8-42 (†) CAN./R.2535
Canadian background unknown. Former prewar Airframe mechanic, accepted for a pilot course. To RAF overseas October 1941. Crashed and killed in bad weather, Dorchester.
F/Sgt : 7-42

McINTYRE, Archibald A. P/O RAF
6-43/1-44 RAF No.123214
Born in India. Sometimes known by his second christian name "*Angus*". Posted from No.54 Sqn in which he was sent to Australia in June 1942, being repatriated to the UK in February 1943. Posted out, serving later from April 1944 onwards with No.222 Sqn until his death.
F/O : 1-44
†28.02.45, Tempest V NV680, No.222 Sqn, Netherlands.

McKAY, Donald A S. Sgt RAF
9-39/10-40 RAF No.740115
Posted from No.111 Sqn, in which he was serving since June 1939. Posted to No.421 Flight (became later No.91 Sqn) in October 1940. Commissioned in October 1941, posted to No.234 Sqn in January 1942 for a second tour of operations until February when he was posted to No.130 Sqn but was sent to Middle East in April, being posted to No.213 Sqn, then to No.33 Sqn in August and No.274 Sqn in November 1942 until the end of his tour. No more operational postings

until the end of war. At least 14 confirmed victories, with No.501 Sqn, Battle of France and Battle of Britain, No.421 flight and Nos.91 & 234 Sqns, Europe, 1940 - 1941. DFM & BAR [both No.91 Sqn].

MESERVE, Robert L.   1ˢᵗ Lt.   USAAF
8-43/9-43   O-442289
American pilot posted to gain combat experience. Probably a pilot of 67ᵗʰ RG. Later served with 353ʳᵈ FS/354ᵗʰ FG for an operational tour from end 1943 onwards, claiming three and half victories with this unit.

MILLER, Bud F.   Flt/Off   USAAF
8-44/10-44   T-1909??
Posted from FIU, he served with in June - July 1944. Previously trained by RCAF and being sent to England in January 1943 as Sergeant (CAN./R.140790), promoted Flight Sergeant in June. Transferred to USAAF in July 1943. Served in Europe with No.605 in 1944. One confirmed victory, No.605 Sqn, Europe, 1944, and eight V-1s destroyed.

MOORE, Eric H.   Sgt   RAF
6-42/10-42   RAF No.656753
Posted from OTU. Commissioned in February 1944. No more details available.

MORELLO, Francis V.*   F/L   RAF
11-40/2-41   RAF No.39256
Known as "*Joe*". Born in India. Posted from No.15 FTS to become B flight commander, succeeding E.Holden on 08.11.40. Posted to No.52 OTU in February 1941 and replaced by C.E. Malfroy at the head of B Flight. Completed his tour overseas in Malta with No.249 Sqn between April and August 1941, then in Middle East with No.33 Sqn (September - October 1941) before becoming CO No.112 Sqn between October 1941 and January 1942. Returned to the UK, became the first CO No.453 (RAAF) Sqn between June and November 1942. No more operational postings until the end of war.

MORFILL, Percy F.   F/Sgt   RAF
5-40/6-41   RAF No.564749
Known as "*Ronnie*" or "*Peter*". Prewar RAF pilot. Served with No.65 Sqn until early 1940 and was posted to No.501 Sqn. Posted to No.58 OTU at the end of his tour. No more operational postings until the end of war, spending the rest of the war as flying instructor in Southern Rhodesia. Commissioned in January 1942. Remained with the RAF after the war retiring with the rank of Squadron Leader in 1958. Seven confirmed victories, one being shared, with No.501 Sqn, Battle of France and Battle of Britain, 1940.

DFM : LG 22.10.40

E.H.MOORE

F.V.MORELLO

C. MROCZYK

MOSSING, Frederick W.   F/Sgt   RCAF
1-44/8-44   CAN./R.132296
    CAN./J.88877
Posted from No.1 TEU. Native of Saskatchewan, Canada. First operational posting. Posted to No.274 Sqn in August 1944, remaining with it until the end of his tour in April 1945. Three confirmed victories, one being shared with No.274 Sqn, Europe, 1945. DFC [No.274 Sqn].
W/O : 4-44, P/O : 7-44
†12.05.45, Tempest V EJ685, No.56 OTU, United Kingdom.

MROCZYK, Czeslaw   P/O   PAF
10-42/2-43   RAF No.P.1727
Posted from No.303 (Polish) with it since July 1942. Posted to No.317 (Polish) Sqn in February 1943, remaining with it until May 1944. Returned with the same unit for another tour between September 1944 and end of war. One confirmed victory, No.317 Sqn, Europe, 1945. DFC [No.317 Sqn].

MUCHOWSKI, Konrad A.   Sgt   PAF
10-40/3-41   RAF No.P.2208 (Off)
Posted from No.85 Sqn, he served in September - October 1940. Prewar PAF pilot. In September 1939 he fought in 42nd Reconnaissance Flight in support of the Pomorze Army, flying PZL.23 Karas light bombers. He went to Britain in one of the first group of Polish pilots at the end of 1939. Posted to No.308

(Polish) Sqn between March - June 1941. Commissioned in April 1943 but no more operational postings until the end of war.

MURRAY, Alan D.   S/L   RAF
9-40/9-40   RAF No.34168
Known as *"Ginger"*. Prewar RAF pilot, being at A&AEE at the outbreak of war. Asked for an operational posting in July 1940, being posted to No.46 Sqn in July. Attached to squadron for one week to gain combat experience before to be posted as CO No.73 Sqn, remaining with it until April 1941. No more opeartionals postings until the end of war. Two confirmed victories, No.73 Sqn, Middle East, 1941. DFC [No.73 Sqn].

MUSGRAVE, John G.   F/L   RAF
12-44/1-45   RAF No.103571
Posted from No.605 Sqn, in which he was serving since January 1944. Commissioned in August 1941. Posted out, tour expired. Twelve V-1s destroyed with No.605 Sqn, 1944.

MUZIKA, Jaroslav   P/O   (CZ)/RAF
4-41/5-41   RAF No.82562
Posted from No.52 OTU. Prewar CzAF officer serving with Air Regiment 3. Posted to No.313 (Czech) Sqn, remaining with it until August 1944. No more operational postings until the end of war. Remained with the CzAF after the war but in April 1949 he escaped to England from Czechoslovakia on board of a Siebel S 204D from Vysokov airfield with other former Czech pilots in the RAF. He joined the RAF again, being awarded an AFC on 01.06.53.

NEWBERY, Richard A.   P/O   RAF
3-41/4-42   RAF No.60104
Posted from OTU. Posted to No.118 Sqn remaining with it until the end of his tour in July 1943. Second tour of operations as CO No.610 Sqn between January 1944 and February 1945. Three confirmed victories with No.118 Sqn, Europe, 1943, and ten V-1s destroyed, two being shared with No.610 Sqn, Europe, 1944. DFC & BAR [No.118 Sqn both].
F/O : 4-42

NEZBEDA, Egon   P/O   (CZ)/RAF
6-41/3-42   RAF No.82565

R.A.NEWBERRY

P.OSTRASZEWSKI-OSTAJA

Posted from No.52 OTU. Czech born in Germany. Prewar CzAF fighter pilot in Air Regiment 2. With FAF 1939-1940 in Toulouse and Blida (North Africa) then escaped to the UK. No.24 Sqn from Summer 1940 until April 1941 where he took a short refresher course before being posted to No.501 Sqn. Posted to No.310 (Czechoslovak) Sqn in June 1941 until March 1942. Tour expired in March 1942 and posted to Czechoslovak Depot. Later posted to Canada as Training CO. After return to the UK became Technical Officer of No.311 (Czechoslovak) Bomber Sqn, later passed his multi-engined rating. Liberator pilot with No.311 Sqn from September 1944 onwards. Transferred to the new CzAF after 1945 as Professor of Air Academy, but after the Communist coup in 1948 he was turned out from CzAF.

Nicol, Stuart E. Sgt RNZAF
3-43/5-43 NZ416573
Posted from OTU. Posted overseas, serving in Middle East, with the Gibraltar Defense flight (GDF). Later commissioned, becoming CO of the Desert Air Force Communication Flight (DAFCF), being also the personal pilot of the General Officer Commanding 8th Army. MBE [1946].

Noonan, Patrick J. F/Sgt RAAF
8-43/3-44 Aus.414074

Posted from No.53 OTU. Native of Queensland, Australia. Posted to No.5 PDC to serve in Far East. Served with No.67 Sqn in India between August 1944 and July 1945. Commissioned in October 1944.
W/O : 11-43

O'Byrne, Peter Sgt RAF
10-40/12-40 RAF No.740334
Posted from No.73 Sqn, in which he served between June and October 1940. Posted out in December 1940, tour expired. No further details.

Orford, Thomas B. Sgt RAF
3-42/3-42 RAF No.1000257
Posted from OTU. Injured in Tiger Moth accident on 20.03.42 and hospitalised. Never returned to the Squadron and posted overseas, serving later with No.127 Sqn from March 1943 onwards.
†06.10.43, Hurricane IIC KZ519, No.127 Sqn, Palestine.

Orr, John B. P/O RAF
10-42/4-43 RAF No.122425
Not much details on this officer. Posted overseas. Flight Lieutenant in May 1944.
F/O : 11-42

OSTASZEWSKI-OSTOJA, Piotr

F/L   (POL)/RAF

8-44/9-44   RAF No.76741

Posted from No.125 Sqn as supernumerary Flight Lieutenant. Prewar Polish pilot. In September 1939 he fought in an ad hoc defence fighter flight formed by WSP instructors. Battle of Britain veteran with No.609 Sqn August 1940 - March 1941. Second tour of operations from September 1942 with Nos.303, 302, 308 Sqns and eventually with No.306 Sqn in June 1943. In August posted for night fighter course, joining No.85 Sqn in February 1944, then No.125 Sqn in April, before being posted to No.501 Sqn. Posted to No.307 (Polish) Sqn in September 1944 until April 1945. One confirmed victory, No.609 Sqn, Battle of Britain, 1940. DFC [No.307 Sqn].

PALMER-TOMKINSON, Anthony

P/O   RAF

5-41/4-42 (†)   RAF No.62286

Posted from No.55 OTU. Known as "*P-T*". Shot down and killed near Cherbourg.

PANTER, Keith V.   F/O   RAF

8-44/1-45   RAF No.162949

Posted from No.25 Sqn, being with it since July 1943. Posted to Fighter Experimental Flight (FEF) in January 1945 until being shot down with his Mosquito and made PoW and 16.02.45. He was released by the Americans early in April. Four confirmed victories, with No.25 Sqn and FEF, Europe, 1944 and 1945 plus five V-1s, with Nos.25 Sqns and 501 Sqns, Europe, 1944. DSO [RAFVR].

PARKER-REES, Alastair**   S/L   RAF

10-44/4-45   RAF No.85665

Posted from No.96 night fighter Sqn, he was serving with since the August 1943 for his second tour of operations. First tour of operations with No.604 night fighter Sqn in 1940 - 1942. Posted to HQ, No.13 Group, Three confirmed victories, with No.96 Sqn, Europe, 1944. Claimed 9 V-1s as shot down with Nos.96 and 501 Sqns, 1944. DFC [No.96 Sqn].

PARKIN, Eric G.   P/O   RAF

5-40/4-41   RAF No.79734

Posted from No.6 OTU. Crashed on approach to Gravesend following engine problems and badly inju-

red, 31.07.40. Admitted to Gravesend hospital and did not return to Unit until 05.02.41. Posted out in April 1941 with a non-operational category, instructing until the end of war.

PARR, Edward J.H.   Sgt   RAF

3-42/3-42   RAF No.1256689

Posted from OTU. Posted from OTU. Injured in Tiger Moth accident on 20.03.42 and hospitalised. Commissioned in April 1944. No further details.

PARROTT, Peter L.   F/L   RAF

5-43/7-43   RAF No.41054

Prewar RAF pilot with a SSC, posted from No.57 OTU for a second tour of operations as supernumerary Flight Lieutenant pending postings overseas. Served with No.607 Sqn between January and May 1940, then posted to No.145 Sqn until September 1940, then posted to No.605 Sqn until the end of his tour in April 1941. Posted to Medeterranea and served briefly with No.72 Sqn, then with No.111 Sqn in August and September bfore becoming CO No.43 Sqn between September 1943 and March 1944, the end of his second tour. Third tour as CO No.72 Sqn between November 1944 and February 1945. Nine confirmed victories, four being shared, with Nos.607 and 145 Sqns, France and Battle of Britain, 1940, No.605 Sqn, Europe, 1940, and Nos.111 and 43 Sqns, Sicily, 1943. DFC [No.145 Sqn], BAR [No.72 Sqn].

PATERSON, James A.   F/O   (NZ)/RAF

6-40/6-40   RAF No.36193

Unofficially attached to No.501 Sqn he performed a handful of operational flights with the unit while based in France, his aircraft being badly shot up by German fighters on 07.06.40. Former New Zealand member of the NZ Army/Territorial Force, before being selected for a SSC in the RAF. Posted to HQ, No.71 Wing in France, then, HQ AASF/Air Component South, performing special duty tasks during this period, including the supply of mail, medical supplies, petrol and despatches. In July 1940 sent to No.7 OTU for refresher course and posted to No.92 Sqn two weeks later, until his death. *†27.09.40, Spitfire I X4422, No.92 Sqn, United Kingdom.*

A.D.Payne

PATTERSON, Leonard J.   Sgt   RAF
9-40/11-40 (†)   RAF No.741219
Posted from OTU. Killed when his aircraft was bounced by three Bf109s off Hastings. Believed to have crashed into the sea.

PATTON, R.   1ˢᵗ Lt   USAAF
10-43/11-43
American pilot posted to gain combat experience. Believed to belong to 67ᵗʰ RG.

A.D.Pickup

PAYNE, Alec D.   F/Sgt   RAF
5-40/6-40   RAF No.745798
Known as "*Jammy*". Very little known about this NCO pilot. Probably posted as reinforcement when the Unit went to France and claimed 5 enemy aircraft between May and June 1940. Contrary to evidence, it is most probably the same F/Sgt A.D. Payne who later served with No.610 Sqn during the Battle of Britain, and later with No.74 Sqn, claiming another victory in 1941. Indeed the chance to have two different fighter pilots F/Sgt A.D. Payne is quite co-incidental.

PEARSON, Geofrey W.   Sgt   RAF
8-40/9-40 (†)   RAF No.742740
Posted from OTU. Failed to return from combat over Ashford. Crashed near Hothfield and buried at Lympne under headstone marked, "Unknown Airman". Grave identified and proper headstone erected, 42 years later!

PECK, George W.   Major   USAAF
7-43/7-43
American pilot posted to gain combat experience. CO 107ᵗʰ TRS/67ᵗʰ RG. Later CO 67ᵗʰ RG between December 1943 and May 1945.

PEGLAR, Warren B.   F/O   RCAF
6-43/9-44   CAN./J.7892
Posted from No.57 OTU. Native of Ontario. First operational posting. Attached to 354ᵗʰ FS/355ᵗʰ FG in August and September 1944. Posted to No.274 Sqn in September 1944, remaining until the end of his tour in December 1944. Sent back to Canada in February 1945. Four confirmed victories with USAAF, Europe, 1944. DFC [No.274 Sqn].
F/L : 10-43

PENNOCK, Thomas   Sgt   RAF
12-42/1-43   RAF No.1482988
Posted from OTU. Posted overseas, serving with No.126 Sqn until his death.
†07.04.43, Spitfire VB EP567, No.126 Sqn, Malta.

PICKERING, Tony G.   Sgt   RAF
8-40/12-40   RAF No.754357
Posted from No.32 Sqn (July - August 1940). Posted to No.601 Sqn in December 1940 remaining with it

J.E.A. POTELLE

Posted from No.257 Sqn, he was serving since beginning 1944. Posted out tour expired. Two confirmed victories, both being shared, with No.27 Sqn and five V-1s destroyed, one being shared with No.501 Sqn.

POTTELLE, Jean E.A. Sgt (BEL)/RAF
10-41/6-42 RAF No.1505870
Posted from No.58 OTU. Prewar Belgian pilot serving with 1ˢᵗ Air Regiment in May 1940 following his unit to France. Returned to Belgium in August 1940. Escaped from his country in April 1941 arriving to the UK in June. Posted sick for four months from January 1942 before returning to the unit in April. Shot down near Cherbourg and became a PoW.

POWIERA, Tadeusz P/O PAF
10-42/2-43 RAF No.P.1646
Posted from No.303 (Polish) Sqn, serving with this unit since June 1942. Posted to No.302 (Polish) Sqn until July 1943. Second tour of operations with No.315 Sqn from August 1944 until his death.
†01.01.45, Spitfire IX MK190, No.317 (Polish) Sqn, Netherlands.

until February 1941. Commissioned in December 1941. Second tour of operations with No.131 Sqn February 1943 - January 1944. No more operational postings until the end of war. One confirmed victory, No.501 Sqn, Battle of Britain, 1940.

PICKUP, Arthur D. F/O RAF
9-39/6-40 § AAF No.90030
Prewar Auxiliary Air Force officer. Remained with Squadron at outbreak of war. Flew with Squadron to France and claimed the squadron's first enemy aircraft on 10.05.40. Returned to England by ship and rejoined the squadron at Croydon before being posted to 4 Ferry Pool at Kemble on 22.06.40. Resigned his commission in September 1940. At the end of war, had the rank of Wing Commander, CO of No.5 (Training) Ferry Pool, Air Transport Auxilliary.

POLLEY, William F. Sgt RAF
2-43/5-45 RAF No.1481712
RAF No.155000
Posted from No.52 OTU. Known as *"Bill"*. Posted to No.165 Sqn. Three V-1s destroyed with No.501 Sqn, 1944.
P/O : 9-43, F/O : 1-44

PORTER, Donald A. F/O RAF
8-44/1-45 RAF No.89236

PRESTON, Ian F. Sgt (US)/RCAF
4-42/7-42 CAN /R.100650
CAN./J.15388
Posted from OTU. American from Illinois. Posted overseas embarking in HMS *Furious* in August 1942 to Malta. Posted to No.126 Sqn on arrival.
P/O : 6-42
†23.09.42, Spitfire VB BR383, No.126 Sqn, Malta.

PROCTOR, John E. Sgt RAF
9-39/7-40 § RAF No.563641
RAF No.44131
Prewar pilot, serving with No.501 Sqn at the outbreak of war. Posted to No.32 Sqn July 1940 - March 1941. Second tour of operations in Middle East as CO No.33 Sqn May - July 1942. Later CO No.352 (Yugoslav) Sqn April - September 1944. Ten confirmed victories, one being shared with Nos.32 and 501 Sqns, France and Battle of Britain, 1940. DFC [No.32 Sqn]. Was awarded a BAR to his DFC during the Korean war.
P/O : 7-40

T.POWIERA

PURCHAS, Turton E.G.   Sgt   RAF
3-42/3-42   RAF No.1177670
Posted from OTU. Posted overseas. Commissioned in May 1943. No further details.

PUTT, Alan R.*   F/L   RAF
8-40/9-40   RAF No.37519
Prewar RAF on SSC. Posted first as supernumary Flight Lieutenant, becoming A flight leader from after G.E.D. Stoney's death on 15.08.40. Posted to No.12 OTU on 12.09.40, being replaced by D.A.E Jones at the head of A Flight. Seems to be his only operational posting. No more details available, ending the was as Wing Commander, rank he received in January 1944.

RABA, Vaclav*   P/O   (CZ)/RAF
4-41/5-42   RAF No.82569
Posted from No.247 (China-British) Sqn. Prewar CzAF fighter pilot in Air Regiment 5. With FAF 1939-1940 serving in Toulouse then escaped to the UK. No.247 (China-British) Sqn April 1941. Became A flight commander on 26.04.42 replacing V.H. Ekins. Posted to No.313 (Czech) Sqn on 20.05.42, remaining until October 1942 ending his first tour at that time.

Replaced by P.J. Stanbury as flight commander. Second tour of operation with No.310 (Czech) Sqn, becoming CO between May and September 1944. No more operational postings until the War's end. Remained with the new CzAF after 1945 but left his country before the Communist coup in 1948 returning to the UK and served with the RAF again.
F/O : 9-41, F/L : 4-42

RALPH, Lloyd M.*   F/L   RNZAF
2-43/5-43   NZ401779
Posted from OTU as A Flight commander replacing L. Scorer on 21.02.43. Posted out on 11.05.43 being replaced by L.S. Black on 18.05.43. Previously with No.485 Sqn between April 1941 and May 1942, serving with this unit again in April - May 1944, and between August and March 1945. Last posting No.66 Sqn until the end of war. DFC [No.66 Sqn].

RANDALL, W.L.F.   F/Sgt   RAF
8-44/8-44   RAF No.1394037
Previous postings unknown. Posted to No.274 Sqn, serving the unit until to be shot down over Netherlands and made PoW on 27.09.44.

RAYMOND, Walter*   F/L   (NZ)/RAF
2-44/2-45   RAF No.36262
    (NZ2428)

Known as "*Wally*". Joined RNZAF September 1939. but transferred RAF April 1940. Served with No.98 Squadron in France, 1940, and No.1 Sqn December 1940 - February 1942. Loaned RNZAF mid-war. Flight Commander, No.16 Squadron, RNZAF. Returned to the UK. Posted from OTU Eshott to No.501 Squadron. Took command of B Flight after O.E. Willis on 29.07.44 until posted to Crosby-on-Eden at the end of his tour. Re-transferred RNZAF April 1945. One confirmed victory, with No.1 Sqn, Europe, 1941.

P.H.RAYNER

RAYNER, Peter H.   F/O   RAF
9-39/5-40 § (†)   AAF No.90022

Pre-war Aux pilot, commissioned in July 1936. Promoted to Flying Officer in December 1937. Crashed and killed after shooting down He 111, 30m N.E. Betheniville.

REES, Charles W.   F/O   RAF
9-39/12-39   AAF No.90050

Prewar Auxiliary Air Force officer with No.503 Sqn having relinquished his commission in 1938. Recalled on active service in September and posted to No.501 Sqn. Posted to No.6 FTS for advanced training. No more details available.

RHODES, John   F/L   RAF
3-45/4-45   RAF No.87042

Pilot commissioned in October 1940. Previously served with No.605 Sqn, flying Mosquitoes. Posted to Transport Command to ferry Mosquitoes. One confirmed victory, No.605 Sqn, Europe, 1944, and two V-1s, with No.605 Sqn, 1944.

RIDGWAY, Donald   F/O   RAF
3-45/4-45   RAF No.156706

No details available on this pilot commissioned in October 1943.

ROBB, Robert L.T.   F/L   RAF
8-44/12-44   RAF No.113877

Known as "*Jackson*" posted from FIU. Commissioned in November 1941, completed a tour with No.85 Sqn in 1942 - 1943. Second tour with FIU in July 1944. One confirmed victory, No.85 Sqn, Europe, 1943. Claimed twelve V-1s as shot down, with FIU & No.501 Sqn, 1944.

ROBERTS, John E.   Sgt   RAF
9-42/10-42   RAF No.1077342

Posted from OTU. Posted overseas and served with No.249 Sqn.
†15.11.42, Spitfire VC EP199, No.249 Sqn, Malta.

ROBINSON, Andrew I.**   S/L   RAF
9-42/5-43   RAF No.39569

Posted in for another tour of operations. Prewar fighter pilot in SSC, serving with No.222 Sqn at the outbreak of war. Battle of Britain veteran with No.222 Sqn, completed his tour at the end of 1940. Posted out at the end of his tour in May 1943. No more known operational postings until the end of war. Three confirmed victories, No.222 Sqn, Battle of Britain, 1940.

ROBSON, J.   Sgt   ?
4-43/12-43   ?

No details available.
F/Sgt : 9-43

ROCOVSKY, Miroslav   Sgt   (cz)/RAF
7-41/4-42 (†)   RAF No.787490
Posted from No.52 OTU. Prewar CzAF NCO. Shot down and killed by German fighters off Cherbourg (France).

ROFFE, Arthur R.   Sgt   RAF
4-43/5-43   RAF No.1331322
Not much detail available, but it seems that this pilot was transferred to Bomber Command as pilot, being later commissioned in August 1944 and awarded the DFC [No.150 Sqn].

ROGERS, Everett B.   P/O   RAF
9-40/10-40   RAF No.81373
Posted from No.615 Sqn. Later in the war served as bomber pilot with No.640 Sqn, ending the war with the rank of Squadron Leader. One confirmed victory, No.501 Sqn, Battle of Britain, 1940. DFC [No.640 Sqn].

ROGERSON, Peter M.   Sgt   RAF
4-43/4-43 (†)   RAF No.1217612
Posted from OTU. Killed in a collision with S.E. Nicol's aircraft and crashed outside Portaferry.

RONDEL, Robert W.   Sgt   RNZAF
11-41/2-42   NZ404411
Known as "*Bob*". Posted from No.61 OTU. Posted to Far East in February 1942. Served with No.67 Sqdn, India, between June 1942 and October 1944. Commissioned in October 1943.

ROSE-PRICE, Arthur T.   F/O   RAF
9-40/9-40 (†)   RAF No.39762
Born in Chile of British parents. Prewar RAF pilot with a SSC posted from No.10 FTS. Shot down the same day of his posting by Bf 109s near Ashford. His body was not recovered.

RYMAN, Royston W.   F/Sgt   RAF
8-44/8-44   RAF No.1314783
Previous postings unknown. Posted to No.274 Sqn. One V-1 destroyed with No.501 Sqn, 1944.
†13.08.44, Tempest V EJ637, No.274 Sqn, United Kingdom.

SABOURIN, Jack A.   F/O   RAF
5-43/5-43   RAF No.115037
Little details on this pilot commissioned in December 1941. Known to have served with No.41 Sqn between October 1943 and beginning 1944.

SAUNDERS, Clason B.   1st Lt   USAAF
7-43/7-43   O-439686
American pilot posted to gain combat experience. Pilot of HQ / 67th RG.

SAVILL, Joseph E.   Sgt   RAF
10-40/10-40   RAF No.740971
Posted from No.242 (Canadian) Sqn, having served with it since September 1940. Previously with No.151 Sqn between July and September 1940. One confirmed victory, No.151 Sqn, Battle of Britain, 1940. No more details available except that he was promoted Warrant Officer in October 1941.

SAWARD, Cyril J.   Sgt   RAF
9-40/11-40   RAF No.748752
Posted from No.615 Sqn (July - September 1940). Posted to No.4 FPP in November. Commissioned in October 1942. Rest of the war mainly as instructor, but served with No.577 Sqn between April and November 1944.

SCHADE, Patrick A.   Sgt   RAF
6-41/7-41   RAF No.785018
Known as "*Paddy*". Born in Malaya of British parents. Posted to No.54 Sqn serving with it until beginning 1942 then posted overseas at Malta serving with No.126 Sqn until August 1942. Returned to the UK and commissioned in April 1943. Second tour of operations in October 1943 with No.91 Sqn until his death. At least 12 confirmed victories, with No.126 Sqn, Malta, 1942, and two V-1s with No.91 Sqn, 1944. DFM [No.126 Sqn].
†31.07.44, Spitfire XIV RM654, No.91 Sqn, United Kingdom.

SCORER, Leslie*   F/L   RAF
12-42/5-43   RAF No.119879
Posted on 19.12.42 from No.602 Sqn to take command of A Flight after A.H.B. Friendship. Replaced on 21.02.43 by L.M. Ralph, taking command of B

Flight instead after P.C. Campbell had left. Posted out on 29.05.43 his command being taken by D.F. Lenton two days later. Previously served with No.43 Sqn, then with No.602 Sqn between July 1941 and May 1942. One confirmed victory, No.602 Sqn, Europe, 1942. DFC [No.602 Sqn].

SCOTT, James A. Sgt RAF
5-43/12-43 RAF No.658046
RAF No.159474
Known as "*Scotty*". Posted to No.9 Group. No more details available. Flying Officer at the end of war.
F/Sgt : 9-43, P/O : 11-43

SCOTT, John M.B. P/O RAF
6-42/9-42 (†) RAF No.119229
Baled out after being attacked by FW190 over Lyme Bay and killed when parachute failed to open.

SEARLE, Gordon H. P/O RAF
6-42/6-42 RAF No.48527
No details available. Later served with No.680 Sqn. DFC [No.680 Sqn].

SEATON, Dunham H.* P/O RAF
9-42/5-44 RAF No.46705
Known as "*Tom*". Joined the RAF in August 1941 from *Wiltshire Regiment (Duke of Edinburghs)*, where he was Lieutenant. A flight leader, replacing L.S. Black on 05.10.43. replaced by W.B. Atkinson on 03.04.44 when he assumed command of the Squadron during S/L M.G. Barnett's detachment to FLS which lasted three weeks. Posted out, tour expired. Second tour as CO No.611 Sqn between January and July 1945. DFC [No.611 Sqn].
F/O : 1-43, F/L : 10-43

SHADBOLT, Ernest W. F/Sgt RAF
7-42/8-42 (†) RAF No.915324
Crashed in bad weather, Dorchester. No more details available.

SHORE, Eric H.L. P/O RAF
8-41/11-41 RAF No.64926
Posted from No.58 OTU. Attacked by Bf109s during

Rhubarb operation; engine failed and force-landed on beach near Ste-Mere Eglise, becoming a PoW.

SING, John E.J. S/L RAF
7-42/9-42 RAF No.37429
Known as "*Jackie*", being posted as supernumerary. Prewar regular officer serving with No.213 Sqn at the outbreak of war. Battle of Britain veteran. Posted out in November 1940. Second tour of operations as CO No.153 Sqn between October 1941 - March 1942. In September 1942, posted to No.152 Sqn as CO relinquishing his command in April 1943. No more operational postings until the end of war. Eight confirmed victories, one being shared, Battle of Britain, 1940. DFC [No.213 Sqn].

SKALSKI, Stanislaw P/O (POL)/RAF
8-40/2-41 RAF No.76710
Posted from No.302 (Polish) Sqn. Former member of Polish AF, born in Russia. Fought with 142 *Eskadra* and shot down six German aircraft in September 1939. Escaped to England and transferred to RAF in January 1940. After his training posted to No.302 (Polish) Sqn and soon posted to No.501 Sqn. Shot down and badly burnt on 05.09.40, returning to the Squadron six weeks later. Posted to No.306 (Polish) Sqn until October 1941. Second tour of operations with No.316 (Polish) Sqn in March 1942, then posted

S. SKALSKI

to No.317 (Polish) Sqn as CO in May 1942 remaining until November that year. Early 1943, he formed the special Polish Fighting Team of volunteers to go to North Africa, attached to No.145 Sqn. Then became CO No.601 Sqn between July and September 1943, becoming the second Pole to lead a British squadron. Returned to the UK becoming CO of No.131 Polish Wing at Northolt, then in April 1944, CO No.133 Wing until September 1944. No more operational postings until the end of war. After the war, he returned in Poland but he was put into jail by the Communist between June 1948 and April 1956. Twenty-one confirmed victories, three being shared in Poland, No.501 Sqn, Battle of Britain, 1940, Nos.306 and 316 Sqns, Europe, 1941 - 1942, Polish Fighter Team, Tunisia, 1943, and No.133 Wing, Europe, 1944. DSO [No.133 Wing], DFC [No.306 Sqn] BAR [No.317 Sqn] 2ND BAR [No.145 Sqn].

SMITH, Desmond J. Sgt RAF
4-42/2-43 RAF No.1194960
RAF No.122928
Posted from OTU. No record of him on the Squadron after February 1943 and probably transferred to Admin & Special Duty Branch in December 1943.
P/O : 5-42, F/O : 12-42

M.F.C.SMITH

SMITH, Michael F.C. P/O RAF
9-39/5-40 § (†) AAF No.90026
Prewar Auxiliary pilot, granted commission as Pilot Officer in January 1938. Shot down following combat with Bf110 near Mezieres, France.
F/O : 9-39

SMITH, Stuart L. F/Sgt RCAF
7-43/6-44 CAN./R.93346
CAN./J.87084
Native of Ontario, Canada. Posted out at the end of his tour. Repatriated to Canada in January 1945 but retuning to England in April before being repatriated to Canada again in August 1945.
W/O : 11-43

SMITHERS, Ronald A. Sgt RAF
2-41/5-41 (†) RAF No.922853
Posted from OTU. Crashed into sea for no apparent reason during convoy patrol near Barry, South Wales.

SNELL, Vivian R. P/O RAF
9-40/12-40 RAF No.41485
Posted from No.151 Sqn, in which he was serving since the beginning of the month. Prewar RAF pilot with a SSC. Posted to No.308 (Polish) Sqn for one month before being posted to No.145 Sqn in January 1941. One confirmed victory, No.501 Sqn Battle of Britain, 1940. No more details available.

SNOWDEN, Ernest G. F/L RAF
10-43/10-43 RAF No.101031
Posted from No.234 Sqn as supernumarary Flight Lieutenant. Posted to No.8 (C) OTU. Battle of Britain veteran with No.213 Sqn, he served with between May 1940 and November 1940 as NCO. Commissioned in June 1941. Five confirmed victories with No.213 Sqn, Battle of Britain, 1940.

SOKOLOWSKI, Eugeniusz F/O PAF
12-42/2-43 RAF No.P.0745
Posted from No.315 (Polish) Sqn, being with it since January 1942. Previously with No.308 (Polish) Sqn for four days in December 1941. Posted to No.317 (Polish) Sqn in February 1943 until March 1943 before being posted to No.309 (Polish) Sqn until the

end of his tour in May 1944. No more operational postings until the end of war.

SOLE, George   Sgt   RNZAF
12-41/1-42   NZ404418
Posted from No.61 OTU. To No.5 PRC prior to a posting to No.258 Sqn at Ceylon in July 1942. Later posted to No.607 Sqn for another tour of duty in January 1944.
†*20.01.44, Spitfire VC MA296, No.607 Sqn, India.*

SOUTER,   Sgt   ?
10-41/11-41   ?
No details were available to help to identify this pilot.

ST-JOHN,   Sgt   ?
11-41/12-41   ?
No details were available to help to identify this pilot.

STANBURY, Philip J. *   P/O   RAF
5-42/9-42   RAF No.104436
Commissioned in August 1941. Posted to Boscombe Down on 30.09.42, tour expired. B flight leader on 20.05.42, succeeding V. Raba. Replaced by C.J. Cox.
F/L : 5-42

`DFC : LG 10.07.42`

STANLEY, Henry W.   Sgt   RAF
1-43/2-43 (†)   RAF No.1330743
Posted from OTU. Failed to return from a night flying cross-country from Eglinton.

STANTON, Norman K.T.   Sgt   RAF
8-41/10-41   RAF No.923987
Posted from No.58 OTU. Posted to No.222 Sqn, serving with it until May 1942. Commissioned later in the war.

STEPHENSON, Andrew J.   P/O   (US)/RAF
9-42/9-42   RAF No.116958
Posted from OTU. American from California. Posted to No.133 (Eagle) Sqn at the end of September to be transferred to USAAF. With 336th FS/4th FG October 1942 - December 1943. Remained with USAAF after the war, retiring in 1966 with the rank of Lieutenant Colonel.

STEVENS,   Sgt   ?
3-42/3-42   ?
Posted from OTU. Posted overseas. No further details.

STEWARD, Russell   F/L   RAF
3-45/4-45   RAF No.124847
Previous postings unknown. Posted out to Transport Command to ferry Mosquitoes.

STOCKBURN, Robert C.   Sgt   RAF
9-42/7-43, 11-43/8-44   RAF No.1126026
    RAF No.143937
Posted from OTU. Known as "*Bob*". Reported as "Missing" from a sweep attacking railway targets near Hazebrouck but evaded capture and returned to England. Began another tour with No.274 in April 1945. One shared confirmed victory, No.274 Sqn, 1945. DFC [No.274 Sqn].
P/O : 2-43, F/O : 12-43

STONEY, George E.B.*   F/L   RAF
7-40/8-40 (†)   RAF No.28119
Posted from No.257 Sqn. Pre-war RAF and civil pilot recalled for active service at the outbreak of war. First trained as bomber pilot but soon volunteered for fighter duties being posted to No.257 Sqn in July 1940 on completion of his training. Replaced E.Holden as B flight commander between 28.07.40 until his death. His flight was later given to J.A.A.Gibson. Shot down by Bf110s near Chilham. Three confirmed victories, one being shared, with No.501 Sqn, Battle of Britain, 1940.

STRACHAN, Bert   Sgt   RCAF
5-42/6-42 (†)   CAN./R.85734
Posted from OTU. Native of Ontario. Shot down and killed by fighters near Cap Levy.

STRANG, Walter N.   Sgt   RAF
7-42/9-42 (†)   RAF No.1370081
Killed when his Spitfire failed to get airborne and crashed into parked Typhoon of No.266 Sqn, Warmwell.

SWEETZER, L.W.   Colonel   USAAF
10-43/10-43

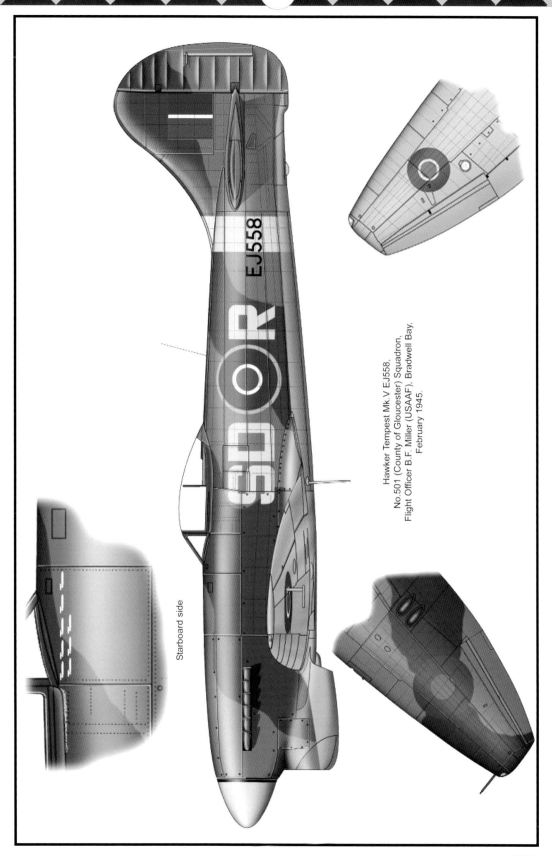

Starboard side

Hawker Tempest Mk.V EJ558,
No.501 (County of Gloucester) Squadron,
Flight Officer B.F. Miller (USAAF), Bradwell Bay,
February 1945.

American pilot from HQ 8th Air Force Support Command. No further details available.

SWENEY, William G. Sgt RNZAF
10-41/3-42 NZ411001
Posted from No.58 OTU. Posted to No.134 Sqn in March 1942, then to No.213 Sqn between August and December 1942. Last posting, No.601 Sqn from January 1943 onwards.
†07.04.43, Spitfire VB ER972, No.601 Sqn, Tunisia.

SYLVESTER, Edmund J.H. P/O RAF
1-39/7-40 § (†) AAF No.90556
Prewar Auxiliary Air Force officer. Commissioned in January 1939. Shot down over Lyme Bay by a Bf109. Three confirmed victories, one being shared, with No.501 Sqn, France, 1940.

TAYLOR, Francis G. Sgt RNZAF
11-41/2-42 NZ41963
Known as *"Frank"*. Posted from OTU. Posted to Far East February 1942. Served with No.67 Sqdn, India, Autumn 1942 and November 1943. Commissioned in October 1943.

TERRY, Peter C. Sgt RAF
8-41/10-41 RAF No.1257673
Posted from OTU. Posted out, later serving with No.185 Sqn over Malta from Spring 1942 onwards.
†07.07.42, Spitfire VC BR317, No.185 Sqn, Malta.

THOMAS, Arthur K. Sgt RAF
10-41/5-42 RAF No.940830
Commissioned in July 1942 and promoted Flight Lieutenant in July 1944. No more details available.
F/Sgt : 2-42

THOMAS, Bryan H. Sgt RNZAF
12-41/2-42 NZ405341
Posted from OTU. Posted overseas. Served with No.260 Sqn between mid-1942 and May 1943, being commissioned meanwhile. Another tour in Italy with No.43 Sqn beginning 1944 until beginning 1945. Three confirmed victories, two being shared, No.260 Sqn, Middle East, 1942 - 1943. DFC [No.260 Sqn].

THOMAS, David S. Sgt RAF
2-41/4-42 (†) RAF No.904947
Posted from OTU. Reported as "Missing" following

E.J.H. SYLVESTER

D.S. THOMAS

Rhubarb near Cap de la Hague peninsula.
F/Sgt : 12-41

THORNTON, Cyril B.   F/L   RAF
8-44/8-44 (†)   RAF No.117692
Posted from FIU, in which he served from July.
Claimed nine V-1s as shot down, three of which were
with No.501 Sqn. MBE [14.03.44]. No more details
available.

TODD, Noel C.   Sgt   RAAF
11-41/3-42   Aus.402892
Native of New South Wales, Australia. Posted from
No.66 Sqn, in which he served two weeks only.
Posted out in March 1942 and repatriated to Australia.
Then posted to No.75 Sqn, RAAF, between October
1942 and December 1943. No more operational pos-
tings until the end of war.
P/O : 3-42

TOFIELD, Alan   F/L   RAF
7-43/8-43   RAF No.42324
Posted from No.222 Sqn, in which he served from
June. Posted to No.1 PDC. Later serving with No.136
Sqn in Far East, before being posted to No.81 Sqn as
CO in October 1944.
†20.10.44, Spitfire VIII MD346, No.81 Sqn, Ceylon.

TOLLER, Alfred A.   Sgt   RAF
8-41/9-41, 9-41/3-42   RAF No.1181831
Posted from No.58 OTU. In September 1941, he was
posted to No.222 Sqn, returning to No.501 Sqn a few
days later. In March 1942, posted to No.601 Sqn and
sent overseas with the squadron. Commissioned in
October 1942. Shot down by Bf109s on 29.04.43 and
made PoW. He was killed a few months whilst trying
to escape. Three confirmed victories, one being shared, North Africa and Tunisia, No.601 Sqn.
†14.08.43, during an escape attempt, Italy.

TOMANEK, Edmund B.   F/O   (POL)/RAF
11-42/2-43   RAF No.76795
Posted from No.164 Sqn, he served a few days only.
Previously with No.315 (Polish) Sqn (November -
December 1941), then No.287 Sqn (May - June
1942), No.81 Sqn (June - July 1942), No.306 (Polish)

Sqn between August and October 1942 then No.501
Sqn. Posted back to No.306 (Polish) Sqn in February
1943 until June 1944. No more operational postings
until the end of war.

TOMKINS, Maurice E.   F/Sgt   RAF
3-42/5-42   RAF No.1169709
Posted in pending being posted overseas. Sent to
Malta and posted to No.249 Sqn.
†26.06.42, Spitfire VC BR382, No.249 Sqn, Malta.

TORNEY, John G.   F/O   RCAF
9-42/10-42   CAN.J/3704
Native of Ontario, Canada, being commissioned in
January 1941. Posted overseas in October 1942.
With No.1435 Sqn in 1943. Repatriated to Canada in
April 1944, serving with No.1 OTU at Bagotville
(Quebec), then with No.7 Photo Wing before being
discharged in December 1945.

TRIPP, Hugh U.H.   P/O   RAF
9-39/10-39 §   AAF No.91069
Prewar Auxiliary officer, commissioned in April
1939. Posted to No.5 FTS to complete his training
pilot course and became a bomber pilot, serving later
with No.44 (Rhodesia) Sqn.
†03.05.41, Hampden I AD864, No.44 Sqn, Germany.

TURBILL, Jack A.   P/O   RAAF
4-42/8-42   Aus.403016
Native of New South Wales, Australia. Posted out to
serve overseas and rapatriated to Australia. Posted to
No.457 (RAAF) Sqn at Darwin in December 1942 but
posted out in May 1943 for medical reasons, being
discharged from RAAF three months later.

TWIGG, Edward   W/O   RAF
3-44/8-44   RAF No.1088331
Posted from No.2 TEU for a second tour of operations. Previously served with No.610 Sqn in October
1942 and No.164 Sqn between November - December
1942 and No.66 Sqn between January and June 1943.
Posted to No.274 sqn, serving with it until the end of
war, being commissioned in February 1945.

J.G.VAISSIER

VAISSIER, Jean G. *Capitaine* FFAF
11-43/8-44 RAF No.F.30638
Posted from No.288 Sqn. Under *Armée de l'Air* Observer training course when France surrendered. Escaped to the UK in June 1940 via Gibraltar. Elected for a pilot course though his age (33 in 1940). First operational posting with No.154 Sqn in February 1942, but posted to No.610 Sqn the following month, remaining only two weeks before being posted to No.616 Sqn. Because of bad eye wounds sustained during his training in England, posted sick. Posted to

A.VAN DEN HOVE D'ERTSKENRIJK

No.288 Sqn in September 1942 for flying duty. Posted to No.274 Sqn in August 1944. Severely wounded in flying accident on 08.12.44. Although J.Vaissier's **DFC** citation is applicable for 274 Sqn, the choice to include it in the Squadron award list only seems to be logical as he spent more time and flew more hours with the Squadron than with No.274 Sqn.

DFC : 31.10.49

VAN DEN HOVE D'ERTSENRIJK, Albert E.A.D.J.G.
9-40/9-40 (†) P/O (BEL)/RAF
RAF No.83699
Posted from No.43 Sqn. Former prewar military pilot serving with Air Regiment No.2 in 1940. Evacuated and arrived to the UK in July 1940. After a refresher course posted to No.43 Sqn in August 1940. Three confirmed victories, with No.43 Sqn, Battle of Britain, 1940.

VENDL, Antonin Sgt (CZ)/RAF
9-41/6-42 RAF No.787685
Posted from No.58 OTU. Prewar CzAF NCO. Posted to No.313 (Czech) Sqn remaining with it until April 1943. Later discharged from RAF and served with 1st Czechoslovak Fighter Regiment in 1944 - 1945 in USSR, flying Lavochkin La-5FNs. After the war he served with Flying Transport Regiment in Prague, but in 1950 he was released from the Czechoslovak Air Force due to political reasons.

VID, Frank J. F/Sgt RCAF
6-43/3-44 (†) CAN./R.69340
CAN./J.86521
Native of Ontario, Canada. Known as *"Frankie"*. Served as Flight instructor for eighteen months in Canada from March 1942, before being sent to the UK in December 1942. Posted missing following recce mission near Le Touquet, France. Commissioned a few days before his death.
W/O : 1-44, P/O : 3 44

VILLA, John W.** S/L RAF
6-42/9-42 RAF No.39768
Known as *"Pancho"*. Prewar SSC pilot. Staff pilot until July 1940 when he was posted to No.72 Sqn, then posted to No.92 Sqn in September, ending his tour in December the same year. Second tour of operations in August 1941 as CO No.65 Sqn until December when he

A. VENDL

R.W. WAINE

was posted sick. Returned to operations with No.501 Sqn in June 1942, continuing to have medical problems. Posted out in September. Later CO No.198 Sqn December 1942 - May 1943. No more operational postings until the end of war due to medical problems. Seventeen confirmed victories, four being shared, Battle of Britain, Nos.72 and 92 Sqns. DFC & BAR [No.72 Sqn & No.92 Sqn respectively].

VINTER, Stanley H. Sgt RAF
3-41/7-41 RAF No.905760
Posted from OTU. Posted to No.92 Sqn.
†24.07.41, Spitfire VB W3381, No.92 Sqn, France.

VRTIS, Karel Sgt (CZ)/RAF
9-41/4-42 (†) RAF No.787447
Posted from No.58 OTU. Prewar CzAF NCO. Shot down and killed near Cherbourg (France).

WAINE, Raymond W. P/O RAF
4-41/4-41 (†) RAF No.61489
Posted from No.56 OTU. Killed when he crashed during low-level "beat-up" near Frampton-on-Severn, two weeks after having been posted.

WARE, Ralph T. Sgt RAF
12-40/12-40 RAF No.516276
Posted from No.3 Sqn, having served with the unit since June 1940. Posted to No.501 Sqn to gain more

combat experience after long months of inactivity in Scotland, pending postings to Middle East, serving briefly with No.112 Sqn. Later ferry pilot. Commissioned in October 1943.
†21.01.45, Mosquito NF.XIX TA439, No.1 OADU, United Kingdom.

WATTS, Edgar J. P/O RAF
2-41/3-41 RAF No.45034
Posted from No.55 OTU. Seems to have been posted to No.151 Sqn in March 1941. Ending the war as Flight Lieutenant, remaining with the RAF after the war until May 1964, retiring with the rank of Wing Commander. No more details available.

WATTS, Edward G.H. Sgt RAF
6-41/7-41 RAF No.1051882
Posted from OTU. Posted to No.145 Sqn in July 1941 and posted the following month to No.485 (NZ) Sqn, then posted to No.41 Sqn in December until his death.
†12.04.42, Spitfire VB W3450, No.41 Sqn, France.

WELLS, H.S. Sgt ?
9-42/10-42 ?
Posted from OTU. Posted overseas and served with No.229 Sqn. No further details.

WESTBURY-JONES, Noel L. F/O RAF
9-39/9-39 AAF No.90018

S.A.H.WHITEHOUSE

Prewar Auxiliary officer, being granted a commission in July 1935. Posted to No.11 Group Pool on 13.09.39. No more details available.

WHELDON, Robert   P/O   RAF
5-41/4-42 (†)   RAF No.62289
Posted from No.55 OTU. Reported as "Missing" following fighter sweep to Cherbourg, France.
F/O : 3-42

WHITEHOUSE, Sidney A. H.   Sgt   RAF
8-40/7-41   RAF No.742922
     RAF No.88438
Joined the Squadron on 26.08.40. Posted to OTU in July 41. Believed to have served later in India-Burma

W.WILCZEWSKI

theatre, ending the war with the rank of Squadron Leader. One confirmed victory with No.501 Sqn, Europe, 1940. No more details available.
P/O : 12-40

WHITFIELD, William H.   Sgt   RAF
10-39/5-40 (†)   RAF No.740692
Known as *"Bill"*. Killed in Bombay crash at Betheniville, France.

WILCOCK, Clifford P.L.   F/O   RAF
7-41/7-41   RAF No.70882
Prewar RAF pilot. Posted from No.610 Sqn in which he was serving since June 1941. Posted to No.54 Sqn. Flight Lieutenant in July 1941 remaining with it until September when he became a supernumerary Flight Lieutenant and posted as flying instructor. No more details available.

WILD, George D.   Sgt   RAF
7-43/2-44   RAF No.1266108
Posted from OTU. Posted out and commissioned in September 1944. No more details available.
F/Sgt : 9-43

WILD, Gilbert   F/O   RAF
9-44/9-44   RAF No.141086
Not much details on this pilot commissioned in January 1943. Posted to No.68 Sqn ending the war as Flight Lieutenant.

WILCZEWSKI, Waclaw   F/O   PAF
12-40/2-41   RAF No.P.0629
Posted from No.145 Sqn, having served with the unit for two weeks in November and December 1940. Prewar Polish pilot, serving in 1939 - 1940 with the French Air Force with GC I/145 and GC I/8 before escaping to the UK. First operational posting with No.607 Sqn in October 1940. Posted to No.316 (Polish) Sqn as founder member of the unit in February, becoming its CO in September. Shot down in combat and made PoW on 08.11.41.

WILKINSON, Bertram D.C.   F/O   RAF
3-39/11-39 §   AAF No.90023
Prewar Auxiliary pilot, being granted commission

in August 1936. Posted to RAF Filton. No more details available.

WILKINSON, Wilfred A.   Sgt   RAF
5-40/8-40   RAF No.518334
Posted from No.6 OTU. Prewar RAF ground personnel member who volunteered for pilot training in June 1939. Following a landing accident at Gravesend on 07.08.40, he was posted to No.1 (C) OTU for conversion to Ansons and posted to No.48 Sqn, a Coastal Command unit, between September 1940 and May 1941. No more operational postings until the war, being instructor until the end of war.

WILLIAMS, Edwards S.*   F/L   RAF
9-39/6-40 §   AAF No.90021
Pre-war Auxiliary pilot. B Flight commander at the outbreak of war. Posted to No.5 OTU in June 1940 when back to England. Replaced by E.Holden in the head of B Flight. No more operational postings until the end of war. Two confirmed victories with No.501 Sqn, France 1940.

WILLIAMS, Ernest L.   F/O   RAF
8-44/11-44   RAF No.80424
Posted from FIU. First tour of operations with No.23 Sqn in Europe and Mediterranean between September 1941 and March 1943. Commissioned in August 1942. Second tour of operations with No.605 Sqn between September 1943 and June 1944, before being posted to FIU. Posted to Fighter Experimental Flight (FEF). Six confirmed victories, Nos.23 and 605 Sqns, and FEF Med and Europe, 1943 - 1945. Claimed 11 V-1s as shot down with FIU and No.501 Sqn. DFC [No.605 Sqn], BAR [FEF].
F/L : 9-44

WILLIS, Oliver E.*   F/L   RAF
3-44/7-44, 11-44/4-45   RAF No.116663
Known as "*Ollie*". Commissioned in December 1941. Posted from No.124 Sqn, serving this unit between June 1942 and June 1943. Injured in flying accident and returned to No.124 Sqn between January and March 1944. B flight leader succeeding B.Fuchs on 31.03.44 until being replaced by W. Raymond on 29.07.44. Returned to the unit in November 1944 as supernumerary Flight Lieutenant. One confirmed victory with No.124 Sqn, Europe, 1943.

WILSON, William   Sgt   RAF
8-41/11-41   ?
Not much details on this pilot. Commissioned in February 1942. Flight Lieutenant in February 1944.

WITORZENC, Stefan   P/O   (POL)/RAF
8-40/11-40   RAF No.76730
Prewar fighter pilot in the PAF. Posted from OTU. Posted to No.306 (Polish) Sqn (November 1940 - May 1941), then to No.302 (Polish) Sqn becoming its CO the same month. In February 1942, Wing Leader of No.1 Polish Wing until September 1942. End of war, CO No.131 Wing. Five confirmed and one shared confirmed victories, No.501 Sqn, Battle of Britain, 1940, No.302 Sqn, Europe, 1941. DFC [No.302 Sqn].

WOJCZYNSKI, Edward L.   W/O   PAF
8-44/3-45   RAF No.794077
Posted from No.307 (Polish) Sqn, the sole Polish night fighter squadron, being with it for his first tour between September 1941 and December 1943. Second tour with the same unit from July 1944. Posted to No.129 Sqn in March 1945 until the end of war. Three V-1s destroyed, No.501 Sqn, 1944.

S.WITORZENC

R.D.YULE

P.ZENKER

WOODSEND, Philip K.　　F/O　　RAF
12-42/1-43 (†)　　　　　　RAF No.62692
Not much details on this pilot, commissioned in March 1941. Crashed in Kirkistown, Eire.

WRIGHT, William H.A.　　F/L　　RAF
6-42/7-42　　　　　　　　RAF No.70834
Previous postings unknown but posted in as supernumary Flight Lieutenant. Prewar RAF officer commissioned in November 1937. Posted to No.66 Sqn as Flight Leader, serving with this unit until December 1942 to become first CO No.193 Sqn between December 1942 and January 1943. No more details available.

YULE, Robert D.*　　F/L　　(NZ)/RAF
11-41/6-42　　　　　　　RAF No.33502
Posted from No.61 OTU to take command of B Flight succeeding R.C. Dafforn on 04.11.41 for his second tour of operations. Prewar RAF pilot, serving with No.145 Sqn when it was formed, Battle of Britain veteran, he was wounded in action on 25.10.40, returning to the unit in February 1941 but sent for rest the following month. Posted to No.66 Sqn as CO in June 1942, replaced by P.C. Campbell at the head of B Flight on 21.06.42. Remained with No.66 Sqn until November 1942. Wing Leader of No.15 Wing/2nd TAF between August 1943 and March 1944. Eight confirmed victories, five being shared, No.145 Sqn, Battle of France and Battle of Britain, 1940, No.66 Sqn and No.15 Wing, Europe,

1942 and 1944. Sqn. DSO [No.15 Wing], BAR to DFC [No.66 Sqn].

DFC : LG 17.04.42

ZAORAL, Vladimir　　P/O　　(CZ)/RAF
10-40/10-40　　　　　　RAF No.81903
Posted from No.310 (Czechoslovak) Sqn. Prewar Czech fighter pilot in Air Regiment 2 of CzAF. With FAF 1939-1940 serving with *Escadrille Légère de Défense* (Defense Flight) at Chartres, then to the UK. Posted back to No.310 Sqn after only ten days with No.501 Sqn. *†19.11.41, Spitfire IIA P7837, No.310 (Czech) Sqn, United Kingdom.*

ZENKER, Pawel　　P/O　　(POL)/RAF
8-40/8-40 (†)　　　　　　RAF No.76714
Former Polish Air Force fighter, with one shared claim against the German in September 1939, while fighting with 142 EM supporting the Pomorze Army. Escaped from Poland arriving in the UK in January 1940 and commissioned. Two more confirmed victories with No.501 Sqn, Battle of Britain, 1940.

Wing Commander E.P.P. Gibbs, CO Ibsley Wing with Flight Lieutenant P. Stanbury, A flight commander, on his right and Squadron Leader J.W. Villa, Commanding Officer of the Squadron. Photo taken in August 1942.
(501 Squadron Association)

SENIOR OFFICERS WHO FLEW WITH No.501
SQUADRON 1940-1945

BEAMISH, Francis V. W/C (IRE)/RAF
5-41/5-41 RAF No.16089
Irish prewar regular officer, veteran of the Battle of Britain with 10 confirmed victories, having served with No.151 Sqn and as Leader of the North Weald. CO No.504 Sqn at the outbreak of war until January 1940. Flew many times during May 1941 with the Squadron while on postings to No.11 Group HQ, but only four were operational sorties. AFC, DSO & BAR, DFC [RAF Station North Weald].
†28.03.42, Spitfire V W3649, CO Kenly Wing, United Kingdom.

GIBBS, EDWARD P.P. W/C RAF
8-42/8-42 RAF No.32225
Prewar regular officer. Flying instructor at the outbreak of war, reaching an operational unit in December 1940, No.232 Sqn, but was posted the next month to No.3 Sqn to become its CO until May 1941, serving briefly with two other units after that Nos.56 and 616 Sqns. He was shot down in July but evaded capture. CO No.130 Sqn between October 1941 and July 1942 and became CO Middle Wallop Wing until October. Two confirmed victories, one being shared, No.616 sqn, Europe, 1941, and CO Middle Wallop Wing, Dieppe, 1942. DFC [No.130 Sqn].

GLEED, Ian R. W/C RAF
5-42/6-42 RAF No.37800
Flew with the Squadron as Iblsey Wing leader. Known as "*The Widge*". Prewar RAF pilot serving with No.46 Sqn at the outbreak of war but soon posted to No.266 Sqn, then No.87 in May 1940 becoming its CO in December until November 1941 when he became CO of Ibsley Wing until July 1942. Later posted overseas and CO No.244 Wing in North Africa in January 1943. Claimed 16 confirmed victories, three being shared, with No.87 Sqn, Ibsley Wing, Europe, France, Battle of Britain, 1940, and Europe, 1941, and No.244 Wing, Tunisia, 1943. DFC [No.87 Sqn], DSO [Ibsley Wing].
†16.04.43, Spitfire VB AB502, CO No.244 Wing, Tunisia.

KINGABY, Donald E. W/C RAF
5-44/6-44 RAF No.112406
Attached to the Squadron whilst being posted to Staff of HQ, Fighter Command. Performed 16 sorties with the Squadron between 04.05.44 and 30.06.44. Previously served as NCO with No.266 Sqn between June and September 1940, then posted to No.92 Sqn until November 1941. Second tour of operations with No.111 Sqn in March 1942, receiving his commission meanwhile, but was posted in April to No.64 Sqn remaining with it until August 1942. Posted to No.122 Sqn and became CO of this unit between November 1942 and May 1943. Then CO Hornchurch Wing between May and September 1943. No more operational postings until the end of war. In all, twenty-three confirmed victories, two being shared with Nos.266 and 92, 64, 122 & 501 Sqns, Battle of Britain, 1940 and Europe, 1941 - 1944. DSO [No.122 Sqn], DFM & TWO BARS [all No.92 Sqn], the only man to receive two Bars to the DFM.

D.E.KINGABY

POSTSCRIPT

On 10th May 1946, No.501 Squadron, AAF, was reformed at Filton in No.62 (Southern Reserve) Group, equipped with Spitfire LF.16Es. Although recruitment was at first very slow, by August 1947 the squadron was declared as operational and continued to maintain its operational efficiency with regular weekend training and summer camps, the first of which was held at St Eval. On 16th December, 1947, H.M. King George VI honoured the Auxiliary Air Force by conferring it with the prefix "Royal" in recognition of its exemplary contribution during WW II.

The following year the Squadron became the second reserve unit to be equipped with Vampire jet fighters when it took delivery of a batch of surplus F.1s in November 1948. These were retained until March 1951 when they were replaced by Vampire FB.Mk.5s. On 1st November, 1949, the Squadron was transferred from RAF Reserve Command to RAF Fighter Command and became part of No.12 Group. With the deterioration of East-West relations following the outbreak of the Korean War, in July 1951 all twenty RAuxAF fighter squadrons were mobilized for three-months full-time service, with No.501 Squadron deploying to Acklington and Tangmere.

In June 1954, the squadron's jubilee year was celebrated when it was allowed to perform the Queen's Birthday flypast over Buckingham Palace for the first time, and in December 1956, the Unit became one of twelve auxiliary squadrons to be awarded the RAF Standard.

However, with the introduction into RAF service of transonic, swept-wing interceptor fighters, the Hawker Hunter and the Supermarine Swift, the argument arose once again that a part-time force was not capable of operating modern high-speed fighters because of their significant advance in aircraft technology and the ever-increasing complexities in air defence. After stiff opposition to a scheme proposed by the Minister of Defence that the auxiliaries should be a reserve element of day fighter pilots, he subsequently modified his plan to allow the auxiliaries to retain their aircraft but switch their role from fighter defence to that of ground attack.

This proved a temporary stay of execution and continued doubts over the future of the RAuxAF. were finally realised on 16th January, 1957 when it was announced that the auxiliary squadrons were to be disbanded and that all flying was to cease immediately as part of the government's proposed defence cuts. Three months later, on 10th March, 1957, No.501 (County of Gloucester) Squadron, R.Aux.A.F was formally disbanded at Filton.

In June 2001, No.501 (County of Gloucester) Squadron, RAuxAF was reformed at Brize Norton from 2624 (County of Oxford) Squadron, R.Aux.A.F., in the Force Protection role to provide a reserve of trained RAF Regiment gunners and Force Protection specialists to reinforce regular RAF units and bases. In 2003 its personnel deployed as part of Operation Telic, the liberation of Iraq.

Formal ties between the "County of Gloucester" Squadron and the County of Gloucestershire were finally recognized on Saturday, 8th April 2006, when the Unit received the Freedom of the County of Gloucestershire. The award is rarely bestowed upon military units by a Civic authority and the Squadron became the first reserve unit to be offered the freedom of a county, rather than a town or city.

Supermarine Spitfire LF.16E, SL620, at Filton in 1946. The Squadron was briefly equipped with the Spitfire before becoming a jet squadron flying Vampire F.1s at the end of 1948. (501 Squadron Association)

Supermarine Spitfire LF.16E, TE474, No.501 (County of Gloucester) Squadron, RAuxAF, Squadron Leader T. James, Filton, 1947.